RECKLESS

★ ★

RECKLESS

THE RACEHORSE WHO BECAME
A MARINE CORPS HERO

★ ★

TOM CLAVIN

NAL
CALIBER

NAL Caliber
Published by the Penguin Group
Penguin Group (USA) LLC, 375 Hudson Street,
New York, New York 10014

USA | Canada | UK | Ireland | Australia | New Zealand | India | South Africa | China
penguin.com
A Penguin Random House Company

First published by NAL Caliber, an imprint of New American Library,
a division of Penguin Group (USA) LLC

First Printing, August 2014

LIBRARY OF CONGRESS CATALOGING-IN-PUBLICATION DATA:

Clavin, Thomas.
Reckless: the racehorse who became a Marine Corps hero/Tom Clavin.
p.   cm.
Includes bibliographical references.
ISBN 978-0-451-46650-1
1. Sergeant Reckless (Horse), approximately 1948–1968.   2. Korean War, 1950–1953—
Campaigns.   3. Warhorses—United States—History—20th century.   4. United States.
Marine Corps. Marine Regiment, 5th—Biography.   5. Korean War, 1950–1953—Artillery
operations.   6. Warhorses—Korea (South)—History—20th century.   7. United States.
Marine Corps—History—20th century.   I. Title.
DS919.C53 2014
951.904'2450929—dc23   2014011593

Printed in the United States of America
1   3   5   7   9   10   8   6   4   2

Set in ITC Berkley Old Style
Designed by Elke Sigal

To Leslie Reingold, who is my champion

CONTENTS

PART III

PART IV

RECKLESS

★ ★

★ ★

August 1952

It looked to be a routine operation. The main attack would be on Bunker Hill that night, and to distract the Communist forces, units of the 5th Marine Regiment were to assault a hill named Siberia. The 2nd Battalion would lead it, accompanied by tanks and armored vehicles carrying high-powered flamethrowers. Even though his mission was to create a reasonably convincing diversion, Colonel Thomas A. Culhane Jr., the commanding officer of the 5th Marines, wasn't taking any chances: He ordered a platoon from the 5th Anti-Tank Company to be part of it. The Chinese hated the recoilless rifles the platoon brought to the fight, and nothing pleased the colonel more than to make life hot and harrowing for the enemy.

Leading the recoilless rifles gun crews was one of the best officers in the regiment. Second Lieutenant Eric Pedersen had assumed command of the platoon in the spring. He was that increasingly rare animal on the front lines in Korea, a Marine who had seen action in World War II. After two years of replacements, most seasoned veterans from that war were back home safe in the States. Pedersen was soon to turn thirty-two, so he was not a gung-ho youngster, and he'd left a wife and two kids back in California. With a string pulled here or there, he could have gotten out of a trip across the Pacific Ocean, or at least have landed a cushy position well back behind the Main Line of Resistance— the series of trenches and defensive works controlled by United Nations forces that spanned the width of Korea near the 38th Parallel—where there were hot showers, hot meals, and movies with Jane Russell and Lauren Bacall.

But here Pedersen was, about to lead his platoon once more into battle. The lanky lieutenant resembled a professor more than a warrior. A slender, beetle-browed man, he had dark, contemplative eyes anchoring a face containing a full-sized, slightly pointed nose and a small mouth that pursed when he was in the midst of contemplation, such as mulling over the best position to place his guns. The way his large ears protruded from his close-cropped dark hair was a bit comical, but none of his men would dare snicker. Pedersen had seen more combat in two wars than all of them combined. They respected him as the finest kind of Marine platoon leader, an officer who wouldn't let his men take any risks he wouldn't take himself. After only a few months together with him, his men would follow him anywhere.

At dusk on that hot summer day, when even a flicked cigarette raised a cloud of dust, the gun crews and guys carrying ammunition were following Lieutenant Pedersen across the thousand yards that separated the relative safety of the MLR from the preselected positions on the hills that looked out at Siberia. On United Nations maps it was officially Hill 58A, a sentinel overlooking a long draw running down the east sides of Hills 120 and 122, part of the Bunker Hill ridge. Marines were already lying in the rocks across a short valley from

Siberia, waiting for the jump-off signal. If the plan the 1st Marine Division staff had put together worked, the attack would cause such a commotion that the Communists would move men and equipment to Siberia from Bunker Hill, and the true assault would take care of those who had remained.

There was enough light left for Lieutenant Pedersen to have a good view of Siberia through his binoculars. He spaced his three gun crews well enough apart from each other that one hit from a mortar or artillery shell wouldn't knock them all out. His gunnery sergeant, Joe Latham, another World War II combat veteran, went from one recoilless rifle to the next and back again, making sure they were secure on their tripods and that the tripods were dug solidly in the hard earth between the rocks of the hill. He wouldn't allow any cowboys firing the gun while standing. It could be done, but the force of the back blast would send any normal Marine flying off the cliff. Well, there was Corporal Monroe Coleman, the strongest man in the outfit—he could possibly fire a recoilless rifle held in both arms, but having the weapon locked tight into a tripod best ensured accuracy.

Beside each gun was a pile of 75-mm shells, each one in a cardboard sleeve. Each recoilless rifle, at more than 100 pounds and almost seven feet long, was tough enough to haul up the hills on every mission the platoon undertook, but those shells weighed 24 pounds each and were an unwieldy two feet long—meaning that a Marine could carry just two of them, one on each shoulder. Coleman, a tall and sturdy young man from Utah, was the only one who could do three, the third shell resting on the back of his neck, wedged between the other two shells. Lieutenant Pedersen had already sent men, including Coleman, back down to the forward ammunition depot for more shells. Getting caught short at the wrong time could mean dead Marines in the valley below.

Pedersen, his lips pursed, watched as the tanks and armored vehicles rolled out, the units of the 5th Regiment in their wake. Seconds later he heard the shrieks of artillery shells streaking overhead, and moments after that clouds of smoke and dirt mushroomed out of the sides of Siberia where the shells struck. The tiny figures of Marines closed in, firing their carbines and BARs as they ran toward the target. Pedersen gave the command and his gun crews joined in, the thrusting back blasts of the recoilless rifles spewing smoke and stones across the flat table of their position. It may have been only a diversionary assault, but it was a damn good show.

Too good, as it turned out. The Chinese forces overreacted. The Marines had sold the distraction so well that the enemy believed it was the real thing. Reinforcements rushed off the Bunker Hill ridge positions toward Siberia. That was the good news. The bad news was that more reinforcements were streaming in from other enemy positions. Within minutes, the Marines on the ground were badly outnumbered and at risk of being surrounded and cut off.

Instead of being able to provide support, the flamethrower vehicles had to pull back lest they fall to the onrushing enemy. Same for the tanks, though they could still provide covering fire. The artillery barrage by the 11th Regiment batteries behind the MLR had to be halted lest the shells fall on friend as well as foe. Pedersen held his breath, watching through binoculars as desperate officers rallied their men to fight a rearguard action while hustling back across the valley. Every few seconds the ground erupted when an exploding mortar shell tossed gritty soil and even bodies into the air. He could hear screaming—or maybe he just thought he did, having heard the agonized cries too many times before.

"We gotta light it up, boys!" Pedersen shouted to his gun crews.

He himself had the best vantage point, being able to see the Chinese positions and attackers as well as the pockets of retreating Marines. Calmly, but loud enough to be heard, the lieutenant gave coordinates, and each recoilless rifle in turn fired, sending off the 24-pound shells. The nickname for the rifles was "reckless" because one had to be reckless to be firing a gun from exposed positions on hillsides. But the guns were often very effective, and now they were firing purposefully, with pinpoint accuracy. They struck enemy troops on the ground, killing clusters of them, and turned mortars and their crews into broken shards of metal and flesh. The devastating fire from Pedersen's platoon passed right over the heads of the Marines, whose chances of survival had just dramatically improved.

As long as the supply of shells held out. Coleman and the other men he had sent for more had already returned, dropped off their loads, and, despite breathing heavily and sweating profusely, immediately set off again. Sergeant Latham estimated that they would not make it to the depot and back in time, no matter how fast they ran. Even the best-conditioned of them would be too slow and carry too few of the precious shells.

But the platoon couldn't quit firing. The destruction issuing from the recoilless rifles kept on, the barrels smoking hot in the cooling air of the evening. Darkness was their enemy too. The lieutenant could direct fire only as long as he could see enemy troops and positions.

Suddenly Pedersen was on his back. Probably a mortar shell had landed nearby. If it had been an artillery shell, he'd already be strumming a harp. He sat up and shook the dirt out of his eyes. A quick glance told him no one else was hurt. It could've been a lucky shot, or a Chinese gun crew had spotted the large back blasts of the recoilless rifles and was targeting them. No matter, the platoon couldn't spare the time to find another position. They had to duke it out until one side won.

The lieutenant staggered to his feet. For a few moments he felt so sick and weak he almost pitched forward onto his face. He was bleeding. He could feel warm blood on his cheek, and he could see that pieces of hot shrapnel had pierced his hip and left leg. Large, strong hands grabbed his shoulders.

"Sir, you need a corpsman."

"Not yet, Joe." Pedersen's vision sharpened and he felt more energy leaking back in than blood leaking out. He told Latham, "Let's give 'em everything we've got left."

The god of war had a sense of humor, all right: It was immediately after one of the recoilless rifles spewed the last shell and just before darkness obscured everything in the valley that Pedersen saw the Marines below reach the safety of the rocks, where a fresh platoon waited, now free to lay down a murderous fire of small arms and mortars, accompanied by the tanks that finally had an open field to fire into. Chinese troops fell like bowling pins. The slaughter became so senseless that even their usually merciless Communist commissars allowed them to retreat.

Lieutenant Pedersen couldn't walk too well on the way back down to the 5th Marines position, so he allowed Coleman to wrap a thick arm around his waist and half carry him. The corporal deposited him in a regimental medical tent. There was nothing to do but wait, as the corpsmen first had to tend to the men who were wounded a lot worse than he was. While Pedersen was waiting, he felt lucky. It wasn't about not being hurt more seriously; it was that the supply of shells had lasted just long enough. Next time, if he and his men weren't so lucky, Marines would die—maybe a lot of them.

It was that hot August night, as he idly heard the sounds of the fight still going on at Bunker Hill, that Pedersen first had the idea of finding a horse.

PART I

★ ★

CHAPTER ONE

Lots of Guts, Little Glory

I f that Chinese mortar shell had landed a couple of feet closer, not only would the Marine Corps have had one less lieutenant, but no one would have ended up hearing about Sergeant Reckless. Two months after the diversionary attack on Siberia, Lieutenant Eric Pedersen prepared to see Colonel Eustace P. Smoak, the new commanding officer of the 5th Marines. That visit and its outcome would begin the journey that would result in Reckless becoming America's own true warhorse.

But the story of that heroic horse could not have become known without her fellow Marines. Pedersen, sure, but there were others too, especially those who fought for their country and their Corps, for whom Semper Fidelis was not just a motto but a way of life. This is their story too, and Reckless, who became the four-legged symbol of "always faithful," would not want it any other way. As much as she was *their* horse, these Marines of the 5th Regiment were *her* brothers.

Pedersen was known for caring about his men, and his sergeants—Ralph Sherman, Elmer Lively, John Lisenby, Willard Berry, and the affable Joe Latham, who at thirty-five was the "grandpa" of the platoon—as well as his corporals and privates thought he was as fine a platoon commanding officer as there was in the 1st Marine Division. That was most of what they knew about their lieutenant. But Pedersen actually had a pretty remarkable lineage, and it was no surprise he was a military man.

His father, John Pedersen, had been hailed as "the greatest gun designer in the world" by another famed gun designer, John Moses Browning. The Pedersens owned ranches in several Plains states and John had been born on the one in Grand Island, Nebraska, in May 1881. Little is known about his early life.

That is not true of the woman he married, Reata Canady, in 1918. She was born in Texas to a Scotsman who built railroads in China. He disappeared there, most likely the victim of a robbery of his crew's payroll. Reata became a violinist, a protégé of Sir Thomas Lipton in England, then a registered nurse at Victoria Hospital. She worked in a field hospital in Belgium during World War I. A German shell hit it as surgery on a wounded soldier was being performed, and Reata covered him with her body to protect his wounds. Both had to be pulled from the rubble. She received a decoration from the British government, and this brought her to the attention of the magazine illustrator P. G. Morgan, who used Reata as a model for now-famous oil paintings of a Red Cross nurse in battlefield conditions.

After the war she became a writer, using the pen name Reata Van Houten. She wrote short stories and articles published by various magazines. She would go on to write pieces on fly-fishing for *Field & Stream* and she had her own program, *The Hostess of the Air*, on NBC Radio. Somehow Reata found time to marry John Pedersen and give birth to two children, Eric and Kristi-Ray, who grew up in homes in Jackson Hole, Wyoming, and Southern California. The marriage did not last, however. Reata later went back to work as a nurse in San Diego, where she died in 1969 at age eighty-five.

John Pedersen's first achievement in the gun business came in 1918 when he invented a device that converted a Springfield 1903 rifle into a semiautomatic, intermediate-caliber firearm. These were mass-produced and shipped off to the Americans fighting in France. After the war, Pedersen designed sporting guns for Remington and collaborated with Browning to create the Model 17 pump-action shotgun, which after redesigns became the Remington Model 31, the Browning BPS, and the Ithaca 37. In all, Pedersen was issued sixty-nine patents for his firearm designs, but because of several business snafus, including during World War II, he was not nearly as successful as he could have been. Pedersen remarried at sixty-five, his new wife being thirty-two; he died five years later, in May 1951, of a coronary while traveling in Arizona.

By that time his son was a commissioned officer in the Marine Corps and a year away from heading for service in Korea. In the fall of 1952, Lieutenant Eric Pedersen and his regiment had been tested not only by battle but also by the wearying, unsanitary, and sometimes downright disgusting conditions of the bunkers that dotted the hills of the so-called Outpost War.

Despite his somewhat prissy name, Colonel Eustace P. Smoak was a tough Marine even among tough Marines and could easily make lowly lieutenants quiver. He had seen plenty of action against the Japanese in the Pacific, and more of the same here in Korea. During the previous war he had particularly distinguished himself while leading attacks against Japanese positions in the Battle of Coconut Grove on

Bougainville in 1943. The suggestion that one of his officers wanted to go off hunting for a horse might be greeted with a growl that Pedersen should have his head examined.

The way this war was going, a lot of people should have had their heads examined. Too many times in the intervening years, the Korean conflict has been referred to as the "forgotten war." Forgotten, unfortunately, was that it was a brutal, nasty, and lengthy one. Some of the fighting there achieved the intensity of such legendary Pacific Theater battles as Tarawa, Saipan, and Iwo Jima in which the U.S. Marines prevailed at great cost. The Korean War was certainly not forgotten by the men who fought in it and their families.

However, it is true that after the first year or so of fighting, there was not a lot reported to the American public to remember or forget. A comparison of *New York Times* headlines, for example, from World War II and from the Korean War indicates that the press and by extension the public had much less interest in events in an undeclared war taking place in a country only the size of Florida on the other side of the world. Plus, it was being waged against the armies of Mao Zedong, who was still relatively unknown and not a full-blown villain like Mussolini, Stalin, Tojo, and Hitler.

The Korean War in American history does not have the epic sweep of the Civil War or World War II, both of which lasted four years and reported staggering body counts. The Korean "police action," as President Harry Truman labeled it, lasted only one year less. By October 1952, the fighting had been going on for twenty-eight months. The Korean War would last a total of three years and one month, and tens of thousands of telegrams expressing sorrow would be sent by the War Department back to the States. Those families have not forgotten.

The combat historian Brigadier General S. L. A. "Slam" Marshall, who would know, referred to Korea as "the century's nastiest little war." The only thing to disagree with is his use of the word "little."

More than 1.3 million Americans served during the war in that windswept gallbladder of a country. By the time of the signing of the truce in July 1953, 54,246 were dead (33,652 killed in action), 103,284 were wounded, 3,746 were taken by the enemy as prisoners, and 8,196 were missing in action, for a total of 169,472. The South Korean Army had more than 800,000 killed and wounded. The enemy suffered an even greater toll, with an estimated 1.5 million casualties, 900,000 of them Chinese Communists.

Another major difference was the slow, dismal grind of the Korean conflict. World War II, for the United States, began with the attack on Pearl Harbor in December 1941 and ended with the Japanese surrender in August 1945. In between, in both Europe and the Pacific, there was one dramatic battle after another, among them Midway, Guadalcanal, Anzio, D-Day, the Battle of the Bulge, Iwo Jima, Hitler's suicide, Germany's surrender, and the dropping of atomic bombs on Japan, followed quickly by its surrender. In Korea, the dramatic battles that inspired the boldest headlines were in the first year—especially the Inchon landing and the Chosin Reservoir campaign—and interest waned after the firing and return to the United States of the swaggering General Douglas MacArthur. His "old soldiers never die, they just fade away" speech to Congress in April 1951, days after he was axed, was his dramatic final act and for many Americans the last truly interesting event of the war.

With the supreme commander of the United Nations forces gone—MacArthur was replaced by the less volatile, and less insubordinate, General Matthew Ridgway—the pace of the Korean conflict slowed to a monotonous, though still deadly, crawl. The events of 1950 had been like the epic battles of Jake LaMotta and Sugar Ray Robinson, each stone-fisted slug seeming to signal sure victory for one or the other. Those blood-filled brawls gave way in 1951 to a grind-it-out sparring match featuring two scarred warriors hoping one would wear down and throw in the towel before his opponent did. It dawned on many if not most officers and soldiers in the field that there would be no knockout blows; instead, there would be feints and some stumbling footwork and an accumulation of points recorded by increasingly disinterested judges and audience.

"The commanders of both armies were largely without illusions—though some illusions might still remain among the political figures above them," wrote David Halberstam. "But from then on it became a grinding war. 'I want you,' Ridgway told a group of Marine officers about that time, 'to bleed Red China white.' It became a war of cruel, costly battles, of few breakthroughs, and of strategies designed to inflict maximum punishment on the other side without essentially changing the battle lines. In the end, there would be no great victory for anyone, only some kind of mutually unsatisfactory compromise."

James Brady, who would go on to fame as a writer and editor, arrived in Korea as a wide-eyed Marine lieutenant on Thanksgiving weekend in 1951. He served as a platoon leader, and when he left the country the following year he did so with both a Bronze Star and a Purple Heart. "In some ways, it wasn't a modern war at all, more like Flanders or the Somme or even the Wilderness campaign" was how he sized up the situation. "There were jets and tanks and warships but you didn't see them very often. Korea was fought mostly by infantrymen with M-1 rifles and machine guns and hand grenades and mortars. There was artillery, of course, quite good on both sides. And barbed wire, lots of that, and mines, always the mines. We lived under the ground, in sandbagged bunkers, and stood watch in trenches. Men who fought in France in 1917 would have understood Korea; Lee's and Grant's men would have recognized it."

Armistice talks had begun in July 1951 at the ancient Korean capital of Kaesong, and those desultory discussions were later moved to Panmunjom, which lay on the 38th Parallel. Whenever there appeared to be some progress, a monkey wrench was tossed into the works. So into 1952 the "grinding war" continued and no one knew how to end it. The war had settled into unbearable, unwinnable battles. There were no more victories, only more death. Both sides wanted to get out, but neither side seemed to have the sense or the willingness to compromise to do so. By mid-1952, the war was ongoing trench warfare, days and nights of living under constant artillery barrages, men caught in the wrong place at the wrong time with not much meaning or satisfaction to be gained from the fighting and dying.

The sarcasm among rank-and-file Marines in 1952 was that they were "dying for a tie." During the last sixteen months of the war, often described as a "stalemate," the Marines averaged twenty-seven casualties a day and more than a hundred dead every month after frustrating month.

There was a lot of courage but little glory to be found in such merciless and squalid surroundings. A hill might be little more than a compilation of mounds of rock-strewn dirt or resemble a small mountain. Most were rugged, steep natural structures containing ridges and gullies and separated by valleys that were often veined by a stream or river. Two hills less than fifty yards apart could belong to opposite forces, though most distances between United Nations and Communist troops were measured in hundreds of yards. The majority of the U.N. troops were U.S. Army and Marine Corps soldiers, who were flanked and supported by South Korean, British, Australian, French, Greek, and even Turkish units.

The Marines were strangers to this kind of reluctant, primarily defensive warfare. During World War II the mission of the Marines, with few exceptions, was to attack and advance and attack again as they carried out the island-hopping strategy. That strategy was often credited to Admirals Chester Nimitz and Ernest King. However, in 1921, Lieutenant Colonel Earl Hancock Ellis of the U.S. Marine Corps drafted "Plan 712, Advanced Base Operations in Micronesia," a plan for war against Japan that first discussed such a strategy. By the time of Pearl Harbor, the U.S. War Department not only had that plan to implement but could refer to Japan's own aggressive strategy that allowed it to conquer much of the Pacific Theater.

In any case, the American strategy throughout the war in that theater from the victory at Midway on had been to capture islands as they fought their way west toward the Japanese homeland. During the first year of the Korean War the combined U.N. forces under the command of General MacArthur battled to gain large swaths of territory as they pushed the North Koreans toward the Yalu River, the border with China. Even in December 1950, as the nearly surrounded elements of the 5th Marines and 7th Marines headed south from the Chosin Reservoir, General Oliver Smith adamantly denied that his troops were retreating, insisting, "We're just fighting in a different direction."

But after that, the war devolved into a much different story. Without enthusiasm, the Marines had to become accustomed to a strategy of digging in and defending positions for an indefinite length of time. That was their mission well into 1952, and as always, they would follow the orders of their commanding officers.

Each side played a chess game. During the daylight hours, the U.N. forces moved their pieces forward, occupying the hills and slopes in front of what was called the Main Line of Resistance. (More specifically, the portion of the MLR in western Korea defended by the Marines was called the Jamestown Line.) When the sun went down, those forces hunkered down or moved backward and the Chinese moved their pawns ahead. It wasn't that the Chinese had better night vision—they feared the airpower of the Americans and the Australians, which was particularly effective during daylight operations. Their MiGs did not match up well with the allies' jets and experienced pilots, some of whom had mixed it up with Japanese Zeros in World War II.

Because of the firepower of the U.N. forces on the ground as well as in the air, Communist troops—overwhelmingly Chinese—relied on stealth, stamina, and intimidating numbers in offensive maneuvers. There was no question about the numbers part of the equation. It was estimated by U.N. commanders that there were forty Chinese divisions, some one million troops, north of the allied positions, complemented by what remained of the North Korean divisions, probably fewer than 50,000 men. The Chinese superiority in numbers did not mean that their ranks were stuffed with raw recruits, failed file clerks, and terrified teenagers. Communist commanders could still count on—among the estimated ten million men in the military—battle-hardened veterans who had defeated Chiang's better-equipped forces, some of whom even dated back to the early days of Mao's revolution and the Long March of 1934.

If only the Chinese had been able to combine superior numbers with smart battlefield tactics, the war might have been over at least a year earlier. The rigidity of the Chinese military was such that field officers from majors on down did not have the authority to change orders during battle. Too often, this resulted in paralyzed commanders unable to prevent the carnage of waves of their men being killed in attacks or other maneuvers that the day before and on paper had looked like winning strategies.

What could also be considered a disadvantage was the blatant disdain the Chinese had for American soldiers. The commissars and commanders apparently ignored the historical fact that a shortcut to defeat is to underestimate your enemy. In a document that had been captured earlier in the war, an enemy writer ranted, referring specifically to U.S. Marines, "We will destroy them. When they are defeated the Americans will collapse and our country will be free from the threat of aggression. Kill these Marines as you would snakes in your homes!"

Dug in on the other side of the Main Line of Resistance were those snakes and their allies: five army divisions, a British division, and an assortment of units from other countries. Anchoring the U.N. defense, however unenthusiastically, was the 1st Marine Division. Given what it had endured and accomplished in World War II and its experiences thus far in Korea, the division, fondly known as the Old Breed, was arguably the toughest division of fighting men any war had seen.

Though both adversaries were subjected equally to the terrible conditions of the freezing Korean winters with the wind blowing south out of Siberia, allied soldiers had a slight advantage during those months beyond having sturdier clothing. Every Chinese soldier wore a flexible two-piece reversible uniform of quilted cotton, a fur-lined cap with thick earflaps, and canvas shoes with crepe soles. Marines learned to listen for the *scritch-scritch* sound of what they called tennis shoes on the snow, indicating the enemy's approach. Their sense of smell came in handy too. Garlic had been a traditional cold remedy in Asia for centuries, and Chinese units had a telltale odor that could be detected hundreds of yards away. This was an even better equalizer in the warm-weather months when the tennis shoes were silent.

To say that conditions for the Marines on and around the hills of the Jamestown Line were "squalid" was often an understatement. "There were times when it was just plumb miserable," recalled Jim Cullom, who in 1952 was a twenty-three-year-old veteran of World War II. The former University of California football and rugby star's nickname was "Truck." He was a second lieutenant, and when he was assigned to lead a machine-gun and rifle platoon consisting of men from Easy and Fox Companies, 2nd Battalion, 5th Marines, there were only eight men left in a unit that should have had a full complement of forty-four men.

"We lived in filthy, rat-infested holes in the ground," said Don Johnson, a member of Fox Company, 2nd Battalion of the 5th Regiment. "Our only hot meals were C-rations heated over Sterno cans. The latrine was so far away, we did our business in C-ration boxes and threw them over the top of the trenches. We didn't shower, shave, and rarely brushed our teeth. At night we were shelled, probed, and forced to listen to Chinese propaganda broadcasts."

Lieutenant Cullom developed a grudging respect for the enemy:

"They were very, very tough from the standpoint that they could tolerate a lot of things that I don't think we could."

They had to. They already had, given that when Chinese troops crossed the Yalu River in the fall of 1950 to join the war, they were only a year removed from ending the long struggle against Chiang Kai-shek. Mao Zedong and his chief lieutenant, Chou En-Lai, had sent Chiang and his forces into exile on Formosa (now Taiwan), and without much of a break their soldiers were fighting again, in possibly harsher conditions.

According to Johnson, "The Chinese soldier was not well equipped. His only protection against the cold was a padded suit—they didn't believe in the layer system. His diet was dried rice and garlic cloves. They carried little sacks containing those two treats. They were bombarded daily, and could rarely stick their heads above the skyline without losing it. They were persistent. They had excellent mortar men." He added: "They were not, however, any match for the Marines."

CHAPTER TWO

★ ★

"Everyone Is Shook"

The summer of 1952 saw more of the same tug-of-war activity, with the Chinese and U.N. forces grappling to take and defend hills and the outposts that had been dug into them. What had upped the ante a bit was a peace proposal that had been submitted to the Communist negotiators at Panmunjom on April 28. Essentially, that was the one accepted . . . though not until July 27, 1953, fifteen months later. But the possibility existed that third summer of the war that it could be agreed to any day. It was presumed that on that day each side would own what territory it possessed—south of the MLR would be South Korea, and north of it would be Communist North Korea. Thus, the most strategic and otherwise valuable pieces of property were being eyed with special interest.

Bunker Hill was prime real estate and had been coveted by the Chinese generals and eventually captured. At 660 feet high it offered an expansive view of the U.N. forces dug in along the MLR, especially the Marines directly in front of it. Technically, what was named Bunker Hill wasn't a hill at all but a ridgeline that ran between Hill 122 in the north and Hill 124 at the southern end. Such subtle distinctions did not matter to the Chinese. Ownership of both hills and the ridgeline connecting them would provide a huge strategic advantage. For that very reason, the Marines could not afford to let the enemy keep it.

There was another reason to take that hill. Kicking the Chinese off Bunker Hill would give the U.N. negotiators more leverage and could hasten a truce. Of course, trying and failing would be embarrassing and allow the Chinese to gain the diplomatic advantage, but Marine commanders would not allow that sort of thinking. Thus, one of the most brutal battles of the war, the first major one fought in western Korea, began.

Though it almost turned into a disaster, on the evening of August 11 when Lieutenant Pedersen led his platoon, the diversionary attack did set the Chinese back on their crepe-covered heels. The tanks and flame-throwing vehicles had created surreal, cinematic scenes—frightening and deadly ones for the Chinese.

Once that assault had drained off enough enemy troops, portions of Baker Company of the 1st Battalion, 1st Marines, commanded by Captain Sereno Scranton, started up Bunker Hill. One platoon had made it to the ridgeline when the Chinese reacted with small-arms fire and hurled grenades. But more Marines made their way up the hill and the defenders began to give ground. By dawn, the Chinese had lost the top of Hill 122.

Marine reinforcements arrived bearing shovels, sandbags, and wire so that a defensive perimeter could be created. Early in the morning of August 12 there was a flare-up of firing by Chinese soldiers who clung to a section of the hill, but that was soon doused. Lieutenant Colonel Gerard Armitage and his 3rd Battalion of the 1st Marines were now responsible for holding on to Bunker Hill.

Maybe the Chinese had finally spilled enough blood on that particular hill—there was little action to speak of as morning turned to afternoon, allowing the Marines to further fortify their position. The quiet was shattered at 3 p.m. when enemy artillery opened fire. By then, the 3rd Battalion and supporting units, about 1,500 strong, occupied Bunker Hill. They provided a rude surprise for the 350 Chinese soldiers who an hour after the barrage emerged from the low ground and headed up toward the ridge. Even under murderous fire they kept coming, until finally their disregard for their own lives wilted.

Captain Bernard Peterson, a forward air controller, had observed much of the brutal battle and the impact on friend and foe alike. He would later write to his wife, "Oh honey, this is a horrible war—worse than anything I have ever imagined possible. Everyone is shook."

During the late-afternoon lull, Major General John Taylor Selden, commanding officer of the 1st Marine Division, brought up reserve units and shifted other units because the entire defensive line was dangerously thin. The Marines on Bunker Hill were resupplied with mortars and machine guns. By 8 p.m., they were ready for whatever the enemy might bring.

As the Chinese had done countless times in the past two-plus years of fighting, they now decided that an attack in the middle of the night would be effective. They were right. An hour into August 13, the Marines came under mortar fire. Minutes later, enemy artillery resumed, blasting the hills and the ridge that constituted Bunker Hill. The artillery of the 11th Marine Regiment answered, and for four hours the American and Chinese positions were a murderous maelstrom as shells gouged hills and blasted humans apart. Every man and every weapon were involved. The prolonged attack was effective in piling up casualties on both sides, but ultimately it failed. Just before dawn, the enemy withdrew.

It had been a busy day for U.S. Navy corpsmen, who provided the immediate on-the-field care for the wounded. And a deadly day too.

Hospitalman John Kilmer had enlisted in the Navy in 1947 in Houston when he was only seventeen. He reenlisted in August 1951, and a year later he was with the 3rd Battalion, 7th Marine Regiment. During the height of the fighting on the night of August 13, Kilmer rushed from one wounded man to another, providing aid. He was exposed to small-arms fire and sniper fire, but mortar fragments got him first. Though seriously wounded, he continued his work, reaching another Marine who had been wounded. As his Medal of Honor citation read, "Undaunted by the devastating hostile fire, he skillfully administered first aid to his comrade and, as another mounting barrage of enemy fire shattered the immediate area, unhesitatingly shielded the wounded man with his body." The Marine survived; Kilmer did not.

The Chinese were back at it before the day was done. At 9 that night, another bombardment of Bunker Hill began. The enemy ground attack that followed focused on the right and center positions of the 3rd Battalion. Once more they almost got through, but the Marines, primarily those in How Company, beat them back with the help of illuminating rounds launched by the artillery of the 11th Regiment. Still, the defensive line was again thinning, and the Chinese seemed to have an inexhaustible supply of men and shells.

During the next day and night the attacks on Bunker Hill were sporadic and not as intense. Maybe the reservoir of even the Chinese soldiers was beginning to run a bit dry. That hope was dashed very early on August 15 when the Chinese artillery opened up, raining bombs on Bunker Hill. It was estimated that during the next three hours, until about 4 a.m., the defensive positions absorbed up to a hundred rounds per minute. During this prolonged thunderstorm of metal, enemy troops probed and massed for a full-scale attack. Then the Americans got lucky. When an M46 Patton tank flicked on its searchlight, caught in the glare was a large group of Chinese soldiers.

Artillery, mortar, and tank fire took many of them out. Preventing that attack may have saved Bunker Hill.

How could the situation become worse? A real thunderstorm, which struck on the afternoon of August 15. Bunker Hill turned to mud and the Marines on it were soaked to the skin. So were the Chinese, but that didn't stop them from sending a company out for another attempt to take the hill. It took an hour to dissuade them. The next day was less than an hour old when the enemy tried again, this time with a battalion-strength force. They kept coming for more than two hours as Marines died in the deepening mud. At one point some enemy soldiers got through the defensive perimeter and Marines killed them with knives and bare hands. At 3:15 a.m., what was left of the Chinese battalion retreated.

Apparently, having come that close to capturing Bunker Hill after five days of furious fighting and not succeeding had demoralized the enemy. While they did not abandon their positions, there were no more attacks that matched those of August 11 to 15. The Chinese did not go on a hiatus—the relative inactivity at Bunker Hill meant that the enemy was devoting more resources and energy to attacks elsewhere on the Jamestown Line, often on the right side, which was manned by Colonel Thomas Culhane Jr. and his 5th Marine Regiment.

Capturing and keeping Bunker Hill was accomplished with forty-eight Marines sacrificing their lives and more than three hundred being seriously wounded. (According to Marine physicians, the total number of wounded topped one thousand.) It was estimated that there were close to three thousand total Chinese casualties.

Casualties meant a crushing caseload for the doctors at the makeshift surgical stations behind the defensive line, even days after the most intense fighting. "Saturday night came, and we'd been up for 36 hours without sleep," reported Lieutenant Birney Dibble, who at that time was a surgeon in the Naval Reserve attached to the 3rd Battalion of the 5th Marines.

By Sunday, August 17, Dr. Dibble and most of the other medical personnel had gone without sleep for forty-eight hours. Sikorskys and other helicopters arrived one after the other bearing those with the most serious torso injuries. When surgery was done, if there wasn't room for a recovering Marine inside, he was brought out and laid gently on the hillside. As the weekend went on there were rows of men, who were checked regularly so the ones who died could be replaced with more of the ones coming out of surgery. They had to be brought water regularly too, because as Dr. Dibble noted, "It was hot, lying there in the sun, and we had to be sure the wounded weren't getting dehydrated."

As was true during and immediately after most of the battles in western Korea that year and for the rest of the war, the main surgical tent was a scene from hell. As sweat poured from their foreheads and chins, doctors hacked off arms and legs and pried open abdomens to stop the bleeding that was draining men's lives away. Kidneys and spleens were removed. The only mercy for the patients was unconsciousness; for the surgeons and nurses it was not having time to think about what they were doing.

Dr. Dibble concluded, "The Marines will never forget Bunker Hill, and neither will we, the doctors and corpsmen who were there on the other end of the pipeline from that bloody hill."

During the next few weeks the Chinese fired mortars at Bunker Hill from time to time, and there were occasional machine-gun bursts and tossed grenades. Robert Simanek, a twenty-two-year-old from Detroit, threw himself on one of them. Fox Company of the 2nd Battalion, 5th Marines, had sent out a patrol, and PFC Simanek was part of it. The Marines ran into a trap. When a grenade fell among them,

Simanek sacrificed himself. The explosion severely wounded his legs, but miraculously, he survived. On October 27 of the following year at a White House ceremony, Simanek became the thirty-sixth Marine to receive the Medal of Honor for his actions in the Korean War.

There was no large-scale coordinated effort against Bunker Hill other than the one from the night of August 25 to August 26, when an assault was repelled. However, smaller attacks could be deadly too. At 1 a.m. on September 5, the Chinese launched mortar shells and soldiers rushed up the hill. They were met by small-weapons fire from the Marines who had survived the mortar onslaught.

Easy Company of the 2nd Battalion, 1st Regiment, took the brunt of this attack. During it, Edward Clyde Benfold, of Staten Island, New York, sacrificed his life to save others. Only twenty-one years old, Benfold was a Navy Hospital Corpsman 3rd Class. Even though he was exposed to intense mortar and burp gun fire, Benfold moved among the Easy soldiers, treating the wounded. At the height of the action, he spotted two wounded Marines in a crater created by an artillery shell. As he went to treat them, advancing enemy troops hurled two grenades into the crater. Benfold grabbed the grenades, leaped out of the crater, and threw himself at the enemy soldiers, who were killed when the grenades detonated. The courageous corpsman was mortally wounded; he received a posthumous Medal of Honor.

Another Medal of Honor was awarded for heroism during this same battle to hold Bunker Hill. PFC Alford McLaughlin, who had joined the Marines right out of high school in 1945, had already earned a Purple Heart the previous month, and on September 4 he was back on the line with his I Company of the 3rd Battalion, 5th Marines. After midnight, as the Chinese blew whistles and bugles and attacked up the hill, McLaughlin stood his ground, shooting two machine guns from the hip until his hands blistered from the overheating guns. He put them aside to cool and withstood the enemy by firing a carbine and hurling grenades, even after being wounded.

To rally his fellow Marines, the twenty-four-year-old from Alabama stood in full view as he took up the machine guns again and sprayed the hill, felling the Chinese as if he wielded a scythe. By the time the decimated enemy broke off the attack, McLaughlin had accounted for well over a hundred dead and wounded. He became one of the few Medal of Honor winners in Korea to live long enough to receive it. McLaughlin would serve as a Marine for another twenty-five years before retiring as a master sergeant.

Despite the high casualty count, as summer drew to a close, the Marines continued to occupy Bunker Hill and enjoy what it represented strategically as well as its value in the Panmunjom negotiations. The hard-fought victory did not appear to change the political situation, though. On the field of battle, commanding officers came and went and that didn't change anything either. On August 29, General Selden, who had been a Marine since 1915, turned over the 1st Division to Major General Edwin A. Pollock, whose orders were no different than his predecessor's had been. Same for General Mark Clark, who that October would replace General Ridgway as commander of all U.N. forces in Korea. "For the first time in modern history, total victory over an enemy was rejected," growled Lee Ballenger, a Marine Corps veteran of the Korean War and author.

Time, however, was not on the side of the Americans fighting in Korea. They were fighting a war of unceasing losses over and above casualties. Unlike the Chinese forces, whose troops were in it until the war ended, the American soldiers had a specific time of enlistment and were subject to rotation when it was time to go home, no matter what was happening on the field of battle. "Rotation" meant combat veterans constantly being replaced by greenhorns who had to learn fast or die.

As far as Lieutenant Eric Pedersen was concerned, Marines wouldn't die because his gun crews ran out of ammunition. With a stick helping him walk and his wounds barking, he had indeed made his way to the command post of the 5th Marines to see a man about a horse.

CHAPTER THREE

★ ★

Flame-of-the-Morning

Life was harsh for eight-year-old Kim Huk Moon and his family, and this one day in 1936 was especially difficult. Grandfather Kim had died, and the boy and his parents, along with Nam Soon and Chung Soon, his sisters, had to work their way from one end of Seoul to the other to attend the funeral. For the parents, navigating the unfamiliar streets choked with carts drawn by horses, mules, and oxen, the occasional automobile, street peddlers, and other travelers was a confusing and possibly dangerous enterprise. For Kim Huk Moon and his younger sisters, it was a frightening experience. They could not even remember their grandfather, so the journey was confusing for them too.

After the funeral—only Kim would retain a vague recollection of it—the weary family had to travel back across Seoul. The trip in both directions was made more harrowing by the presence of occupying

Japanese troops, who always had the right-of-way. On the way back, when Father Kim tried to get his footsore family onto a streetcar, an irritated Japanese officer beat him. Japan had annexed Korea in 1910 and had maintained an intimidating, sometimes brutal military presence there for almost three decades.

Tired, thirsty, and hot, the Kims sought shelter in the shade of a grandstand at the Sinseul-dong racetrack. The young boy could see that there were horses being exercised at the track. One of them, a red sorrel with four white stockings and a broad white blaze from her forehead to her nose, was brought to the outer rail and its rider called for water. Kim was mesmerized by the beautiful horse. However, his father was in a hurry to return home, so he led his family away.

The Kim house was typical of many Korean homes, an L-shaped structure with a roof of rice straw and walls of baked mud. Inside, a raised floor covered the majority of one wing. The other wing was a *kong*, or sleeping area. The baked-mud stove was in the first wing, but heat from it coursed through tunnels in the sleeping area as well as under the raised platform, providing a strong defense against the frigid winter cold. Each wing had one window; it was without glass, and was covered by a rice straw mat in the winter. Mrs. Kim tended to the house and supervised her children while her husband worked in the fields of a rice grower.

One day soon after the grandfather's funeral, Kim managed to find his way back to the racetrack, and again he saw the sorrel mare. Though his sisters feared that he would become lost or run afoul of the wrong Japanese soldier, Kim continued to return. He became a familiar presence at the racetrack and was tolerated, sometimes treated kindly, by the Japanese officers who visited to watch the horses being run for their amusement. The reddish mare appeared to be a favorite for her speed and appealing looks.

While on his way to the racetrack one day Kim encountered a

Japanese man atop a stallion. Suddenly, the horse became agitated and almost crushed its rider. Kim grabbed the horse's reins and prevented a serious injury to the Japanese man. He introduced himself as Kan, and grandly explained that he was the lead rider for a colonel who was commander of the Imperial Cavalry and thus in charge of the horses kept at Sinseul-dong. One of them was the horse whose coat looked aflame when she galloped in the bright sunlight. Her name was Yuen, which means "happiness" or "merriment." Seeing the joy in Kim's face as he absorbed this information, and grateful for his quick thinking, Kan hired the boy to assist a trainer named Takeo, also Japanese, every day after school.

One day a few weeks later Kim, not realizing how impertinent he was, announced that he had renamed the horse Ah-Chim-Hai, or Flame-of-the-Morning. The others at the track, even old Takeo, thought it was fitting, and over time everyone at Sinseul-dong used the new name.

The boy was paid in yen notes, which he had to hide in a glass jar so Father Kim wouldn't discover that he worked at the racetrack. The Kims believed that their oldest child, their son, was staying at the school for extra lessons, and they saw him as the one who would end the cycle of generations of Kims existing by a life of backbreaking labor. They were quite proud of him, and he did return every evening happy and excited by what he was learning.

Young Kim's secret was safe until the following summer. Kan took his horses, including Flame-of-the-Morning, to race in Japan, and when he returned a couple of months later, he sought out Kim at his home. It was there that he met Father Kim for the first time. The father was not happy with the subterfuge or that Kan wanted to make his son an apprentice for five years. However, he had to hide his hurt and anger because he could not possibly risk irritating a Japanese man of some importance. And he could not refuse the fifty yen that Kan paid him. He did persuade Kan to promise that Kim would continue to attend school.

For those five years Kim was an apprentice trainer and rider. An early highlight in his career was when Flame-of-the-Morning raced to victory in the Governor-General Cup Race, held at Sinseul-dong. There were many other wins after that, which endeared him to the colonel as well as to the jocular Kan and the wizened Takeo. Another highlight for the boy was at least one visit to Japan. When he returned home, even Father Kim marveled at the descriptions his son offered of a land that might as well have been on the other side of the world.

Kim's apprenticeship ended in 1941, when a new war was raging in Europe. He had turned thirteen, Takeo had retired, and Kan gave Kim the opportunity to ride Flame-of-the-Morning in what was to be her last race before she was sent to a breeding farm in Japan. That race also ended in victory. However, soon after, the Japanese attacked Pearl Harbor. Many of the Japanese military and public officials in Korea were called home, including Kan. He told his favored apprentice and rider that arrangements would be made to ship Flame-of-the-Morning and the other horses to Japan. Until then, Kim was in charge of caring for them.

Several months passed with no arrangements being made. Kim learned that Kan had traded riding horses for piloting planes for the emperor. The teenager dutifully took care of the horses left behind at Sinseul-dong. Father Kim was shipped off to a labor camp of workers building a dam, even though he was suffering from tuberculosis, as was Kim's mother. One day a police officer appeared at the stable to tell Kim that he was to take the horses, including Flame-of-the-Morning, to a farm where they would work the fields and haul rice to ships in the harbor in Inchon that would carry the cargo to Japan. The police officer also reported that the colonel, who had taken a shine to the young and eager apprentice, had been killed in a battle with the "Yankee big noses."

Kim and the horses made the journey to the farm, which was adjacent to a prisoner-of-war camp housing American soldiers. There, Kim befriended a POW named Bill Duffy, a Marine sergeant. Kim managed to secretly give rice to him and the other half-starved Americans. Every day was the same, with Flame-of-the-Morning and the horses working the fields, the oppressive monotony broken only by the torturous trips to Inchon with heavy bags of rice.

One day, Kim was discovered giving rice to Sergeant Duffy. The boy was beaten unconscious and tossed into a cage used to punish POWs. He was released only because during his absence Flame-of-the-Morning was in such an agitated state that the other laborers could get no work out of her, even after Japanese overseers whipped her. Though Kim was not beaten again, over time he suffered from agonizing headaches and the vision in his left eye dimmed.

One of his sisters got word to Kim that Kan had been killed in battle. He was almost paralyzed by sorrow, but he also had to hope that the Japanese on the farm would not learn this information. The prospect of Kan's one day returning to reclaim Kim and Flame-of-the-Morning as part of his racing team was what kept the cruel overseers from heaping further abuse on the boy and the horse. Still, Kim and the sorrel mare were far from coddled. They were assigned to haul the night cart through the POW camp as prisoners emptied buckets from the latrine into it. The contents had to be deposited outside of the camp.

This turned out to be a minor blessing in disguise. Hauling the soil cart was indeed a disgusting chore, but not quite as hard on the horse's legs as dragging plows through fields that were sometimes choked with mud and stones. Also, emptying the cart allowed Kim to go outside the farm and POW camp. This provided him with new ways to collect and sneak rice to Duffy and the other American prisoners, who were becoming more gaunt and weak.

When he discovered a field that had been harvested of rice and was awaiting a new planting, Kim requested and received permission to take Flame-of-the-Morning running through it in the evenings. The boy had faith that the war would end, peace would come to Korea, and with it racing would resume, and he and Flame-of-the-Morning, still in reasonably good shape, would be competing and winning again.

Amazingly, that is what happened. One day most of the Japanese camp guards and farm overseers were gone. Rumors ran amok that Japan had surrendered. The American POWs opened up the prison gates and storerooms and found the food left behind by the Japanese. Sergeant Duffy proclaimed that it was thanks to Kim that some of them had survived, and as far as they were concerned the seventeen-year-old could have anything he wanted. Kim wanted to be the owner of Flame-of-the-Morning. Duffy had one of the prisoners, an Australian who spoke Korean, write up a letter to that effect and the sergeant signed it.

This was a dubious document, but no one challenged it as proof that Kim Huk Moon was the owner of this cart horse. He and Flame-of-the-Morning made their way back to Seoul. He found his mother at their home—by this time, Father Kim was presumed dead—and his two sisters, Chung Soon and Nam Soon. The latter had two young children and hoped that with the war over her husband would return from wherever he was with the Korean labor crew that had been forced to work for the Japanese.

Kim found that the Sinseul-dong racetrack had fallen into disrepair, had been vandalized numerous times, and was overgrown with weeds. He still had faith that there would be racing there, so he told no one that he was now completely blind in his left eye.

The Korean political system gradually pulled itself together, and Kim went to see an official about his sister's husband. "Your brother-in-law was with the Japanese forces on the island of Iwo Jima," he was told. "There were no Korean survivors from that battle." Nam Soon was overwhelmed by grief—so much so that one day, leaving her children behind, she trudged to the Han River and threw herself into its frigid waters. Kim and his other sister were left to raise the children and care for an ailing Mother Kim.

And there was Flame-of-the-Morning. The good news was the formation of the Seoul City Race Club and other clubs like it. Repairs were made to the racetrack and the first postwar day of competitions was scheduled, which would also be a day of celebration of Korean freedom. Kim exercised and trained the horse and learned how to compensate for having just one good eye. It was a triumphant moment indeed when Flame-of-the-Morning, with Kim in the saddle, won the featured race at Sinseul-dong.

But the sorrel mare suffered several injuries during the race. None were fatal, but they were enough that combined with her being at least twelve years old, they meant she would never race again. When Kim recovered from this disappointment, he saw this as an opportunity to find a mate for Flame-of-the-Morning before she got any older. After a long search he found a suitable match, a stallion from Pusan. As Flame-of-the-Morning's pregnancy progressed, Kim continued to race on other mounts to earn enough money to feed his family and his horse. Every night Kim stayed late in the stall to keep Flame-of-the-Morning company.

At dawn one day in what was probably June 1948, Flame-of-the-Morning gave birth to a filly. She was identical to her mother except that she had one red stocking instead of all four being white. Kim was glad for this because it would allow him to tell mother and daughter apart once the filly was fully grown.

But a week later Flame-of-the-Morning was dead. Chung Soon found her brother stroking his beloved mare's head in his lap. The horse had contracted a fever four days earlier, and being an older horse that had just given birth, she was too weak to recover. Another blow was the news that the elderly Takeo had died. Now Kim was the only survivor from the original prewar racing team.

He turned over care of the filly to a fellow rider at Sinseul-dong, a young man named Choi, whose mare had foaled shortly before Flame-of-the-Morning did. His grief for her meant that Kim could not bear to be with the filly, nor could he compete in races. But when his sister informed him that the family had run out of money, Kim roused himself and resumed racing. He often won—even with one eye—because he was spurred on by a natural talent and mouths to feed. But his years with Flame-of-the-Morning, now represented only by the filly, were in the past.

CHAPTER FOUR

* *

Holding the Hook

As one of the more intelligent as well as experienced officers in the entire 1st Marine Division, Eric Pedersen knew that a breakthrough of the Main Line of Resistance and the occupation of Seoul—only twenty-six miles south of the left flank of the MLR—would have been catastrophic for the United Nations forces. True, the capital city of Seoul had been taken before, but the timing of such a capture by the Communists in the fall of 1952 could not have been worse.

Surely, enemy negotiators at Panmunjom would have pressed that advantage, and in the wake of such an embarrassment those on the U.N. side might well have been more inclined to accept the terms offered. It would be understandable if the majority of Americans back home—some of them still weary from the world war that had ended only seven years earlier—would then have viewed the sacrifices of the past two years as wasted. So the line of defense in western Korea had to be held.

Most of that responsibility fell to the 1st Marine Division . . . meaning the line was in excellent hands. It had done just about everything else asked of it for almost forty years. The original unit had been activated two days before Christmas in 1913 in Philadelphia as the 1st Advance Base Brigade. It was deployed to Vera Cruz, Mexico, while that country endured political turmoil involving Pancho Villa and his rivals. Over the years the brigade had several deployments, including Haiti; then while in Cuba in February 1941 it was redesignated as the 1st Marine Division.

It shed a lot of blood in the Pacific Theater in World War II. First it was sent to Guadalcanal, then Eastern New Guinea, then New Britain, then Peleliu, and finally Okinawa. For two years after Japan's surrender the 1st Marine Division participated in the occupation of North China, and then finally it was sent home to the States, arriving in June 1947 at Camp Pendleton, just north of San Diego. It was deployed—in a hurry, and piecemeal—to Korea in September 1950. During those first few months, commanded by Major General Oliver Smith, it participated in Douglas MacArthur's finest hour of that war, the landing at Inchon, and then famously at the Chosin Reservoir.

It was during this campaign that one of its companies, Fox, of the 2nd Battalion, 7th Regiment, achieved legendary status by holding off an overwhelming Chinese force at Toktong Pass. For five days and nights the 246 Marines withstood attacks by an estimated 10,000 Chinese troops, buying time for elements of the 5th Marines and 7th Marines to put some distance between themselves and the Chosin Reservoir. Medals of Honor went to the Fox Company's commanding officer, Captain William Barber; to PFC Hector Cafferata, who almost single-handedly rejected a powerful enemy assault on what became known as Fox Hill; and to Colonel Raymond Davis, who led a battalion of "Ridgerunners" over snow-packed hills to the relief of Fox 2/7.

But the entire division distinguished itself at the Frozen Chosin. That November, ten Chinese divisions had swept down from the surrounding mountains with the directive from their leaders to destroy the entire division. When Smith had said, "We're fighting in another direction," what he meant was that it successfully withdrew—fighting every step of the way—over seventy-eight miles of mountain roads to reach the port of Hungnam. The cost was high, with an estimated 4,000 casualties, but the division dished it out too, with an estimated 25,000 in Communist casualties.

The division anchored the east-central front of the MLR in 1951; then the following year, in what was called Operation Mixmaster, it was shifted to the western front to protect Seoul and be close to Panmunjom. Smith had been temporarily replaced by Brigadier General Lewis "Chesty" Puller, but then he was back, giving way in April 1951 to Major General Gerald Thomas, who in turn gave way to General Selden in January 1952.

In the fall of the year the division's commanding officer, the man who would ultimately find himself as Reckless's top commander, was General Edwin A. Pollock. Though in portraits he has a bit of a hangdog look, the fifty-three-year-old from Augusta, Georgia, had the background that the leader of the 1st Marine Division should have. He graduated from the Citadel with a degree in chemistry, became a second lieutenant in the Marine Corps, and was part of expeditions to the Dominican Republic, Nicaragua, and the Pacific. Soon after World War II broke out, Pollock was a lieutenant colonel and CO of the 2nd Battalion in the 1st Marines. He led his men in the fierce fighting on Guadalcanal and earned the Navy Cross. A couple of years later, he added the Bronze Star during combat on Iwo Jima.

When the call came in August 1952 to assume command of the 1st Division in Korea, Major General Pollock was the commanding officer of the 2nd Marine Division at Camp Lejeune in North Carolina. Going overseas to help fight a war that was not receiving enthusiastic support at home was far from a plum assignment, but Pollock was a true Marine, and he went where his superiors told him to go.

Lieutenant Pedersen and his "reckless rifles" platoon were routinely attached to the 5th Marines, a regiment that had practically been born fighting. Little wonder that it became the most highly decorated regiment in the Marine Corps. Like the division, it had been born in Philadelphia, in June 1917, and it was straightaway sent to France. In the seventeen months leading to the November 1918 armistice, the 5th Regiment was in the thick of such campaigns as Aisne-Marne, Meuse-Argonne, Marbache, and St. Mihiel.

It had actually arrived in Korea on August 2, 1950, a month ahead of the rest of the 1st Division. The war was going very badly for the South Koreans, and when the 5th Regiment landed at Pusan, it became the first Marine ground unit to enter the conflict. The regiment was in the forefront of the drive to hold on to what became known as the Pusan Perimeter and thus prevent the North from having control over the peninsula. For much of 1952 the commanding officer of the 5th Marines had been Colonel Culhane, and by the fall, the CO was Colonel Smoak.

He would be replaced toward the end of the year by a thirty-nine-year-old Kansan, Lew Walt. He became a Marine second lieutenant in July 1936 and saw service in China. With a wide, seemingly jovial face and a winning smile, Walt would become one of the handful of Marine officers to see combat in World War II, Korea, and Vietnam. Along the way, he was awarded two Navy Crosses and two Distinguished Service Medals, and he was a four-star general when he retired. Walt collected some of that hardware while leading the 2nd Battalion, 5th Regiment, on Guadalcanal, where he was wounded, and on New

Britain and Peleliu. He was a full bird colonel when he was assigned to be the commanding officer of the 5th Marines in Korea.

As that war dragged on, the outposts along the Main Line of Resistance in western Korea evolved into defense stations manned by a platoon or sometimes only a squad or two. In between the outposts were minefields and stretches of barbed wire to deter the enemy from attempting to filter through the gaps. The 1st Division section of the MLR was a series of long, sinuous trenches six to eight feet deep dotted with bunkers, weapons emplacements, and what were simply called "fighting holes."

Every day—or, more accurately, concerning the enemy, every night—the MLR defenses were probed, and such forays were interspersed with outbursts of small-arms or mortar fire. The Chinese would let loose some artillery from time to time too, though such assaults were usually reserved for supporting all-out infantry attacks. Despite being closest to the enemy, the Marines manning the outposts had an advantage—if the action got really hot and the outpost was in danger of being overrun, they could fall back to the MLR and the much greater firepower it issued. The men on the MLR did not have such a "luxury," because retreat and allowing the defense to cave in was just not an option.

Many of the Marines at outposts on the hills and ridges slept in collections of bunkers and tents that resembled what a hundred years earlier had been frontier mining camps near where gold had been found in Montana or the Klondike. The bunkers consisted of timbers anywhere from six to twelve inches thick, with the walls buttressed by sandbags. Doing the construction were Korean Service Corps workers, who would use picks and shovels to dig the hole and carry the timbers uphill. There was an effort to use prefabricated bunkers, but it proved not too practical to haul them and install them while the enemy, especially sharpshooters, was watching.

There was little comfort in these structures that—in theory, anyway—could survive a hit from a 105-mm or even a 120-mm shell. A typical bunker could accommodate four men snugly. If it had to contain a fifth, his bunk was a sort of shelf cut into the earthen wall that previously had held canned goods and maybe grenades and racy magazines. A Marine better not be claustrophobic, because this sleeping berth was only two feet high, so after he had wriggled himself in and was lying down the earth was only a foot or so above his face. It was common to hear curses muttered during the night after a Marine got up to relieve himself and banged his head into the dank roof in the process. Worse, a heavy enemy shell landing near enough to the bunker could shake everything loose and bury all of a bunker's occupants. Mother Nature could be considered an enemy too because enough of a soaking rain could loosen the earth under a bunker.

This was life for the Marines in the fall of 1952. It was hell to stay, but they couldn't go forward or backward. There were no defining battles or even moments that caused an irrevocable change in the war. As one senior Marine explained to his younger officers, "In this kind of stable warfare we've got right now, you don't really think in terms of a major offensive. That's for spring. But even in winter you can't go to ground. That's no good for morale, no good for Marines. You keep on the prod, jabbing away at them, keeping them off balance and nervous, bringing in prisoners, maintaining the aggressive spirit of the men. This is the sort of patrol you will be sending out, leading yourself in some cases, just getting out there and snooping around without a shot. It's a game for young officers, tough young men who stay cool and think fast."

There were flare-ups at Bunker Hill, but so far the concentrated combat of August had not been repeated. Among the other hills the Communists coveted were Carson, Reno, and Vegas. They were well forward of the MLR, giving the observers of the 2nd Battalion, 7th

Regiment, opportunities to track Chinese movements. The position, though, also made them more vulnerable to attack. It was crucial that these hills not fall into enemy hands because then the Chinese could fire down upon the MLR defense positions.

The three hills had been so named by Lieutenant Colonel Anthony Caputo, the commanding officer of the 2nd Battalion in the 7th Regiment. "When I looked at how they were positioned and being forward of the Main Line of Resistance like that, I figured it would be a gamble to hold on to them," recalled Colonel Caputo during an interview in May 2013, on the eve of his ninety-fourth birthday.

The New Jersey native had already had an illustrious Marine Corps career, which included being a groundbreaker in racial equality in the military. After graduating from the University of Pennsylvania in 1941, he enlisted and was sent to the Officer Candidates School in Quantico. Caputo went from there to the Marine base at New River, North Carolina (which later became Camp Lejeune). Montford Point was part of the camp, and that was where a new program began—to train black men for combat service, the first ones allowed to join the Marines. "I felt that I had a part in history," he said more than seventy years later.

He certainly did. From the initiation of the program, with Caputo, a newly minted captain, being given the first company that came through the gates to be schooled in the ways of war, 20,000 African American recruits were trained at Montford Point. More than 13,000 served overseas during World War II, and Caputo was with some of them. In January 1944, when a contingent of these new and now highly trained Marines who were designated the 51st Defense Battalion were deployed to the Pacific Theater, they went from island to island, wherever they were most needed. (During his tenure at Montford Point, Caputo married Mary Bowen of Burgaw, North Carolina, a newspaper reporter. The couple celebrated their seventy-first anniversary in November 2013.)

Caputo went on to be part of the bloody invasion of Okinawa. After the war he held assignments at Camp Lejeune and Quantico. He was with the 1st Marine Division when it shipped out to Korea. Even though he had faced fierce Japanese fighters, the enemy in Korea impressed him. "The Chinese were tough and they fought without regard for their lives," he remembers. "They were relentless, and they simply just charged ahead. You had to give everything to stop them. Thankfully, that is what Marines did."

One of the outposts that Caputo named, Reno, was the farthest from the Main Line of Resistance and the most difficult for the Marines to get to. Workers of the Korean Service Corps had dug a trench across saddles, and it was through this trench, and only at night, that supplies and replacements reached the outpost. Marines were dug in on the reverse slopes because Chinese-held high ground looked down on the hill. The outpost could accommodate only thirty-six Marines, not enough to withstand a full-scale attack. Every night, Lieutenant Colonel Caputo sent a platoon to take a position behind Reno—it became known as the Reno Block—so it could provide support fast. It was only a matter of time before the enemy made its move for all three hills. Possessing them would be a big chip at the Panmunjom poker table.

The most vigorous attempt to take those outposts was still several months away. Arguably the fiercest fighting of the fall was the battle for an area known as the Hook. It was a bare crescent-shaped ridge on high ground that intersected the Jamestown Line where it curved south. Two outposts, Warsaw and Seattle, had offered some protection for the Marines guarding the Hook, until the latter was grabbed by the Chinese. The Hook was the key to keeping possession of the Samichon and Imjin valleys. If it fell into enemy hands, the 1st Marine Division and the British Commonwealth Division next to it would have to retreat and take up new positions two miles to the south, closer to Seoul. For the U.N. forces and truce negotiators, a lot of precious real estate would be lost.

In the third week of October, the Chinese gathered as many as ten battalions of artillery, and their gunners set their sights on the Hook and the MLR on either side of it. The enemy also amassed seven thousand troops. Bracing for the attack were the 7th Marines, with four thousand men, accompanied by a tank company and thirty-eight pieces of artillery. Winter was on the way. By October 26, the low temperature dropped to twenty-eight degrees. It would get much colder than that for the Marines on alert . . . if they survived that night.

Days earlier, a few units of the Chinese artillery had begun to speak. Twelve hundred rounds rained on the Hook on October 24. Marine and enemy artillery traded salvos on the following day. There was more of the same on the 26th, with the intensifying Chinese fire covering for its troops moving forward and staying concealed while the sun was still up. When dusk arrived, so did the enemy assault.

The nearby outposts Ronson and Warsaw were hit first. Both positions were taken by the overwhelming Chinese attack, and only three of the Marine defenders survived. But the Hook was the main target, and the position was manned by Charlie Company, 1st Battalion. "A veritable avalanche of explosives and steel began to saturate trenches on the Hook" was one description of what occurred next. A Marine after-action report estimated as many as thirty-four thousand artillery and mortar rounds were fired by the enemy.

It was too much for the company to withstand. The Chinese reached and cleared out trenches. In short order they brought up laborers to begin constructing defensive positions. The strategy was not just to take the Hook but to keep it. And while they were at it, the Chinese sought to seize the opportunity of punching a big hole through that entire section of the MLR.

In darkness, after another artillery and mortar barrage, a large force—one account stated that it was a "charge of thousands of Chinese troops"—hurled themselves at the Marines. Some Chinese troops advanced far enough that they overran a forward observation post manned by a unit of the 2nd Battalion. The officer in command was Second Lieutenant Sherrod Skinner Jr. The Connecticut native and Harvard University graduate—as was his twin brother, David, who also joined the Marine Corps—was three days shy of his twenty-third birthday.

Skinner had been busy well before this latest assault. For hours he had been exhorting the men in the trenches to hold. Once, when the Chinese threatened to overrun his command, Skinner called for an artillery strike so close to his position that it was something of a miracle that he and his men survived. His radio hadn't survived the shelling, though, so trying that desperate tactic again was no longer an option. There was no choice but to hold with the men and weapons available. Lieutenant Skinner repeatedly exposed himself to the enemy so he could direct machine-gun fire, and he dashed behind the lines to grab and carry fresh ammunition and grenades. Twice enemy bullets found Skinner and he was losing blood from those wounds.

Finally, at the height of the attack and with their ammunition spent, the observers' position was overrun. Skinner just managed to order his men to feign being dead. They pretended so well that enemy soldiers didn't detect the deception even when searching the "bodies." Unfortunately, one would soon be truly dead. When a grenade was tossed into a bunker, the selfless lieutenant threw himself on it to save the two other Marines lying next to him, "fully absorbing the full force of the explosion and sacrificing his life for his comrades." His family would receive the posthumous Medal of Honor, and in 1991, Skinner Hall at the U.S. Marine Corps headquarters in Quantico, Virginia, was dedicated to him.

In the early hours of October 27, the Marines managed to stall the enemy's advance. However, the Chinese had obtained a solid foothold in a breach of the MLR, including most of the Hook, and they were digging in for the duration. The best way to ruin the enemy's plan was to counterattack right away, no matter how exhausted the Marines were. The responsibility fell to Able Company of the 1st Battalion, 7th Regiment.

The 2nd Platoon set off first, right before dawn. As the Marines advanced they were subjected to the fire coming from Charlie Company's old positions as well as from newly captured outposts. The remaining men of Charlie were also part of the attack, as were tanks, 11th Regiment artillery, and air strikes delivering 1,300-pound bombs on the Chinese defenders. Able Company advanced as far as it could; then How Company of the 3rd Battalion was ordered to join in. When they got as far as they could, it was the turn of Item Company, from the same battalion. Their attack began at 1350, or 1:50 in the afternoon. Later that afternoon the Marines of Baker 1/7 were also ordered to retake the Hook.

With artillery, mortar, and tank shells plunging into the Hook as well as Marine F-4U Corsairs flying through the air, the fighting raged all day. It continued after the sun set because the Chinese were determined not to retreat and the Americans were at least equally determined to make them retreat. There was a pause shortly after midnight. Ground troops waited while the Chinese positions were pasted by artillery; then at 3:40 a.m. Baker Company resumed the advance. Grudgingly, the defenders gave way. By dawn, Marines had regained the Hook.

The loss and immediate recapture of the Hook from October 26 to 28 saw some of the fiercest fighting of the entire war. And it was the first time that the Jamestown Line, the Marines' section of the MLR, had been breached and held for any length of time. The Battle of the Hook had to be fought to its full conclusion, whatever the cost, because it simply could not be yielded to the enemy.

That cost was a high one—at least seventy Marines dead and more than four hundred wounded, taken prisoner, and missing. The Chinese had paid an even higher price for ultimately no gain, with 532 reported killed and an untold number of wounded.

There would be no end of hostilities for the rest of the year, but both sides had to pay more attention to preparing for winter. During the same month as the battle for the Hook, a certain lieutenant in the 5th Marines, wounded a few days earlier in a separate action, had lain awake thinking about a horse to help in combat by transporting ammunition up the hills to beleaguered outposts and firing positions.

If he could find the right one, Eric Pedersen believed, the relative lull of the winter offered an opportunity to train it. Given more than two years of warfare, for all he knew there wasn't a decent horse left in Seoul, but he aimed to find out. The lieutenant could not have imagined he would find a racehorse who had been on her way to becoming a champion.

CHAPTER FIVE

★ ★

The River Crossing

When Kim Huk Moon had returned to racing to support his family, he did so with the help of Choi Chang Ju. He was a fellow rider at the Sinseul-dong track who in previous races had tried to beat the courageous Flame-of-the-Morning. He had been thwarted by the unbeatable combination of Kim and his horse. Choi was more friend than rival, though, and when Flame-of-the-Morning died it was he who provided the mare to nurse the motherless filly.

Choi went beyond that generous gesture. With Kim so filled with grief that he could not even look at the copper-colored filly, Choi took care of her. He and his mare raised the "twins," as he called the two young horses, asking nothing in return. And when Kim said he needed to earn money, Choi, whose stable had expanded to several horses, hired him as his main rider. Even with vision in only one eye, Kim won more than he lost, and for the two friends there was money to be made in horse racing as South Korea's economy improved in the late 1940s.

Kim could not forget the filly, but he avoided her because seeing her would bring fresh pangs of grief. It was a surprise, then, that when he encountered her sixteen months after her birth, he was filled with wonder rather than sorrow. One morning Kim arrived at Sinseul-dong and saw Flame—since she was the spitting image of her mother, everyone there simply called her that—in the center field of the track with several other young horses. Suddenly, she broke away from them at a gallop. To the young man, it seemed that his beloved Ah-Chim-Hai had come back to life, but with three instead of four white stockings. Kim knew of the Buddhist teachings about reincarnation, and there could be no better evidence of it than the new Flame.

Grief was gone, replaced by amazement and joy. A few moments later, what Kim felt was fear. Flame had run to one corner of the field and was just turning to come back when three growling dogs appeared from under the railing. Flame galloped faster, but the dogs were at her, nipping at her legs and rump. If the vicious animals brought her down, they would tear into her and possibly cripple her, or worse.

Kim leaped over the railing and ran to intercept Flame and the dogs. His waves and shouts caught the dogs' attention. Two stopped in their tracks as Flame veered toward Kim, terrified. She halted behind him. The third dog had stayed in pursuit, but a kick from Kim per-suaded it to reevaluate its plans. The grateful horse leaned her head against him, and Kim put an arm around her neck. It was, indeed, like having his best friend in his life again, and all the love that he'd thought had evaporated came flowing back.

Kim and the beautiful, swift Flame would become a new winning team.

He knew it deep in his bones, and this is what he told the frisky filly as he rubbed her down in her stall. Kim also apologized for ig-noring her all this time, for blaming Flame for her mother's death. He had not been strong enough to see past his grief. Things would be different now.

And they were, in ways that Kim could not have anticipated. During the next few months, Flame took easily to the training to be a racehorse—quicker, in fact, than he would have thought possible. Hard to believe, but Flame seemed to be more intelligent than her mother. Conceivably, some intelligence could have been passed along from her father, but Kim knew little about that stallion in Pusan. He suspected that indeed Flame had been reincarnated with a stronger, healthier brain as well as body. Whatever she had of the stallion, he could not see it.

It would have been too much too soon for Kim to ride the horse so early in her training, but he had a willing volunteer who could: Yon, the son of his late sister, Nam Soon. The boy sat atop Flame as Kim led her around by a rope. Finally, though, Kim's turn came. Flame had what was described as a sort of "rocking horse gait," and feeling her strength and easy rhythm under him, Kim knew he had a horse that could be even a greater champion than her mother.

There was more evidence of this in races that the Sinseul-dong track hosted. Flame easily outran the competition, which included a few of Choi's horses. Good-naturedly, he would mutter in Kim's presence the Korean equivalent of "No good deed goes unpunished." After every victory, Flame pranced with pride. She had a humanlike confidence in her abilities. In the eyes of everyone who worked at the racetrack and who had cheered from the stands, Flame was a champion and would go on to national glory.

And there was national glory to be had. Horse racing in Korea dated back to the 1890s, when a foreign-language institute run by the national government held a horse race on its annual day of sports. It was not until 1914 that there was a day of racing that the public could attend. What is considered modern horse racing in Korea began in 1922, when betting on contests was introduced and the Chosun (or Joseon) Racing Club was formed. It was soon followed by other racing clubs—with pari-mutuel betting introduced the following year—and they all were collected under the umbrella of the Chosun Horse Affairs Authority. The Sinseul-dong racetrack opened to the public in 1928. It would not be the only track for horse racing in Korea, but it was an especially popular one, since it was located in Seoul, the capital city, and the most well-known horses competed there.

In 1945, as World War II was winding down, the new umbrella organization was the Korean Racing Authority, which, according to the *Horse Racing News*, was designed "to restore the national identity in horse racing." This goal was waylaid when the Korean War broke out five years later. The physical, emotional, and financial toll on Korean citizens robbed them of any interest in horse racing, with simple survival becoming of much keener interest. The racetracks constructed during more prosperous times were turned into sites for military training or abandoned altogether. Most of the horses were abandoned too, stolen by desperate families for plowing or other chores, captured and taken away by North Korean troops, or meeting worse fates.

But in the years after the war, horse racing and its popularity were up and running. Successful horses and their jockeys were stars. By the time Flame turned two years old, in June 1950, she was on her way. She waited patiently enough right before a race began, perhaps focusing herself mentally as well as physically. Aboard her, Kim was coiled like a spring, the nervous one of the two. Suddenly, the horses sprang ahead. Sometimes, bored with the efforts of the other horses, Flame ran with abandon and ended the race quickly. But there were times when Kim felt Flame ease up so she could toy with her rivals. Most remarkable was that she seemed to know in some way about Kim's blindness because she would never let another horse get up close to her on his bad side.

Kim and everyone at the Sinseul-dong track, including the big-hearted Choi, were excited about the beginning of the summer racing season. More spectators would see Flame for the champion she was, and Kim would make enough money to comfort his family for quite a while.

On June 25, without warning, the Communist North Koreans invaded South Korea. Suddenly, only five years after the Japanese occupiers had been banished, the country was at war again. Worse, it was once more being overrun by enemy forces bent on enslaving the people. Obviously, Seoul was an immediate target of the ruthless invaders.

Choi's reaction was to arrange to send his horses south to safety to be cared for by his Chinese father. Then, he said, he would enlist in the Republic of Korea Army to help repel the Communists. Kim realized he would have to move his family and Flame to safety, and quickly. Once that was accomplished, he too would join the army. He was familiar with Pusan and it was, he assumed, far enough to the south, so that was where they would go. Already in the distance, like an approaching storm, the thunder of artillery could be heard.

The Kim family and Flame escaped just in time, but it wasn't easy. As humble as it was, the mud hut had been the Kims' home since Mother Kim had married her husband, and she could not bear to leave it. She simply refused to go, no matter how much her son reasoned with her. What changed her mind was the frightening sound of the big guns drawing closer and seeing her neighbors, some of whom had lived there longer than she had, gathering their possessions and heading south.

The family's transportation would be a night soil cart someone had left behind, with Flame pulling it. If Kim had had the time to think about it, he would have been bitterly disappointed at how his dreams of racing championships had been dashed, and the humiliation of having Flame be nothing more than a cart horse, as Flame-of-the-Morning had been at the Japanese labor camp. But such painful ruminations would have to wait. The Communists were certainly not waiting to capture his country's capital city and everyone who was not swift enough to leave it.

Kim loaded the family's meager possessions in the cart and placed his mother, niece, and nephew atop them. His sister, Chung Soon, sat beside him at the front. He flicked the reins and Flame began pulling. Kim's love and admiration for the horse grew at the way she took on the burden of carrying his family to safety. He could not have anticipated that the journey would be so harrowing, and tragic.

It was slow going. Even with Kim leaving the cart to walk beside Flame, with the burden of hauling four people the horse could only plod along. And the rutted roads were choked with thousands of others evacuating the capital city, who were in turn nearly suffocated by the dirt and dust kicked up into the hot and sultry summer air. There was some relief after the sun set, but weariness was setting in, especially for Flame, though she made stubborn progress one step after another. Kim could not help but recall the persistence of her mother—she too would never quit.

At the ferry station on the bank of the Han River the journey almost ended—Kim and his family were confronted by thousands ahead of them waiting to cross. It might be days before their turn came, and by then they could be overtaken by the Communists. They could not even get past the throng of people to go farther down the river and reach the Yeongdeungo Bridge. Yet turning back meant death, or a living hell created by the cruelty of the Communists.

Kim had an idea. Its success, though, depended on Flame being an even more amazing horse than he knew she was. He turned the cart back upriver, away from the crowd of desperate refugees. Above the village of Chusong-Jong, he found a place where the river was narrower. He unhitched Flame and led her to the water's edge. "We must swim across," he told her.

She understood instantly. Her body quivered, excited by the challenge, and she nodded her head and flared her nostrils. Kim led his sister off the cart and to Flame. He instructed Chung Soon to hold Flame's tail and to not let go until they reached the other side of the dark river. He took hold of Flame's mane and the three of them entered the water. Thankfully, because of the dry conditions of summer, the river was shallow enough that Flame's hooves could dig into the bottom for some distance. When the time came to swim, the red filly did so easily. After what seemed like hours, they all could feel the bottom again.

In the darkness, Kim's eyes searched for flat, smooth ground on the south side of the river. When he found a welcoming spot, he told Chung Soon that he would go back across the river and send their nephew next. There would be no choice but to send Flame across the river once more with their niece by herself because the terrified Mother Kim could not be left alone in the dark.

Flame was used to having Yon on her back, though under her would be a track, not water with no bottom. After the boy slid off into Chung Soon's arms, Flame and Kim reentered the water without hesitation. Kim marveled at the young horse's strength—was there nothing Flame couldn't do? Next she transported Nam Soon. The child was frightened, but the strength and calm of the brave filly were reassuring. Nam Soon didn't even seem to notice that Kim had stayed behind on the north bank of the river.

Finally, it was Mother Kim's turn. The horse breathed more heavily after returning this time than on the previous trips. The loads she carried were not heavy, but battling the river currents during six treks back and forth was exhausting. This would be the last one, at least. The only question was if the horse would be carrying Mother Kim.

The old woman was panicking. Crossing a gurgling river in the dark on a horse held countless terrors for her. She insisted on being left behind. Kim tried to explain how Flame had carried the others across without incident, but his mother was beyond reasoning. He had no choice but to take Mother Kim off the cart and into the water. He held her with one arm while his other hand held fast to Flame's tail. Once more the small horse set off.

This was the slowest crossing of them all. Flame was clearly tiring. She struggled against the current to keep on a straight line to the waiting Chung Soon and children. And the water had not felt as cold before. Flame stumbled emerging from the river, and was breathing heavier than before, but she had delivered her cargo safely. Even though Mother Kim was shivering and whimpering from the shocking experience, the family had left Seoul and thousands of refugees behind on the other side of the Han River. They were safe.

Or so Kim thought. Without the cart, he and his sister and Yon had to walk beside Flame, who carried Mother Kim and the young Nam Soon. They could go only as fast as the boy's legs went, except when Kim summoned enough strength to carry him. They could still hear the sound of artillery, as though the Communists were pursuing them. They were slowed further when Mother Kim needed to rest, and these pauses became more frequent. The old woman was ill. The fright and the cold water had overwhelmed her fragile system.

She did not survive to see Pusan. Kim buried his mother north of the city, on a hillside that looked down on the Nakdong River. He had only Chung Soon and his young nephew and niece left. And, of course, Flame. She was a member of the family too.

Reaching Pusan, Kim was able to find the man who owned the stallion that had sired Flame. He saw immediately how tired and underweight the sorrel horse was and he was kind enough to provide food and shelter for Kim and his diminished family. As he had vowed to Choi, Kim tried to enlist in the army. But as hard-pressed for men as his country was, he was rejected because of his blind eye. Kim was not too disappointed, because he had no answer for how his family could fend for themselves if he was off to the north fighting the invaders.

While remaining in Seoul might have been a death sentence, Pusan almost turned out not to be a refuge at all. The South Korean army melted like spring snow before the relentless Communist advance of an estimated hundred thousand troops. There was one defeat after another as the south fell under North Korean control. Any hopes that the loss of Seoul would be the worst event of the new war faded fast as the Communists neared Pusan, in South Korea's southeast corner.

The government begged the United Nations, and the United States in particular, for help. But there was none immediately available. American forces across the board in Southeast Asia had experienced reductions in the years following the Japanese surrender. All that was left to call upon to save South Korea was the 24th Infantry Division of the 8th Army, and that was in Japan. Though it was below strength and the soldiers had to contend with aging weaponry, the division was ordered to Pusan. From there it marched north on what could be a suicide mission. Its mandate was to engage the much larger Communist force and try to slow it down while other allied units arrived and got organized.

For weeks, the 24th was on its own to face the onslaught. Though defeated in the Battle of Osan on July 5, the brave men of the division gave ground grudgingly. They also took it on the chin in battles around Chochiwon, Chonan, and Pyongtaek. The sheer numbers of the North Koreans were too much for the Americans . . . almost. They were doing what they had to do: slowing down what had been during the first two weeks of the war an uninhibited advance.

The 24th made one last stand in the Battle of Taejon in the third week of July. Again it was battered and bruised—but the division had finally bought enough time and thus saved Pusan from at least immediate surrender. The rest of the 8th Army had arrived, as had various U.N. units, and elements of the 1st Marine Division were on the way. The number of allied troops was now roughly equal to that of the North Koreans.

But the fact remained that for the Kim family and all the other terrified civilians, the region, except for the port in Pusan, was surrounded. During the first week in August, the enemy confronted what became known as the Pusan Perimeter, the three-sided, 140-mile-long last line of defense. If it broke and the North Koreans captured Pusan and its port, the war would be over, having lasted barely six weeks. Such a stunning defeat, with the loss of tens of thousands of troops killed and captured, would have been spoken of in the same breath as Gallipoli and Dunkirk. If the United Nations tried to continue fighting, without the port to accommodate troops and equipment, the allies would have had to storm the Korean beaches and try to gain footholds against an entrenched enemy. The Marines had learned what a bloody job that was in the Pacific Theater during the previous war.

Maybe it helped to realize that the only alternative was being pushed into the Korea Strait and having to swim for Japan, because the allies stood their ground. The perimeter was manned mostly by units of the U.S. Army, the British Army, and the Republic of Korea Army. For six weeks the North Koreans threw themselves at the long defensive line, needing just that one punch powerful enough to break through. They didn't have it. The allied commanders recognized that time was on their side. By controlling the Pusan port, they could continue to add troops, including units of the 1st Marine Division, and supplies to compensate for losses. The North Korean troops were far from home and their main supply bases, and as their savage attacks were repelled, the high body count took its toll on personnel that could not be replaced that far south. The allies' superiority in the air blew holes in the attackers too.

Finally, the combination of dwindling men and resources and the completely unanticipated landing at Inchon to the north proved to be too much for the enemy to tolerate. The North Koreans turned their backs on Pusan and hurried north. They would not stop for weeks more, and their retreat became a rout with General Douglas MacArthur's forces from several countries in hot pursuit.

With Pusan safe and all the reports proclaiming that the North Koreans were on the run, some Seoul residents yearned to return to their homes. Kim was among them. In his view, every Marine was like his POW friend Sergeant Duffy, and if there were thousands of them, the enemy stood no chance. That had certainly been a huge victory with the successful invasion of Inchon, perhaps breaking the back of the Communists. In his most hopeful moments, Kim envisioned the Sinseul-dong track being unscathed by the fighting, the war ending in just a few weeks, and him atop Flame in races in the following year. When word arrived that Seoul had been recaptured by the U.N. forces, Kim was more than hopeful.

But the war did not end in a few weeks, even though the allies swept up through South Korea and into North Korea. There were rumors that November of 1950 that Supreme Commander MacArthur would lead an invasion of China, escalating the war, or that to preempt that, and to prevent North Korea from being removed from Communist control, the Chinese would stream across the Yalu River, as plentiful as ants, and fight the allies south of it. With the immediate future being so uncertain and winter approaching, Kim decided that he and his family would remain in Pusan.

The absence of fighting there was the only real advantage. Food was scarce. Every day for Kim was a new adventure in foraging and pleading for scraps from soldiers to feed his family and Flame. With her, he took whatever work he could find, which included hauling food and munitions from the ships in the harbor—increasingly, they were American ones—to supply dumps around the city. But when Kim heard the news of the allied advance being reversed at the Chosin Reservoir and soon after that the combined Communist forces of North Korea and China had retaken Seoul, he knew that his decision to stay had been the right one.

CHAPTER SIX

★ ★

Return to Seoul

Before setting off to see Colonel Smoak, Eric Pedersen rifled through his possessions and managed to come up with a total of $250 cash. If this had been Wyoming or Southern California, he'd have had a pretty good idea of the value of a strong, healthy horse, and $250 wouldn't come even close. But this was Korea after more than two years of devastating war, it was all he had, and maybe it would be enough.

When he arrived at the 5th Marines command post, Pedersen had to cool his heels for a while, but eventually he was ushered in to see the colonel. Smoak heard him out. He knew Pedersen was one of the regiment's best officers and had been a "mustang" in World War II, meaning he had distinguished himself so well as an enlisted man and noncommissioned officer that he had been given a battlefield promotion to lieutenant. And what the heck, it seemed a benign enough activity for the young man to spend a day or two out of harm's way scouring Seoul for a horse. And whatever nag or candidate for the glue factory he found, Pedersen was paying for it with his own money.

Colonel Smoak shrugged and gave his permission. He could not possibly have known what he set in motion with that shrug.

Pedersen requisitioned a jeep and recruited Sergeant Berry and Corporal Philip Carter from his platoon to accompany him. After hooking a two-wheeled trailer onto the back of the jeep, the three Marines left for the capital city.

Lieutenant Pedersen was certainly not the first officer in a twentieth-century conflict to think that some kind of pack animal could be of use on the front lines. In the First World War, as many as sixteen different kinds of animals were deployed. These included thousands of camels in the British Imperial Camel Corps, and that kingdom's cavalry boasted close to a million riding horses. Horses also pulled artillery and other heavy guns along with carts of ammunition and various supplies, as did thousands of mules and oxen. There were winged warriors too, with hundreds of thousands of homing pigeons employed. (In World War II, G.I. Joe, a British pigeon with American training, flew twenty miles in twenty minutes, arriving at an American air base with a message in time to prevent bombers from taking off to destroy an Italian city that British forces had just occupied.) But Pedersen was the first officer to actually do something about it in the Korean War, when for the American military, at least, three decades after the end of World War I, animals were in the process of being discarded, not embraced.

Every Marine who had to run back to get more ammunition was one less Marine fighting on the front lines; a pack animal would resolve that problem. The recoilless rifle had proven to be an enormously effective weapon against the Communists, and even with men spending time fetching instead of fighting, there were times when the gun crews ran out of shells. Several times in the six months that Pedersen had been in Korea he'd had to watch through binoculars with mounting frustration as emboldened enemy troops and tanks gained ground in the absence of recoilless rifle fire.

Given his family background, if anyone knew weapons it was the lanky lieutenant. And as an experienced combat Marine and platoon leader, he also knew that at the most basic level Marine units were organized to deliver firepower most effectively. A rifle platoon operated on a very simple premise: One man cannot be expected during a fight to control the actions of more than three other men and still keep a keen eye on what the enemy is doing. Thus, a rifle platoon consisted of three squads, usually commanded by sergeants, and in each squad were three fire teams, each with a corporal in charge. It would be terribly inefficient, and deadly, for a platoon leader to try to give orders to close to forty men while under fire. So the lieutenant gave orders to his three squad leaders, and each in turn gave orders to his three fire team leaders. Woe to the sergeant or corporal who screwed up that low-level chain of command.

With weapons, the vast majority were ones that could be carried and used effectively by a single Marine and that were made in the United States. The primary rifles were the M-1 Garand, a .30-caliber, gas-operated automatic weapon with an eight-round internal clip, weighing 9.5 pounds (add a pound for a bayonet), firing thirty rounds per minute, and with a range of about 600 yards, and the less-desirable M-1 .30-caliber carbine, which at 6.5 pounds was easy for a Marine to carry, but its range was only 325 yards, and with a shorter barrel it had less accuracy and velocity. The pistol of choice was the M-1911A1 .45-caliber, a semiautomatic that carried seven rounds in a detachable box magazine, weighing three pounds and with an effective range of 30 yards.

The typical fire team had the M-1918A2 Browning Automatic Weapon as its core dispenser of destruction. At strength in Korea, a Marine platoon had six BARs. The gun had the effective combination of being able to fire fast and accurately. It weighed 19.4 pounds and had a range of almost a thousand meters, which was actually farther than a Marine could see a target to shoot at. The BAR used the same .30-caliber ammo as the M-1 Garand, could fire semi- or fully automatically, had a 20-round detachable box magazine, and could expel three hundred to six hundred rounds per minute from the shoulder or supported by a bipod.

The combination of this kind of firepower and the way a unit was organized at its foundation made a Marine Corps company the best fighting unit in the world.

Was a BAR more effective than a recoilless rifle? Both were very effective, serving different purposes. A BAR could harass but not stop a tank. And a Marine with a BAR couldn't expect to kill an enemy soldier he couldn't see. A 75-mm recoilless rifle shell could go through things, such as any kind of structure or defensive works shielding the enemy as well as disable a tank or piece of artillery.

The look of a recoilless rifle, which some old-timers still referred to as the "recoilless gun," was something like a combination of rifle and bazooka. Like a bazooka, the gases that propelled the shell rushed out of the rear of the tube. Unlike a rocket launcher, a recoilless rifle launched actual artillery shells, and for much longer distances.

The rifle was developed as a weapon to use against tanks and was introduced into combat by the Germans in World War II. Late in the war the Japanese developed a similar weapon as they prepared for the anticipated invasion of the mainland by American forces. By the time the Korean War began, the American military had recoilless rifles of its own.

The American version had a range of several thousand yards, so enemy soldiers and equipment could be punished before they even spotted a Marine position. So as effective as a BAR was, recoilless rifles were essential to countering the firepower the Chinese and remaining North Korean units directed at the Main Line of Resistance outposts. The "fire curtain" that the intense use of the rifles could create could intimidate even the most loyal or zealous Communist soldier being ordered to charge forward.

But there were a couple of drawbacks. One was that despite what the manufacturer's manual stated, there was a back blast when a recoilless rifle was fired. The smoke and dust and small rocks kicked out and up by the back blast was a giveaway to the enemy of the gun crew's position. Marines had learned early on that after firing only a few rounds, they had to hustle to a new position before being targeted by Communist artillery or mortars. The other drawback, of course, was having to keep the weapon supplied with shells.

That summer of 1952, Kim Huk Moon began to think that it finally would be safe to return to Seoul. The city had been recaptured in March by the Americans and their allies. After a few months, it seemed that not only would the war not be so far south as Pusan again but his home city was secure enough to risk returning.

Though it had been a hard time living in Pusan for almost a year, he and Chung Soon had always been able to work to provide food and shelter for Yon and Nam Soon and Flame. The work Flame had to do was unrelieved drudgery, but the iron-willed horse never shirked or complained. However, she was excited the morning that Kim hooked her up to the battered old cart and placed the children and their few possessions in it, as though she knew they were going home. And home, they all hoped, meant racing, where the red mare with the white blaze could truly shine, to fulfill her destiny as a champion, and not be just another workhorse.

As harsh and humiliating as life was for the former racehorse in her much-reduced circumstances, that Flame was still being cared for by a family of civilians was something of a miracle. As the summer of 1952 waned, many civilians in Korea could barely care for themselves. More than two years of war had robbed families of fathers and sons as well as homes and other possessions. There were few jobs in the urban areas, and in rural regions farmers eked out a living with the greatest difficulty. And there was always the fear that a war that had gone back and forth across the country during the first two years could return to areas in the south and devastate them all over again.

The many casualties cannot be attributed to simply the fortunes of war, with citizens being collateral damage as the two sides slugged it out. A shocking number of Koreans had been victims of massacres. Not just the Communists were perpetrators. On June 28, 1950, only three days after the war had begun with North Korea's invasion, the president of South Korea, Syngman Rhee, ordered what became known as the Bodo League Massacre. Right-wing groups were let loose to eventually murder as many as 100,000 suspected Communists and sympathizers.

Not to be outdone, when the North Koreans had taken over more and more territory in the first weeks of the war, their political officers had rounded up and killed every educated person they could find. It was believed that without academic and religious leaders (among others), the occupied Koreans would be unable to put up much resistance. North Korean officers also executed males who refused to join the Communist army. It is estimated that these mass executions and the South Korean males simply kidnapped and brought north as the North Koreans retreated in the fall of 1950 totaled as many as half a million men.

Two years later, few families remained intact. Women had been subjected to atrocities too, including rape and murder. Older family members died from exhaustion, malnutrition, and even hopelessness, which had surely contributed to Mrs. Kim's death. Children grew up in what passed for "households" that often were fatherless and that struggled to provide basic necessities. Some areas of South Korea had been turned into wastelands by battles, still littered by buried mines and unexploded artillery and mortar shells. This, in addition to the physical toll exacted by such abysmal surroundings and fractured families, made for cruel conditions for children to grow up in.

This was the environment that surrounded Flame and the remnants of the Kim family. Perhaps, once they got back to Seoul, life would be better.

But the prospect of a better life that would include the return to racing became more remote the closer the Kims got to Seoul. Each day as they plodded north, Kim observed the devastation of the countryside. The North Koreans had already taken what they could on their way to Pusan, and the battles that had accelerated their retreat north had destroyed roads, bridges, and even entire villages. Kim wondered if this had been Seoul's fate too.

Almost, as it turned out. The sturdy cart had to cross a rickety makeshift bridge over the Han River because the Yeongdeungo Bridge had been blown to bits. Buildings and entire blocks had met the same end in the city. Some streets were covered with rubble. A few buildings and landmarks remained intact, but some sections of the city where Kim had grown up were unrecognizable. This was worse than after the Japanese had left.

Miraculously, he found their home . . . or what was left of it. The roof was gone, as was one wall. Still, it was all they had. In the war-ravaged city there was material from collapsed buildings to scavenge, and before too long, with Chung Soon's help, Kim had made the small structure habitable. They couldn't help thinking about the years in the past when their parents and sister were alive. This made Kim even more grateful to have Flame, because she too was a connection to the past. He couldn't bear the thought of losing her, which was much the same way he thought about his sister and his nephew and niece.

And then he almost did lose Chung Soon. This was because the work she did turned out to be much more dangerous than either of them could have anticipated.

Rice not only sustained the family but provided brother and sister with work. While Yon looked after his sister at the family hut, Chung Soon went to work in nearby rice fields just outside Seoul, and Kim, with Flame hauling the cart, transported rice from the fields to government warehouses in the city. That Flame would ever race again, let alone return to her champion status, now appeared impossible.

As it was after the Japanese occupation, the Sinseul-dong track was in disrepair. It probably would have been in even worse state after two years of war and being used as an ammunition dump by the Communists during their occupation of the city, except the Americans had done some fixing up so the interior could be used as an airfield. The only horses that remained were, like Flame, employed as pack animals. Still, Kim and his horse liked to stop by the racetrack on their way home from work—maybe Flame remembered her triumphs with Kim astride her.

It was a wonderful surprise when during one visit they found Choi at the track. Kim marveled that his friend had survived the fighting. He had not returned unscathed, though. His battalion had fought with the U.S. Army's 2nd Division, and during a battle at Wonju his left arm had been so badly wounded that an Army surgeon had amputated it just below the elbow. Choi, always one to look on the bright side, thought it was a pretty good deal that his battle injury earned him a signed document giving him access to care at American military hospitals as well as a prosthetic arm when his stump was ready for the fitting.

It also earned Choi a daily ration of rice from the South Korean government, but he still offered to go to work with Kim and Chung Soon to help any way he could. It was on one of those days, as summer waned, that Chung Soon almost died.

With a group of others, she had been working a new section of the field. Suddenly, there was a powerful explosion. Bodies were tossed into the air, and parts of bodies too. One of the workers had stepped on a land mine, probably one of who knew how many such mines that the North Koreans had planted in that once-abandoned field. Other workers converged cautiously, wary of other land mines. Carefully, they dragged the ones who had survived the blast away from the smoking crater, leaving behind the four workers who clearly were dead. Chung Soon was among the survivors, but her left leg was badly mangled. A tourniquet was applied to stop the flow of blood.

She was put in a cart and carried home, where a doctor had been summoned. He saw immediately that the leg could not be saved, so he amputated what was left of it. Yon was sent to find Kim and Flame as they hauled rice, and Kim arrived shortly after the surgery. That his sister had been badly injured was agonizing enough for him, but the doctor explained that the amputation by itself might not save Chung Soon's life. She should be cared for in a hospital, but they were over-flowing with wounded soldiers. She should have painkillers and drugs to reduce the risk of infection. However, the doctor had none, and even if Kim could find where such drugs were available to Korean civilians, he could not possibly afford to purchase them.

As Chung Soon lay perspiring and whimpering, Kim felt more helpless than he had ever felt during all the previous trials of his life. Because he could do nothing, his beloved sister was doomed.

CHAPTER SEVEN

★ ★

The Empty Stall

Lieutenant Eric Pedersen and the two men from his platoon drove slowly along the rutted, explosion-damaged roads toward Seoul. The potholes were bad enough, but the Marines were unaccustomed to driving a military jeep with a trailer attached. How difficult might it be if on the return trip they actually had a horse in it? Or a mule?

The lieutenant had asked the colonel for a couple of days, but he hoped to be lucky enough to find one of the animals at an old racetrack or other facility where they were still kept, work out a deal with its owner, and be back to his regiment before sunset. The second half of October meant there were days that could still be full of sunlight with a tolerable temperature, but the nights could be below freezing. Most of the men on the MLR had already made the switch from warm-weather to cold-weather clothing.

The Sinseul-dong track was known to most Americans who had

spent any time in Seoul, and since it was being used by the American military, Pedersen decided to make that his first stop. If there were horses there, maybe he could find one that was not too broken-down, one that still had some mileage left to give. He hoped for a younger horse because an older one might not take to training too well or might not have the necessary stamina. In any case, if there were no horses at that racetrack, he could get directions to the next one.

A part of Pedersen wondered if this was a wild-goose chase. Even if it was, this journey was a day away from the war. There hadn't been many of those this year.

Chung Soon survived, thanks to Choi. Once again, he had come through for his friend's family.

When Choi heard of the land mine accident, he went to the Kim home as fast as he could. Seeing his friend helpless and the young woman in misery, Choi had an idea. He went out into the family's small yard, found a stick, and began beating the stump of his left arm with it. Kim tried to stop him, but Choi explained his plan. Then he staggered off to the nearest American military hospital.

Kim visited him there the next day. Choi's arm was so inflamed by the beating that he would have to remain in the hospital for several days. Most important, though, were the medications prescribed to him. He slipped some of his ration to Kim for his sister.

It was even better when Choi was discharged because he arrived at the Kim home with an American military doctor in tow. In a re-markable coincidence, this doctor, whom Choi had encountered in a hospital hallway, was the same one who had amputated Choi's arm in Wonju. The doctor examined Chung Soon and gave her medicine. He returned almost every day to treat her, and he brought food for the family as well. When the young woman was able to stand, the doctor had crutches waiting for her. By the time the doctor told them that he was being rotated home to America, Chung Soon was well.

Over the next few weeks, Chung Soon became accustomed to the crutches, and she could do normal household chores, but she could no longer work in the rice fields. Kim wondered about an artificial leg, but Choi told him that they were available to soldiers only, unless one had a lot of money, possibly as much as $200. Choi might as well have said a million dollars, especially with Kim now being the only wage earner in the family, though Choi contributed what he could from his labors.

One day in the third week of October the two young men and Flame stopped at the Sinseul dong track to give the copper-colored horse the kind of exercise that delighted her. Kim put an old saddle on her and off they went around the track. Flame was practically chortling with joy because of the freedom of galloping. Cheers arose from American soldiers lining the railing. When the ride was finished and he was rubbing Flame down, Kim had a wonderful vision of the war being over, the racetrack being filled with awestruck people, and his beautiful mare winning the big race. If that day ever came, maybe then he could buy a leg for his sister.

When he and Choi came back outside to go home, Kim saw three American Marines waiting for him. He was disappointed that none of them resembled his old friend Duffy, who had granted him ownership of his beloved Flame-of-the-Morning.

Lieutenant Pedersen and his two companions had arrived in time to see the last few minutes of the horse's run. Pedersen was not looking for a racehorse, but he had been impressed by the horse's energy and strength. And by her demeanor too, as she acknowledged the cheers of the aircrewmen on her way to the stable. This was a young horse who wouldn't quit when challenged.

Pedersen approached the two young men. The one who looked more Chinese than Korean spoke English. He displayed his arm and proudly explained how he had lost part of it fighting alongside American soldiers. He introduced his friend, Kim Huk Moon, who shook Pedersen's hand, smiling nervously. Choi explained that the horse, Flame, was owned by Kim.

Pedersen told Choi, who translated, his name and that he and his men every day fought the Communists north of Seoul. The platoon he commanded had oversized rifles that fired big, heavy shells. He was looking for a horse to carry those shells for the special rifles.

Choi hesitated before he translated to Kim, then concluded, "He says he wants to buy Flame."

The uneasy smile on the young man's face melted completely. Lieutenant Pedersen saw this and reached into his pocket. He took out the wad of green bills and told Choi, "Tell Kim Huk Moon that I can pay $250."

That didn't need to be translated. Kim knew that was a lot of money. From what Choi had told him weeks earlier, that would buy a leg for his sister with enough left over for food for a few months, and for improving the hut and purchasing clothing for the approaching winter. But to lose Flame . . . again?

There were a few other horses in the stalls behind them in addition to Flame. Kim almost said, "Tell the Marine to go look at them." But he didn't. This stranger was here to buy a horse for $250. By the end of the day, if Kim did not sell Flame, that money would be in someone else's pocket.

His heart breaking, Kim motioned for Choi to wait. He returned to the stalls to see Flame.

The red mare nuzzled him as he whispered to her that he was very sorry, but she was going away to live with and work for the American Marines. They were good men, like Duffy, who her mother, Flame-of-the-Morning, had known and helped to survive. The Marine named

Pedersen looked like a good man too, and Flame would belong to him now.

The horse was quiet, gazing solemnly at him. Kim knew she understood, and that now she would face a new challenge in her life. He whispered one more apology, caressed Flame's face and neck, and led her outside.

One can only speculate about what would have been the fate of this young Mongolian mare had she remained in the care of Kim Huk Moon and his family. No one knows what happened to them after Flame was purchased by Pedersen. Very likely, as the family continued to struggle and the war continued for close to another year, taking an ever greater toll on Korean civilians, Flame would have been sold—for a lot less money—and put to work. The worst-case scenario is she would have been starved or otherwise mistreated and would not have lived for as many years as she did.

So even though when Lieutenant Eric Pedersen arrived he was looking for a horse that would be put in harm's way, the best thing that happened to the future Sergeant Reckless was to be taken away to become a member of the 5th Marine Regiment and with it to continue this brutal war. Flame had found a new family.

But for Kim Huk Moon, it was one more reduction of his family— his father, Ah-Chim-Hai, his mother, his sister, and now Flame. This time, at least, there was a choice, and he knew he had made the right one.

After he helped to steer the horse into the two-wheeled wooden trailer and watched the Marines drive away with Flame, he retreated to the stalls where he could not be seen, fell onto a pile of straw, and cried.

PART II

★ ★

★ ★

CHAPTER EIGHT

A Four-Legged Female Marine?

As the jeep carrying Eric Pedersen and his two companions from the recoilless rifle platoon towed the trailer bearing Flame north to the 5th Marine Regiment's position on the Main Line of Resistance, the lieutenant, being an educated man with years of service in the military, may have reflected on the use of animals in war, especially those who had distinguished themselves.

In the Civil War, a few horses gained some renown because of the men they bore into battle—such as General Ulysses S. Grant's Cincinnati, General Stonewall Jackson's Little Sorrel, and especially General Robert E. Lee's Traveller. Pedersen may have known the saga of the Confederate commander's horse. His original name was Jeff Davis when he was born in 1857 in Blue Sulphur Springs, Virginia. He was an American Saddlebred of Grey Eagle stock, and as an adult he was a full 16 hands high and weighed 1,100 pounds. In the spring of 1861 he was commandeered by a Confederate Army unit and renamed Greenbriar. When the officer in charge of the unit, Robert E. Lee, was transferred to a new command in South Carolina the following February, he took the horse with him, with another name change, to Traveller.

In battles during the Civil War, General Lee and Traveller were inseparable. The horse not only had extraordinary stamina but appeared to the troops to be fearless. Lee rode him during every campaign of the Army of Northern Virginia through the surrender at Appomattox Courthouse in April 1865. Soon after, Lee wrote to his daughter Margaret that his horse looked like "a plucked chicken" because on the former general's journey to his new position at Washington College in Lexington, Virginia, people pinched hairs out of his horse as souvenirs.

General Lee died in 1870. During his funeral procession, Traveller was led behind the caisson bearing his owner's body, his saddle and bridle draped with black crepe. Only a year later, the fourteen-year-old Traveller was dead, having developed tetanus after stepping on a nail.

The horse's "afterlife" took him traveling almost as much as he had during his lifetime. Four years after Traveller's death, grave robbers stole his bones, and they were bleached and exhibited in Rochester, New York. They remained there until 1907, when they were returned to Virginia, mounted, and displayed in the Brooks Museum at the renamed Washington and Lee University. During the next twenty-two years the skeleton was repeatedly vandalized by students who carved their initials in it, with Traveller considered something of a good luck charm. The remains were moved to the basement of Lee Chapel, where the enemy was exposure to dampness and mildew, and the remains continued to deteriorate at the time of the Korean War. (Finally, in 1971, what was left of Traveller was buried on the university grounds, only a few feet away from where his owner is interred in the Lee family crypt. Modern students have shown a tad more respect to the horse, designating Traveller as the namesake for the Safe Ride Program, part of the university's efforts to reduce drunk driving.)

The most notable animals in World War I were Crump, a Brussels griffon, who also had the dubious distinction of smoking a pack of cigarettes a day; Prince, an English dog who journeyed two hundred miles to a trench in France where he found his owner; Sergeant-Major Mac, whose acute sound sensitivity allowed him to hear enemy aircraft approaching from far enough away that he served as an early warning system for his British unit; and the canine that American editors christened Stubby the Hero Dog.

In World War II, however, horses played a prominent role for several countries, primarily in the early years in the European theater. They were used to transport troops, artillery, supplies, and what remained of cavalry units in several countries. The Soviet Union and Germany led the way by employing a combined six million horses. Despite his heavy losses in more than six long years of war, Hitler could still field six cavalry divisions as late as February 1945. Actually, he had little choice, because by then the German military had more horses than it had oil supplies to power trucks, tanks, and other vehicles. The Soviet Union did not face such shortages.

But the United States was putting horses in its past. In 1920, there were 25 million horses in the country; twenty years later, there were 14 million left. In December 1939, the famed U.S. Cavalry had fewer than 10,000 horses. The military was converting to being fully mechanized, and after the attack on Pearl Harbor those efforts were accelerated. It was a fitting symbol that in 1942 the Army's 1st Cavalry Division consisted only of infantrymen. Even though General George Patton lamented the lack of true cavalry during the campaigns in North Africa and Italy—"Had we possessed an American cavalry division with pack artillery in Tunisia and in Sicily, not a German would have escaped"— the only real action that Americans mounted on horses saw during World War II was when the 26th Cavalry Regiment, known as the

Philippine Scouts, held off Japanese invaders on Luzon and repelled tanks in Binalonan so allied forces could retreat.

Thus, in the fall of 1952 in a war being fought by an even more mechanized American military, Eric Pedersen's idea that an animal could play a role in it was a unique one. And while he had been impressed by Flame's exhibition of racing at the Sinseul-dong track, he could not have imagined how unique a horse she was.

She was part stallion, but in every other respect she was a Mongol mare and thus came from especially sturdy stock. The Mongol breed is little changed from the time of Genghis Khan, whose hordes rode them to create by his death in 1227 the largest empire the world had known, one that would not be surpassed until the British Empire centuries later. (Khan once declared, "It is easy to conquer the world from the back of a horse.") It is estimated that there are three million such horses in present-day Mongolia, more than the human population. The Mongol horse's smaller stature can give the impression that it is a pony or unable to bear heavy burdens. It is twelve to fourteen hands tall, with strong legs, large hooves, a long mane and tail, and a head that might seem a tad too big for its body.

Though Flame was born in Korea, not Mongolia, her DNA carried the enduring strength of dozens of generations. In their native country, where temperatures can plunge to 20 below zero Fahrenheit, the horses live outdoors year-round. They are used for both riding and work—and for racing. They have been known to gallop for 20 miles at a time. In Mongolia, horse racing is the most popular sport after wrestling, so a breed that succeeded at it was particularly prized. But a Mongolian didn't have to care at all about racing to benefit from such a horse—the animal could also walk more than 50 kilometers a day while carting a weight of more than two tons.

Two other attributes of Mongol horses would allow Reckless to play a crucial role in the biggest battle of her young life: the ability to tread safely in rough terrain, and to keep charging even if the rider has fallen.

But if it was a horse that Eric Pedersen returned with from Seoul, it didn't have to turn out to be a hero; it just had to go from Point A to Point B carrying ammunition. Real heroism was for the Marines, the two-legged kind.

If pressed, Pedersen might have copped to another motivation for the trip to Seoul and back: He simply loved horses. He and his sister had grown up during their father's more successful years and had even spent a few years in England when his father was an executive with a company there. Then the Pedersen children lived in Jackson Hole in Wyoming and Prescott in Arizona, both in horse country. The boy spent as much time as he could riding.

His own family now lived in Southern California, not far from the Marine Corps base at Camp Pendleton, and he hoped they would own a ranch and raise horses on it. When Pedersen had set off for Seoul, he might have been content to return with a good, solid mule. But he really wanted a horse. And that is what he got—though, sadly, he left its former owner sobbing in the racetrack's stalls.

Given all the tribulations Flame had already endured in her young life, standing in a moving trailer was probably not an upsetting experience. For once, she was being hauled instead of the other way around.

Lieutenant Pedersen and the other two Marines drove back to their position in Changdan on the Main Line of Resistance. There, after the sun had set, they were greeted by the other men in the platoon. At that particular time, the platoon was attached to the 1st Battalion of the 5th Marines.

That night, the new four-legged recruit received a new name. The Marines first called her Recoilless, but that sounded too awkward and clumsy for the sorrel mare with a somewhat dignified demeanor. What about the nickname for the unique rifle they employed? The impression was that you had to be a combination of careless and fearless—equaling reckless—to man such a weapon because of the notable back blast from it that alerted the Communists to your position. That seemed like a more suitable name for the horse, and thus from then on she was Reckless. The earning of ranks and the stripes that followed the name change were still several months ahead.

Lieutenant Pedersen knew that two men in the platoon had some experience with horses. Corporal Monroe Coleman, who had spent part of his youth in Utah on a ranch and certainly knew horses, was appointed one of two caretakers of Reckless.

Sergeant Joseph Latham, the oldest Marine in the platoon, was a native of Alabama and had also been raised around horses. He was a Marine Corps lifer, having enlisted way back in 1938, and he'd seen action in the Pacific Theater during the last war. When the Korean War broke out, it was back to the battlefield for him. Fourteen years in the Marines and getting shot at in two wars sure wasn't any easy life, but Latham was a man with a genial face, a hard man when he had to be, but with a pretty soft interior. He was the one the younger guys could go to. Now he was being given a horse to train. The gruff but kind sergeant would be the one to put Reckless through "hoof camp," teaching her what she needed to know about a battlefield.

First, though, Pedersen and his men had to figure out how they and Reckless could all live together. They immediately requisitioned a supply of wood planks, usually used to build bunkers for Marines who were manning the outposts, and constructed a behind-the-lines bunker where Reckless could sleep. The first meal they cobbled together for her was a crumbled-up loaf of bread and some uncooked oatmeal. The next day the Marines found a suitably flat area nearby and fenced it in so Reckless would have her own pasture. The resourceful Latham went out foraging, and came back with a load of barley, sorghum, hay, and rice straw. A few days later, he even managed to find a block of salt for her. With no immediate objection from the recruit, it looked like she was going to stay a while.

Reckless's new living situation and the treatment she received were surely a step up from what her life had been like the past couple of years, after her budding career as a championship racehorse had ended. The comforts and the attention of all the men—who, obviously, had to be intrigued by this new creature in their midst as well as enjoying the break in the daily routine drudgery of life at the front—no doubt distracted Reckless from thoughts of Kim Huk Moon and his family. There had to be some knowledge that they were missing from her life and that the special bond between her and Kim had been broken. But Reckless would not be the least bit lonely with the men of the recoilless rifle platoon. They were her family now.

CHAPTER NINE

Yak Yak Town

Reckless and the band of leathernecks she had come to live with set out to get to know each other. During their first few weeks together there was no lack of volunteers among the Marines to attend to her. No one had a curry brush, so an old shoe brush had to do for grooming. Especially for the men who hailed from cities back home and had little or no experience with horses other than seeing one pull a milk cart, Reckless was a sudden and exotic presence in their lives here on the other side of the world.

She seemed to have a sense of entitlement about being rubbed down and stroked and otherwise cared for, as if such signs of affection were her royal due. She wasn't a large, imposing horse, but the Marines were impressed by her strength and a sense that she could endure almost anything. Lieutenant Pedersen described how he had seen her run with power and grace at the Sinseul-dong track, conjuring up memories in the men's minds of the stories about great racers like Seabiscuit, Citation, and the colt on its way to being named Horse of the Year of 1952 back in the States, Native Dancer.

There was enough concern that Reckless might abruptly bolt, maybe make a run for it back to her old family and home in Seoul, that her first few nights in camp she was tied in her bunker. However, she appeared so completely content in her new and unfamiliar surroundings that the men allowed her to stroll about whenever she wanted, and she slept soundly at night. Clearly, for Reckless, this was home.

The recoilless rifle platoon was also impressed by her appetite. So were other men from the 1st Battalion who stopped by to visit, as word spread that a horse had joined their ranks. Reckless easily packed away her meals. They were supplemented by snacks of apples and carrots. She had never before tasted these and other fresh foods because with the Kim family her diet had been nothing more than hay and some grain.

"I would feed her, so every time she'd see me, she'd trot over," recalled John Meyers. A gunner with the 5th Regiment's Anti-tank Company, he often doubled as a cook. "I gave her an apple a day. She knew exactly where I slept and she'd come in the tent and lick my face to wake me up, so she could eat."

Reckless also displayed an eager curiosity about what was on the Marines' plates. When she wandered near the galley tent and saw a mound of scrambled eggs, Meyers didn't have to do anything because she helped herself. The mare was perfectly willing to expand her diet. After she finished gobbling up her morning eggs, she went to work on bacon and buttered toast. She then washed the robust meal down with a cup of coffee. After dinner, dessert could be a chocolate bar or a piece of hard candy, and at any time of day she liked to snack on shredded wheat and even mashed potatoes.

If the Chinese had ever considered enlisting a horse to haul ammo, all they would have had to do was observe Reckless for a few days to realize they wouldn't have sufficient supplies to feed one.

Or to tolerate some other consequences. According to John Meyers, "The Marine Corps had this terrible chocolate pudding that was just horrible stuff. All the guys would just dump it in this big fifty-five-gallon garbage can. Well, who gets into the can but Reckless. She eats the pudding, and then she got the worst case of diarrhea you've ever seen."

In addition to being fascinated by Reckless, the Marines indulged her because they knew that at some point she would be exposed to danger. They could still hope, though, that she would never have to be deployed. As Christmas had approached in 1950, 1951, and now in 1952, whispers spread about a truce being hammered out and the troops heading home to America, England, Australia, Turkey, and other United Nations countries that had taken up arms against the Communists. Once again, though, there was little genuine cause for optimism. The Truman administration was stuck in neutral, not willing to pursue the war more aggressively, yet unable to end U.S. involvement by pulling out.

For many of the men on the Main Line of Resistance the stalemated combat situation in Korea had become a frustrating, depressing, no-win routine. Even the daily appearance of an enemy pilot in their midst provided no real relief.

"A guy we called 'Bedcheck Charlie' used to come around every day right after dark," recalls Ted King of Minnesota, who in the fall of 1952 was a corporal and a radio operator. "We figured he was Korean because he knew every hill. Sometimes we'd be up on a ridge and he'd be flying below us."

When Bedcheck Charlie flew behind the MLR with Marines below him, he pulled the pin on a grenade, put it into a fruit jar, and dropped it out his cockpit window. King said he didn't think the raids ever caused an injury. Charlie could still be irritating, though. On the few remaining mild nights that fall, movies were projected onto a suitable hillside.

"We'd be sitting there on sandbags like being in an amphitheater," says King. "The lights were out, we're watching the movie, and then we hear Charlie coming. The guys would be shooting into the air with pistols and M-1s, then we had to just sit there with the lights out grinding our teeth until he got bored and flew away."

Despite such modest distractions, knowing that there was not much support back home made the mission even more difficult. That the war was interminable and perhaps unwinnable had become a significant issue in the 1952 presidential campaign.

A majority of the men stuck in Korea wanted Dwight Eisenhower to be elected president that November. He had been a soldier, like them, and one of the heroes of World War II. He knew what fighting was like and he knew how to win. At the Republican Convention, the other leading contenders were Robert Taft of Ohio and the reluctantly retired Douglas MacArthur. In any other election during a war, MacArthur, with his gargantuan reputation (and ego), might well have triumphed, but Eisenhower trumped him as a national and less polarizing figure and was nominated on the first ballot. He would face off against the Democratic nominee—not Truman, who had accepted that he didn't stand a chance and bowed out, but Adlai Stevenson, the governor of Illinois.

The most that Eisenhower would say about the war to the press was "I shall go to Korea," which he repeated during a speech in Detroit in October. He won the election in early November, and late that month he was on his way. Eisenhower spent three days in Korea. (One of his landing areas was the field at the Sinseul-dong racetrack.) "America will see it through," he declared about the war. But when he returned to New York and huddled with his advisers, the game plan they devised was to work out a cease-fire and get out of Korea. That would mean real progress had to be made in the truce negotiations.

That would not be easy to do, no matter who was president. Marines, who took pride in their irreverence, referred to Panmunjom as "Yak Yak Town"—all talk, no action. Actually, some good news would have been that there was any talking going on at all. Negotiations remained deadlocked over the exchange-of-prisoners issue. By the fall of 1952 there were more than 130,000 Communist soldiers residing in POW camps in South Korea. According to a survey conducted by the United Nations, the number of those who did not want to return home had swelled to 60,000. The dilemma for the U.N. was that agreeing to exchange all of their prisoners, as the Communists insisted, would mean forcing roughly half of them to return, and the United States would not sign off on that.

Finally, in mid-November, India introduced a resolution suggesting "voluntary repatriation." A repatriation commission consisting of both allied and Communist members was to be established, and it would figure out which prisoners would end up going where. While this appeared to be a logistical and bureaucratic nightmare, it did provide a way out of the stalemate at Panmunjom. The U.N. adopted the resolution by a 54-to-5 vote. This would result in the resumption of negotiations. Still, as had been true in the previous years of the war, nothing would happen overnight.

As Lee Ballenger, a Korean War veteran and historian, explained, Korea was America's first limited war, one in which military victory was prohibited. Statesmanship was the prevailing goal, and armies were restricted from gaining ground. "A military victory, as defined by one side decisively defeating the other, was neither sought nor achieved."

Ironically, the lack of momentum to achieve a goal, an alien feeling in the Marine Corps culture, could lead to a dangerous apathy. The strategy of conducting no major offensives did not equal a low-risk situation, but some men had to find that out the hard way, such as when a sniper's bullet suddenly punctured a helmet or a mortar shell landed on a large flat rock where seconds before a handful of leathernecks had been sunning themselves on one of the few warm days remaining in the fall.

"We could become so damn blasé about being there," recalls Fred Donovan, a 5th Marines corporal who arrived in Korea as a replacement that autumn. "One day I went out with a fire team, four guys, to protect a convoy, and I remember going out with just two grenades and a .45. That's how stupid I was. We just figured what the hell, we've got to walk up that hill anyway, so we might as well be as light as we can. Yeah, we pulled some dumb stuff over there."

For a few more months, most Marines could get away with being lackadaisical. But lying ahead were the fiercest and deadliest battles that the Marines in western Korea would experience.

Normally, early winter was a pretty quiet time along the Main Line of Resistance. There were still probes into the Chinese and U.N. lines, skirmishes sometimes flared up into firefights, artillery would suddenly rumble, grenades were tossed, mortar rounds landed indiscriminately, and men on both sides were killed and wounded. The enemy had a slight advantage when the days were short because that meant less time being exposed to American and Australian fighter jets, and the Chinese had more experience conducting night raids. With snow sometimes suffocating the sounds of the enemy's approach, the men of the 5th Marines and their brothers in the 7th Regiment had to be extra vigilant. That kind of weather meant that there was little downtime, because almost every day snow would suddenly spit out of the gunmetal gray sky, and when the storm moved on, it left behind several more inches lying atop the previous day's deposit.

One stark example that the war was not as dormant as nature came on the night of December 8. A Marine reconnaissance unit suddenly found itself under attack, with the Chinese wielding burp guns, their weapon of choice. This was a Soviet invention, a submachine gun rushed into production after the USSR was invaded by Germany early in World War II. The PPSh—the designer was George Shpagin—utilized a simple blowback action and fired from an open-bolt position. It was a reliable weapon with a high rate of fire and a large magazine capacity. Another weapon that the Communist troops relied on was the 7.92-mm Mauser rifle, which China itself had been manufacturing for almost thirty-five years.

The only problem for the Chinese forces was that they didn't have enough burp guns, rifles, or even ammunition to go around. There were simply more men than munitions. During assaults, some Chinese soldiers carried guns while others toted bags of grenades. Also, leaders would coldly calculate the expected casualties when they were about to attack a fortified U.N. position. Burp guns and Mauser rifles as well as fewer than one hundred rounds of ammo would be given to troops in the front lines, and those behind them would have no weapons at all, other than the bamboo-encased potato-masher grenades—there never seemed to be a shortage of those. However, some dated to before World War II, and there was no guarantee that they would explode seconds after the fuses were lit by tapping them on rocks and harder ground surfaces.

With snow on the ground it could be difficult to discern a Chinese advance. The typical winter uniform was a thick, two-piece jacket that was reversible, white on one side and yellow on the other. They also wore fur-lined caps instead of helmets, which led to a disproportionate rate of deaths from head wounds. Marines realized that some of the shots from their carbines could not penetrate the quilted uniform jackets, so word was passed to shoot for the head only. Enemy soldiers could blend in with the snow and walk quietly in their canvas shoes and thus could be almost on top of the Marine position before they were discovered. Then all hell would break loose. As the attack progressed and the Chinese in the front were cut down, the ones behind them would keep moving forward, grab the guns and unspent ammo from the dead and wounded, and press ahead. At some point the Chinese units might run out of ammunition, but the expectation was they would never run out of soldiers to be slaughtered.

On that night of the 8th the moon and stars were obscured by brooding storm clouds. The enemy appeared out of the oppressive dark in droves and broke through a hastily formed defensive perimeter. That was when Sergeant Lloyd Smalley took over. The Boston native, only twenty-two years old, directed the fire of his squad while he himself poured it on as well. Chinese troops were dying left and right, and finally the withering fire proved too deadly even for them and they withdrew.

Sergeant Smalley moved ahead of his squad to where the perimeter had been, looking for dead and wounded Marines. He found one who had been hit badly. PFC Howard Davenport might not last long enough for a corpsman to get to him, and he was lying dangerously close to the re-forming enemy line. The sergeant picked Davenport up and headed back to his squad. This earned renewed attention from the enemy and they opened fire, lobbing grenades too. Smalley was hit twice by shrapnel, but not stopped. He had just arrived and handed Davenport off to his men when he was hit again, this time fatally.

Sergeant Smalley's family received his posthumous Navy Cross, the highest honor a Marine and a member of the U.S. Navy can receive. (The highest honor anyone in the American military can receive is the Medal of Honor, available to members of all branches of the service.) Davenport, who had to undergo many surgeries, survived. He sent flowers to Mrs. Smalley every Mother's Day after that.

For the most part, though, with snow falling more frequently and the ground freezing, the dropping temperatures and bulky winter clothing (more so for the allies), December was not a good month for any kind of sustained offensive. A temperature of fourteen degrees on the night of December 7 was actually welcomed because just a few days earlier it had been four degrees and accompanied by a prolonged snowfall.

But November and then December were busy months for Reckless and her chief handler, Sergeant Joe Latham. As much as she might have liked to, the chestnut-colored mare couldn't simply wander around the camp and eat all day. This was a time for training. Horses were not inclined to stand their ground, let alone continue the job given to them, when there were explosions and other forms of fighting around them. If there was any possibility of training Reckless not to turn tail and run away when shooting started, that had to be done months before the heavy action resumed in the spring. The tasks she was given to learn had to be practiced over and over again.

Every day, Sergeant Latham took her into the hills. To do that, he first had to help her learn how to get in and out of her two-wheel wood-slatted trailer without damaging it or herself. It was only thirty-six inches wide by seventy-two inches long, and even for a Mongolian mare of barely fourteen hands and nine hundred pounds there was no extra room. However, Reckless was agile enough that it was not a problem. As Latham reported, "She'd jump in the trailer and go in catty-cornered, and I'd tie her down."

Once in the hills, he taught Reckless how to navigate the terrain. The horse had to dig her hooves in on some steep hillsides, especially when the soil and rocks were slippery from snow. The occasional mild day actually made training trickier because the melting snow wasn't any better than a sheet of ice for climbing on. Latham arranged with a few other Marines to be in a position to fire BARs, carbines, and .45s when Reckless came near. She would be hearing a lot more noise than that when things heated up, but at least this demonstration gave her a taste of it.

The terrain Reckless would encounter would be difficult for more reasons than the weather and some hills having inclines as steep as forty-five degrees. There would be holes in the ground gouged out by artillery and mortar blasts, and dead and wounded men to avoid stepping on. A huge danger was barbed wire, which could entangle Reckless and rip her flesh open. Day after day Sergeant Latham instructed the horse on how to recognize barbed wire and step over it or at least locate a gap in it.

The same went for communication wires—not as dangerous, but they could trip her up and be severed as Reckless tried to free herself, putting units out of touch with commanders. Sergeant Latham and Corporal Coleman, who after Latham spent the most time with Reckless, noticed a trait she had of lowering her head and sizing up a situation for a few moments before deciding how to proceed. This intelligent caution, the men hoped, would allow her to avoid dangerous obstacles. In their own experience with horses, they couldn't remember one with such a combination of strength, gentleness, and smarts.

And there was the primary job she had to do. Flame had done more than her share of hard labor before, so a new name wasn't going to change her ready, willing, and able attitude when called upon to carry objects. The two trainers began slowly, attaching two recoilless rifles on her saddle, one on each side, and leading her up and down hills that were far enough away from enemy observers (and snipers), then repeating that process with a shell attached to each side. Every week or two, depending on how much practice the weather allowed, another pair of shells was added.

Lieutenant Pedersen and his men wondered how many shells it would take before the weight would be too much for Reckless. Ten would add up to something like 240 pounds, and no one thought she could handle that. Reckless was, after all, a small horse, and a mare, not a stallion. Pedersen may not have known that Reckless had been sired by a stallion, the one in Pusan. If he had known Flame-of-the-Morning, he would have been amazed to see that Reckless was a carbon copy of her. So even though technically Reckless was part stallion, she was viewed and would always be referred to as a Mongolian mare.

For the undersized horse, every trip during a battle would require climbing uphill, the load feeling heavier with each step. Would the sixth shell be the proverbial straw that broke the camel's back? Were eight shells even possible? Lieutenant Pedersen didn't want to put that much of a burden on her, and told Latham and Coleman to have Reckless carry no more than six shells.

Reckless was also taught how to protect herself. It had to be anticipated that she would be exposed to enemy fire where there was no immediate cover. Latham instructed her on how to lie down to reduce her exposure to snipers and shrapnel. "Putting my hand on her hoof meant she should fall down," he said, and Reckless would imitate the sergeant's abrupt crouch. Also valuable was learning how to kneel and crawl into a shallow bunker. What might not work too well was Reckless lying down or hiding in a bunker while she was supposed to be carrying shells. Sergeant Latham had to hope that when the time came, a horse as intelligent as Reckless would know the difference.

She had to be taught to protect herself behind the lines too, because Chinese gunners didn't want any of the Marines to relax. "We'd get incoming there too, and they'd lay it on you," Latham recalled. "If Reckless was back in the back, she'd go to a bunker. All I had to do was yell, 'Incoming, incoming!' and she'd go."

Because she was such a bright animal, it shouldn't have come as any surprise that she had a sense of humor. Some mornings, when she was having breakfast—which, inevitably, was whatever the other Marines were having that morning—Latham would approach her to get going on that day's lessons. The sorrel mare let him get to within a few feet; then she would pretend to be frightened and dance away. When the sergeant, playing along, came near again, Reckless would bare her teeth and make to charge at him, then dance farther away. After a few minutes of such theatrics, Reckless would be persuaded by a piece of candy to begin her school day.

At the end of every day, Sergeant Latham reported on her progress to his platoon leader. Though $250 was not chump change, Pedersen must have considered himself pretty lucky to have found and purchased what was obviously a special horse. He hoped that specialness would extend to when the real shooting began and the lives of his men as well as Reckless's life were at risk.

An unexpected benefit soon became apparent, completely unanticipated—Reckless lifted the spirits of his platoon. Most of his men had been together in Korea for months, some since the summer. They were certainly veterans now, and tough guys whether they were twenty-two or twenty-five years old, or an "old-timer" like Latham. Now in winter's full grasp, these men hadn't bathed in weeks—a latrine was a luxury. They were unshaven and hollow-eyed, and missing girlfriends or wives and families every single cold and dangerous day.

Yet he observed when some of the sergeants played poker—Latham and Ralph Sherman, John Lisenby, and Elmer Lively, and whoever else wasn't too tired on any given evening—how their faces lit up when the horse's name was mentioned. These tough Marines became kids again. And how they laughed when Reckless poked her handsome head into the tent to watch the cards be dealt and the chips be tossed. Pedersen recognized that no matter what she did in battle, Reckless was becoming a legend and there would be stories told about her back home. One of the first ones would have to be what occurred one night when a lucky Latham had just finished raking in $30 worth of chips and Reckless, wondering what kind of different snack this was, essentially cashed him out by reaching her head forward and eating them.

It was certainly abnormal for a Marine recruit to be inspected by a major general, but that was what happened when one day a jeep arrived bearing the commanding officer of the 1st Marine Division. Word of the recoilless rifle platoon's horse experiment had spread up the ranks, and General Edwin Pollock was curious enough that he came to see her for himself. It must not have been totally a surprise inspection because her copper-colored coat sparkled in the morning sunlight thanks to an extra-diligent brushing by Corporal Coleman. The general knew horses, having ridden them as a youngster, and he thought Reckless a fine animal.

"When I first saw Reckless she was behind the 5th Marines line in Panmunjom—Hill 229—Bunker Hill Sector," the general recalled. "She was not doing anything exceptional beyond receiving praise, food, and adoration from a group of Marines. Naturally at this time I did not visualize the extent of her fame and fortune. I did realize, however, that any little morale factor would be a help and I considered the purchase of Reckless such a factor. This was at the time that we were being hit hard and regularly by the Chinese. Anything to maintain the already high morale was most welcome."

The division commander noticed, however, that Reckless needed new shoes. (No doubt a few wags commented that the CO hadn't expressed nearly as much interest in the quality of *their* boots.) He told one of his aides, Lieutenant Eugene Foxworth, to find a blacksmith.

He did so, but without doing any homework first. That same day, Lieutenant Pedersen received a call from Foxworth informing him of a Korean blacksmith in a nearby village. Sergeant Latham put Reckless into the trailer and off they went.

The errand turned out to be a disaster. Inside the blacksmith's hut, Reckless was tied to a pole that held the wooden structure up. That was the first mistake. The blacksmith was a rough man who, oddly, seemed to have little patience. The situation was made worse because the horse had apparently forgotten Korean, so the man's commands were unintelligible. Reckless resisted when he tried to examine her hooves, and that made him angry. (It was just Latham's luck that Foxworth had found a blacksmith who actually did not like horses.) He became angrier yet when the sergeant told him to be more gentle with the mare. He dragged out a chain and tried to tie Reckless down.

The proud horse would have none of that: Reckless turned and showed the blacksmith her business end, and with a well-aimed kick he was sent soaring, taking half the hut with him, which in turn caused the center pole to fall over. It struck the luckless Latham in the head and he collapsed. With a toss of her mane, Reckless exited what was left of the hut. Once the stars around Sergeant Latham's head stopped spinning, he enticed the horse back into the trailer and off they went.

Back in Changdon, the punchy sergeant told of their adventure, and the Marines grew more fond of Reckless than ever. She had given the surly blacksmith what he deserved. And the spunk she showed would serve her, and them, well in battle.

CHAPTER TEN

★ ★

Baptism by Fire

Sooner than Lieutenant Pedersen and the men anticipated, Reckless was to be tested. Not content to ease up for the rest of the year, Communist troops were digging trenches in a section on the Main Line of Resistance known as Hedy's Crotch. The Hollywood star Hedy Lamarr may have been aware that Outpost Hedy had been named after her, but the naughty nickname of this area adjacent to it might have been kept under wraps.

If the digging project were left unchecked, the trenches would approach the MLR and make a surprise attack more effective. Thankfully, sharp eyes had detected the furtive activity. Lieutenant Pedersen and his recoilless rifle platoon were given the task of destroying the trenches that had already been dug and were now being fortified. Hedy's Crotch was more than two miles away from the platoon's position with the 5th Regiment.

When the gun crew the lieutenant designated for the job, led by Sergeant Sherman, moved out, Reckless was with them, riding in her two-wheeled trailer. The Chinese occupied a hill known as the Yoke, and from it they could see the road that went north from Kwakchon, a Korean village that had been battered by artillery and other fire enough times that all its inhabitants had fled south. The enemy would shell the road if they saw indications that a mission was under way. Wisely, Pedersen ordered the three vehicles carrying his men, weapons, ammunition, and Reckless to set off toward the north spaced ten minutes apart and to be in no apparent hurry. They did not arouse the enemy's interest, even though one of the vehicles hauled a horse trailer. When the squad arrived at the base of the hill, they looked up five hundred yards, to the ridgeline. They had to climb that to get the recoilless rifles in position, but they were experienced climbers by now and it did not take long.

Both Sergeant Latham and Corporal Coleman were with Reckless on her first mission. They got her out of the trailer and secured six shells to her packsaddle. Pedersen, Sherman, and the other Marines began the trek, and they were soon followed by Coleman leading Reckless. From the mouths of all of them chugged puffs of vapor in the cold air. When horse and handler arrived at the ridgeline, they received a cheerful greeting from the Marines already in position.

The men knew that the recoilless rifles were the best way to destroy those trenches, and under a pale white sky that refused to let the sun penetrate they prepared for the job straightaway. Standard procedure: They would fire just a few times and move, fire and move, so the Communist gunners couldn't target any one position after observing the back blasts. Usually, though, the enemy fired anyway, and that meant incoming for the Marines stuck in place.

The first load of a half-dozen shells was taken off the mare's back, and Coleman led her down for another load. They were halfway up the hill with six more shells when Sherman's gun opened up. Coleman later reported that the sudden "wham" of the recoilless rifle, even from two hundred yards farther uphill, caused Reckless to jump right off the ground, despite the almost 150 pounds of metal in her load. The next shell was fired, and one after that. Reckless's eyes were white and she snorted and shook her head. She was terrified.

"She had to get used to the gun firing," recalled Harold Wadley, a sergeant in the 5th Marines, six decades later. "The first time, she went straight up into the air, and when she came back down, she collapsed into a shaking fit. The second time, she went up again, but not as high, and she calmed down more quickly. But the third time, she was fine. From then on, explosions didn't bother her."

Soon her biggest concern was food. The operation made her so hungry that Sergeant Latham found her trying to eat an abandoned helmet liner before going back down from the ridge. Still, this was more firing than she had experienced before. Would she break away and run down the hill?

No. Instead, with Corporal Coleman's gentle persuasion, they traveled back and forth from the ridgeline several more times. Reckless shook whenever the guns were fired, but she stood her ground. She moved only when the gun crew members changed position. The shells were taken off her and it was downhill for more. She had started uphill once more when the Chinese artillery began pounding the ridgeline. She began to perspire and there was some fear, but not enough to stop her in her tracks. When they next got to the bottom of the ridge, Latham made sure to run his hand down her neck and speak softly to her. Then it was time to load up again.

During the noisy and risky interval while Sergeant Sherman's crew ruined the enemy's trench-building achievement, Reckless did not quit. She and Coleman made half a dozen trips up to the firing positions on the ridgeline, delivering a total of thirty shells. The Chinese were unhappy to be the recipients of each one.

Back at camp with the 1st Battalion, to celebrate it was beer instead of water in a helmet for Reckless, the newly minted combat veteran. The result was the same, the beverage being lapped up, but this time it was followed by a hearty belch. She wanted more—her usual signal for seconds was to nudge or pinch Joe Latham's arm—but the men figured they had better check with Doc Mitchell, the corpsman who had been designated as her personal physician.

Reckless was rubbed dry, had a blanket draped over her, and was led to her bunker. But because the night turned quite cold, and even though she was half Mongolian mare, she soon left and strolled into the tent Sergeant Latham shared with two other Marines. "Here's Reckless," the men muttered, and shifted accordingly. There, worn-out but warm, she fell asleep beside the stove.

Before the year ended, the 1st Battalion had a new commanding officer. Lieutenant Colonel Edwin Wheeler was a thirty-four-year-old native of Port Chester, New York, who had left law school to enlist in the Marine Corps when World War II began. He had been a rifle platoon leader in the unit known as Edson's Raiders against the Japanese in the previous war, and he counted the Silver Star earned in the Solomon Islands campaign among his medals. He would go on to become the only officer to lead every kind of Marine Corps unit—platoon, company, battalion, regiment, and eventually the 1st Marine Division in Vietnam—into battle.

Officially, Wheeler was not the CO of Lieutenant Pedersen's platoon, but he technically was for as long as the recoilless rifle team was attached to his battalion. Wheeler's men kept their eyes peeled for any activity around Outpost Hedy and Bunker Hill, and Pedersen's men and Reckless roamed that section of the MLR to be available if they were needed. This gave more men of the 1st Battalion an opportunity to marvel at the horse that appeared to have the calm disposition of a veteran Marine. A few times the platoon went far enough to the east to bump up against units of Lieutenant Colonel Caputo's 2nd Battalion of the 7th Regiment, who continued to face the enemy from Outposts Reno, Carson, and Vegas.

It was around this time that the platoon almost lost its lieutenant. Again. Lieutenant Colonel Wheeler decided that the Chinese in front of Bunker Hill needed to be reminded that the Marines had them in their sights, and a few recoilless rifle shells would do the reminding. Because reaching the preferred firing position required navigating barbed wire and that day the ground was especially slippery from a quick spike of the temperature above freezing, when Pedersen and a gun crew moved forward, Reckless was left behind. That decision might have saved her life.

The lieutenant and his men arrived at their position. They didn't come under fire, but it was still a painful part of the mission. In the winter and spring, most Marines on the front lines, especially those who went out on patrols, had knuckles, knees, and elbows tattooed with bloody scabs because they were continually slipping on the frozen or thawing slopes. It always seemed that just when the aggravatingly sore injuries were close to healing, it would be time to go out on a mission again. Predictably, Sergeant Sherman and his crew did their share of grumbling on the way up the ridge. Pedersen let them vent. A Marine who didn't complain was one who didn't care.

Bleeding sores or not, with brisk efficiency the men set up. After Pedersen sighted new encroaching trenches through his binoculars and spoke quietly to his men, the big gun began firing. As usual, after three or four detectable back blasts, they moved to another position. This time, however, the enemy didn't react in the usual way. Instead of trying to target the back blasts, the Chinese gunners let loose with a barrage to baste the ridgeline with artillery and mortar shells. Shrapnel from the latter bit into Lieutenant Pedersen's hip and leg. He had to be carried back down and then driven to the battalion aid station.

His wounds weren't too bad, but they were bad enough. By that evening the lieutenant's wounds had been dressed and he was back with his platoon, but it was the third time since his arrival on the MLR earlier in the year that he had been wounded. When the news made its way up to General Pollock, he ordered that Pedersen's combat days were over, and with it his command of the recoilless rifle platoon.

When Pedersen learned of Pollock's decision, it added insult to injury. His wounds hurt, *and* like an old horse he was being put out to pasture. When his men heard about the division CO's order, they weren't happy either. They were not only losing their lieutenant, whom they admired and trusted with their lives, but they expected they would be losing their lieutenant's horse as well. Pedersen had paid for Reckless out of his own pocket and he had assumed, as had his men, that when it was his turn to go home it would be her ticket to America too.

The next day, the lieutenant hobbled over to see Colonel Smoak, looking for an exception to what was essentially a three-strikes-you're-out policy about being wounded in combat. The colonel, whose replacement as CO of the 5th Marines was on his way, was sympathetic. However, it was not a regimental matter, but a 1st Division one. At least there Pedersen had a card to play. Major Charles Lamb, the division adjutant, was a friend of Pedersen's. Pedersen pleaded his case to Lamb, pointing out that he was back on duty the same day after the last scrape, so that really shouldn't tip the scales. Lamb said he would get his friend in to see General Pollock.

It was Reckless who made the difference. The next day, when Lieutenant Pedersen was ushered in to see the commanding officer, Pollock pondered and then rescinded his previous order. He recognized that the lieutenant's most recent wounds had been minor and that if he were sent home the 5th Anti-Tank Company would be losing a fine and experienced leader. But what kind of message would it send down the ranks to make this exception? Sure, there were officers who would be okay with a piece of shrapnel or a flesh wound as a ticket home, but there were plenty of others who would resist leaving a job unfinished. Lieutenant Pedersen, with a long-suffering wife and two children waiting for him in California, could be a poster boy for that.

When General Pollock asked about the horse, the lieutenant saw his chance. He explained that if he was ordered back to the States and took Reckless with him, all the training would go to waste. She had shown a lot of potential in the Hedy's Crotch mission and would be ready for more when spring arrived. Plus, the men in the 5th and 7th Marines would sure miss her. On the other hand, if Reckless was left there in Changdan . . . well, that would make it a really tough pill for Pedersen to swallow, having to give up his horse as well as his command.

That argument was icing on the cake for General Pollock. He didn't want to lose Reckless. Or this plucky platoon leader. The sorrel mare was treated that night to a snack of bread and strawberry jam by grateful Marines.

In case any of the men in Lieutenant Pedersen's platoon doubted his report of Reckless's racing talents, she gave a persuasive presentation at the expense of an unfortunate private first class named Arnold Baker. With the potential for more combat looming, the lieutenant had assigned Baker to be backup to Latham and Coleman. If anything happened to one or both of them, Reckless would not have an unfamiliar caretaker and guide.

With the Sinseul-dong demonstration in October still fresh in his mind, the platoon CO had issued orders that Reckless was not to be ridden. But Baker apparently thought he knew horses pretty well and could get along with any of them. Reckless, he learned the hard way, was not just any horse.

One sparkling clear afternoon when a Marine could kid himself that winter in Korea wasn't so bad, Baker believed that Reckless needed more exercise to stay fit, especially with her appetite. He led the filly out to an open area in the Hwajon-dong Valley, protected by

Fox Company of the 2nd Battalion and far enough away from the front line that Reckless would not be in danger.

But Baker was the one in jeopardy when he decided to climb aboard and take her for a brisk stroll. Reckless remembered suddenly how it felt when Kim was her rider, or she felt the freedom to let loose—either way, off she went.

Baker bounced up and down and all around, gamely hanging on to the halter rope with one hand and the sorrel mare's mane with the other, his legs gripping her muscular sides. He yelled "Whoa!" and anything else he could think of, which Reckless interpreted as encouragement. She reached the end of the pasture area that had been designated for her and kept going, blurring past tanks and trucks and Marines with gaping mouths, some of them veterans of combat who thought they had already seen it all. Reckless wheeled around when she reached the road and headed toward the front.

Baker was pretty desperate by this point. The sentry at a gate on the road heard him screaming as he and Reckless flashed by. Seconds later, "Reckless is loose!" the sentry yelled into the phone. Sergeant Latham was summoned. His first thought was a scary one—that even before Reckless and her petrified rider approached Chinese positions, they might gallop through a minefield on the other side of a fruit orchard.

Latham jumped into a jeep. Safe lanes were available for Marine patrols, but that would mean nothing to a hurtling horse with four legs flying. The sergeant floored it and the chase was on.

To Baker's chagrin, Reckless was inexhaustible. Lookouts atop hills on the MLR reported Reckless's approach, and that on her was a Marine clinging for dear life. If Baker survived this, he'd gladly accept whatever punishment Lieutenant Pedersen meted out for this ill-conceived excursion. He heard some shouting, the voices getting closer. Actually, he was the one getting closer—to the men of Fox Company on the front line, who one by one stood and gestured and yelled, "Go back! Reckless, stop!" She ignored them and charged into the minefield.

Baker prayed, his eyes squeezed shut. He was far from the only Marine praying, but the others had their eyes wide-open, expecting any moment to see an explosion and horse and human flesh being hurled into the cold air. But Reckless must have realized where she was—or maybe she simply had gotten enough excited energy out of her system. She slowed, turned, and trotted out of the minefield, ambled through the fruit orchard, and headed back to her platoon.

Along the way, she rendezvoused with Sergeant Latham, who immediately noted her sweaty coat and bright, happy eyes. Baker was like a limp dishrag on her back, begging to be put out of his misery.

What was his punishment? Well, the specifics are not known, but Marine platoon sergeants have their own way of taking care of thoughtless young men who disobey orders. It is known that PFC Baker never sat atop Reckless again.

A year earlier, the 5th Marine Regiment, along with most of the 1st Division, had been on the front lines in eastern Korea. The weather had been worse there, with more snow and an especially cruel wind coming out of Siberia. Conditions weren't as hard on the western front as the winter of 1952–53 began. The bad news, though, was that because of the proximity of Panmunjom, that was where a surprise early-winter attack would take place if there were to be one at all. The Marines had to be on constant alert. It was especially welcome, then, when the regiment, including Lieutenant Pedersen's platoon, was relieved by units of the 1st and 7th Regiments and could spend a few weeks in the relatively low-tension environment of the division reserve position.

Reckless continued to be trained, but if there was a little too much snow, much of it became encrusted with ice, so she was put to work stringing telephone wire. Instead of shells, wire reels were tied to her packsaddle. Here the platoon discovered another unexpected benefit of the chestnut mare—she could string as much wire as a dozen men.

As 1952 came to a close, Reckless seemed quite content with her surroundings. Weeks earlier, whenever it had rained, even though she was covered by a blanket, she would step out of her open-faced bunker and into one of the nearby tents. She did the same in December, when it snowed. As soon as her slender head poked through the tent flap, one of the occupants offered the mantra, "Here's Reckless," and they would shift sleeping bags and themselves to make room for the rest of her.

This was especially true on those nights when the wind blew hard. It wasn't from Siberia; it was more out of Manchuria, but by the third week of December it was difficult to tell the difference. It was all the same to Reckless, who the year before had been with the Kim family in Pusan to the south and of course was accustomed to Korean winters by now.

Some mornings, it was time to strap the saddle on again and return to hoof camp. Where had that saddle come from? California—specifically, Vista, northwest of San Diego. Lieutenant Pedersen had written his wife, Katherine, and asked her to send a packsaddle. She went to a local veterinarian, who donated one that some time ago had been given to him in lieu of paying cash for treatment. When the saddle arrived in Korea, it was something like an early Christmas gift for the four-legged Marine.

When Christmas itself arrived, Reckless was given the day off. She was provided with some extra food as well as a couple of beers, as was the rest of the platoon. Same for New Year's, a quiet and cold day. Unfortunately for the Marines of the 1st Division, what the dawn of 1953 meant was continuing to be away from their families . . . and entering the fourth year of war, with no real end in sight.

CHAPTER ELEVEN

★ ★

A Korean "Clambake"

In January 1953, a new president arrived in the White House. On the 20th, Dwight Eisenhower was given the oath of office by Chief Justice Frederick Moore Vinson, just moments after his vice president, Richard Nixon, had been sworn in. There was hope among many of the thirty-four million American citizens who had voted for Ike that he would end the conflict in Korea. Initially, however, he would be no more successful than Harry Truman had been.

Indeed, that January the war seemed even more forgotten, almost as if a country other than the United States was doing most of the military heavy lifting. Lee Ballenger, the future author and a Marine stationed in Korea who was as frustrated as anyone, would later write, "The bulk of the American press and many military historians tended to ignore the continuous small-unit battles that occurred on a daily basis as not newsworthy. The cumulative effect of this small but tediously regular fighting made little impression on reporters. Disasters and triumphs came piecemeal, in miniature doses too small for headlines. For a lack of reporting by the military and civilians alike, the conduct and outcome of most battles were lost to history."

Events in Korea fought for headlines with news closer to home— the University of Southern California defeating Wisconsin 7–0 in the Rose Bowl, the death of country music star Hank Williams, the arrival of the new cruise ship *Andrea Doria* in New York Harbor, Dizzy Dean's election to the Baseball Hall of Fame, the convicted spies Julius and Ethel Rosenberg's appeal to Truman a few days before he left office for a stay of execution, and the projection that the national budget deficit would hit a whopping $10 billion.

With many homes still without televisions, millions of people continued to routinely go out to theaters to see movies starring Glenn Ford, Kirk Douglas, Gregory Peck, John Wayne, Clark Gable, Ava Gardner, James Stewart, and a handful of exciting newcomers including Marlon Brando, Audrey Hepburn, and Marilyn Monroe, whose potboiler *Niagara* released that month promised "a raging torrent of emotion that even nature can't control." (Arriving replacement soldiers carried news to envious Marines that the voluptuous Monroe was dating Yankees legend Joe DiMaggio, and indeed the star-crossed lovers would be married a year later.) Heard in nightclubs and streaming out of jukeboxes across America were tunes sung by Rosemary Clooney, Eddie Fisher, Doris Day, Johnnie Ray, Patti Page, and Frankie Laine with the still-popular "High Noon" from the Gary Cooper and Grace Kelly Western that had been such a big hit the previous year.

What would later be called the baby boom was continuing, and all those parents had mouths to feed and jobs to do. A faraway war in the middle of winter in a country only the size of Florida was being given less and less attention.

The depth-of-winter conditions in Korea were where its resemblance to Florida ended. Below-zero temperatures plagued the higher elevations, bruising winds swept down from the north, and snow buried the combatants on both sides of the Main Line of Resistance. The Marines had an advantage in sturdier cold-weather clothing, but they couldn't be complacent. The Chinese were not hibernating—they continued their attempts to find holes in the MLR that could be exploited with swift, strong action. The snow on the hills, especially after a blizzard-like storm, resulted in fewer lessons for Reckless, and longer lessons on the days when the weather was tolerable.

Early in the new year Reckless was introduced to a beverage that would become a favorite indulgence, or at least as much so as beer. As Sergeant Latham led her back into camp after one of those long days of training, they passed the division PX just as a supply truck was unloading a couple of cases of Coca-Cola. What the heck, Latham thought, and he grabbed a bottle and poured some of its contents into his helmet. After only one tentative taste, Reckless lapped up every drop. If the company had been looking to reach four-legged consumers, Reckless would have been an enthusiastic endorser of the sweet, fizzy product.

The Marines who observed this got a big laugh. But when Doc Mitchell was told about it, he advised that Reckless be limited to two Cokes a day. He had once read something about carbonated water and a horse's kidneys. The patient's only comment was a lusty belch after each bottle.

Daily life could never be considered cozy for the men of the 5th Regiment, but it did become even less comfortable that month. The 5th Marines were ordered to a new position, replacing the units of the 7th Regiment that guarded the outposts of East Berlin, Berlin, and the Nevada Cities—Carson, Reno, and Vegas. This would place the Marines and their Mongolian mare at the epicenter of the first major battle of the 1953 campaign.

For Reckless, the new position meant there wouldn't be the same comforts as there had been in the platoon's previous position on the

MLR and especially in reserve. No bunker or pasture awaited her on the line, and with the frozen ground covered with snow, neither could be created. She spent more time in tents next to stoves at night. That was fine enough, but there weren't as many food treats on the front line either; it was more a diet of C rations like the other Marines ate.

Reckless was also at the center of a sort of controversy. When she was near the front line and the Chinese decided to remind the Marines that their artillery was still operational, during an attack some of the men of the platoon as well as in the 1st and 2nd Battalions shrugged out of their flak jackets and draped them on the horse's back and neck. Their officers grumbled, but no one went as far as to order the Marines to cease the protective practice.

The popularity of Reckless grew. After she had been with the regiment almost three months, more and more stories about her circulated among the men. Only some of them were true. The rest were products of the minds of bored, shivering Marines grateful for any news that distracted them from the cold and the distance from home. The stories spread just as fast, though, because returning to the front line in a new position meant Reckless was coming into contact with more of the 5th Regiment, especially the 2nd Battalion. Lieutenant Pedersen's platoon was attached to it now—he established his command post next to that of Fox Company—and the Marines of this battalion came to feel that they had adopted the sorrel mare.

Members of the platoon scouted out a pasture nearby that was shielded from Chinese observers by Hill 120. Even though the enemy couldn't see this section of the valley that had once featured Panggi-dong, now a destroyed village, they would occasionally toss a few mortar rounds into it just to let the Americans know they were still keeping their eyes open. The Marines built an open-face bunker to provide Reckless with some protection.

Sergeant Latham and Corporal Coleman taught Reckless the route between the ammunition depot and the MLR. The plan devised was that during an attack, Reckless would go to the depot located over three hundred yards southeast of her pasture. There, six shells would be strapped onto her packsaddle, and with that load of about 150 pounds of shells plus saddle, Reckless would march to the front lines. In addition to the Nevada Cities outposts, the 2nd Battalion guarded the Berlin and East Berlin outposts. Beyond them were the outposts Frisco and Detroit. They had been captured by the Communists, and most Marines believed that an attempt to retake them was inevitable.

It was expected that when called upon, Reckless would carry the recoilless rifle shells to Hill 120. Lieutenant Pedersen had placed some of his men on the ridgeline there because it overlooked the MLR and Berlin and East Berlin, and the guns could reach the two enemy-controlled outposts too if necessary. The Chinese also occupied Hills 190 and 153 facing Vegas, so if that outpost was attacked the enemy would find it raining recoilless rifle shells.

Whenever the January weather allowed, Reckless made practice runs. After the first two hundred or so yards, a narrow, twisting trail took her on a forty-five-degree incline to the Hill 120 ridgeline. Reckless was no plodding plow horse—she gave herself a running start, easily carrying the weight of the saddle and shells as she trotted the first two hundred yards and then threw herself up the hill. She waited on the ridgeline, filling her lungs, until Latham or Coleman caught up.

After she got the hang of it, Reckless didn't even wait—she made her way straight to the gun crews who exchanged the shells on her back for pieces of candy in her mouth. She worked on those hard treats all the way back down to the ammunition depot. The Marines on Hill 120 were glad to see the horse abruptly appear with a last lunge at the top the hill, but they knew Reckless would be an especially welcome sight in the heat of battle. They hoped, though, that she wouldn't make an inviting target for enemy sharpshooters.

————

A couple of weeks later, Sergeant Latham was the first to notice that Reckless had lost weight to the point where her ribs began to show. He noticed too that she became fatigued sooner on the practice runs. She wasn't sick; she was simply not getting enough to eat. The pasture in winter was not a good provider. The Marines were out of hay and grain, and with the roads being in such poor condition, it wasn't practical to send a truck all the way to Seoul or anywhere south of the Imjin River, in addition to having to explain to the 5th Regiment brass the decision to send a couple of men away from the front lines. However, the sergeant noted that there was still grass on the slopes of Hill 120 not covered by snow.

A few days later when Colonel Lew Walt—who before Christmas had taken over the 5th Marines from Colonel Smoak—came to visit Fox Company, he found several Marines on their hands and knees yanking grass out of the ground. He was told, rather nervously, that before dinner and while there was still some light left in the day, the men on Hill 120 took turns grabbing grass and bringing a good mouthful to Reckless.

The new regiment CO was fine with this display of how much affection his men had for the horse, but he realized that most likely the winter would outlast the supply of grass. The colonel sent word back that the first truck to cross the Imjin from the division supply camp was to contain food for Reckless. What helped in the meantime was that a new member of Lieutenant Pedersen's platoon arrived with a crate of Wheaties and graham crackers, which Reckless enjoyed. Soon the outlines of her ribs faded.

She would need her renewed strength right away. Lew Walt was not a frontline commander who was content waiting for snow to melt. The colonel's large round face, quick to break into a smile, didn't hint at all the hard bark on him that no enemy bullet or bayonet could penetrate. To hell with the politicians—if he had to fight, he would do it to win.

Colonel Walt believed—correctly, as it turned out—that the Communists were using the deepest part of winter as a way to lull the allies while they carved new trenches out of the frozen ground and in other ways prepared to surprise his men with new offensives. Colonel Walt wanted to launch a couple of attacks to disrupt any progress the enemy had made, and grab a few prisoners who could be interrogated about what else the Communists were up to. He received approval from General Pollock, and thus "Tex" and "Clambake" joined the Marines' lexicon.

The crucial positioning of the recoilless rifle gun crews atop Hill 120 became apparent in the first operation, and even more so in the second. Both were successful raids against a familiar target, Ungok, the observation and listening post about a thousand yards north of the MLR. The hill overlooked rice paddies and offered Chinese snipers a good view of any Marines who made the mistake of exposing themselves.

During Operation Tex, the recoilless rifles targeted enemy positions and provided cover for the Marines in Dog Company of the 2nd Battalion as they attacked the Chinese troops on Hill 139 just north of Outpost Berlin. The operation lasted most of the day, and Reckless not only kept the guns supplied but did not hesitate on her trips up and down Hill 120 when the firing on both sides came fast and loud.

The raiders in Operation Clambake—which did not get under way until February 3—also benefited from fire from that hill. Two reinforced platoons from Able Company of the 1/5 launched the assault. In addition to Lieutenant Pedersen's gun crews, the attack was supported by tanks, heavy machine guns, a battery of 105-mm howitzers courtesy of the 11th Regiment, and Marine jets warming the Chinese positions with high-explosive bombs and napalm.

One of the pilots engaged in the action that day was Captain Ted Williams. The Splendid Splinter, who hailed from San Diego but was better known in Boston, had exchanged his Red Sox jersey for a Marine Corps uniform, as he had done during World War II. Williams had not seen combat in that war but he was making up for it in Korea, where he would fly a total of thirty-seven missions, often as the wingman to a future astronaut, Captain John Glenn.

At dawn on the 3rd, with the temperature two degrees below zero, allied tanks rolled across the snow-covered ground toward Kumgok, a sister hill. The plan was for the Chinese to see this move as the real attack and react accordingly. Encountering barbed wire, the tanks simply blew it away. The enemy scrambled, shifting troops and guns away from Ungok. This made life a bit easier for the two Able platoons. They were already across the frozen paddies and starting up the hill when the frantic Chinese began to rush troops back from Kumgok. The Marine pilots dove out of the morning sun at the scampering soldiers.

As Ted Williams described his run at the enemy, "I released my bombs, and as I did, it seemed that every [gun] in Korea opened up on me. Machine guns, burp guns, even rifles, you name it, they were all zeroing in on me and they all didn't miss." His plane was so badly damaged that flames erupted and Williams barely managed to land it on the first friendly airstrip he found behind the MLR.

Meanwhile, the men of Able Company made their way uphill and into the caves the Chinese had dug in Ungok. The 3rd Platoon had been held in reserve, but when the two-hour battle neared its peak, 2nd Lieutenant Raymond Murphy and his men were ordered to join the fray. They were subjected to blistering fire from rifles, burp guns, and mortars. Almost all of the officers and sergeants in the first two platoons were casualties. Lieutenant Murphy, who had just turned twenty-three, and his men now fought for the survival of the entire company. There was nothing else to do but attack where the enemy appeared to be the strongest.

It worked. While his men kept the Chinese pinned down, Murphy carried wounded Marines to safety. He was showered with shrapnel when a mortar round landed next to him, but the young officer didn't quit. When a group of Chinese suddenly approached, Murphy killed them with his carbine. He then ordered Marines off the hill, and picked up a discarded BAR to cover them with withering fire. As the bleeding lieutenant started down the hill, holding one end of a stretcher, he was again slashed by shrapnel.

Back at the MLR, a weakened Lieutenant Murphy allowed his wounds to be treated only after corpsmen had cared for the other Marines who had come back with him. Just over eight months later, a recovered Murphy was in Washington, D.C., having the Medal of Honor bestowed upon him by President Eisenhower.

The only real good news about the war for the Marines in January 1953 was that casualties were down. Only forty-two were killed, 523 were wounded (more than half seriously enough to be evacuated), and five were missing. Some comfort for a Marine on the coldest days was that with fewer offensives in winter, he was less likely to die.

More comfort would have been not to be in a position to be killed at all. William Janzen of Charlie Company in the 1/5 was nineteen when in a letter home he wrote, "Everybody over here is thoroughly disgusted with those peace talks. It makes you wonder sometimes just what the hell you're fighting for anyway. We are doing nothing but holding on to what we already have and fighting to get back what we lose. Then, after getting it back we sit down and wait for them to try and take it away again. We should be pushing on and getting this war over and done with."

Operation Clambake that first week in February indicated that maybe aggressive senior officers like the almost cherubic Colonel Walt and the dour-faced General Pollock were about to do just that.

But the raid also showed the price would be high, with fifteen men killed and seventy-three wounded. The Marines on the ground and in the air had destroyed the Chinese defenses on the hill and killed close to four hundred enemy soldiers. Clambake implied that the new year would be as bloody as the previous three, and perhaps more so.

Given that few, if any, of the prisoners taken during the Tex and Clambake raids were high-ranking officers, interrogators at best learned about the size and strength of only specific units near the MLR. For example, the equivalent of a Chinese sergeant may have had a vague idea about his battalion, but nothing above that, and certainly not what strategies were being devised by senior officers. Perhaps that was just as well. If the men of the 1st Division had known what it was up against, letters home would have had a more apprehensive tone.

Communist leaders may have had more confidence that the negotiations in Panmunjom would be successful in 1953 because they indeed used the winter to prepare to grab ground that would remain theirs when a cease-fire was declared. The digging, constructing, and fortifying of trenches was just one activity. Despite the distance to the Yalu River, the Chinese had moved vast amounts of supplies to their side of the MLR, consisting mostly of ammunition and easily portable food. And there were a lot more of the enemy to be fed. The Communists had reinforced their positions on the MLR, especially in western Korea, and many of the troops had been battle-tested in the three previous years. It was a different situation on the American side, where nearly all the replacements were new to combat.

As of February 1, the Chinese and North Korean forces totaled close to 1.1 million men. That the U.N. forces had 932,000 on duty in Korea might not appear to be a significant difference, but this number included air forces and naval personnel, with typists, clerks, and others who kept the behind-the-lines bureaucracy operating. As far as armed soldiers ready to fight, there were a lot more of them on the north than on the south side of the MLR.

Whether or not he had an idea about enemy numbers and strength, Colonel Walt wasn't done with rousting the Chinese that his 5th Marines faced and taking some more of them prisoner. To that end Operation Charlie was born. It would consist of the most intense action of the still-new year.

The goal was to retake Hill 15—which every Marine referred to as Detroit. The Communists had conquered it the previous October, and their continued occupation of it had to stick in General Pollock's craw like pieces of jagged glass. The last week in February was the time to do something about it. An assault would also be the time for many Marines, including Reckless, to distinguish themselves.

With support from 5th Regiment tanks, two platoons from Fox Company of the 2nd Battalion, commanded by Captain Dick Kurth, would lead the attack. They would have to cross more than three hundred yards of open terrain, most of it frozen rice paddies, and then go up the hill to get to the Chinese positions. The enemy had the benefit of having possessed the hill for five months, and during that time the Chinese—or more accurately, with the slave labor of Korean workers—had not only fortified the defenses but had also constructed a series of caves and tunnels. A 2nd Battalion report noted that the "defense of the hill was organized in such a manner that all bunkers and fighting holes were mutually supporting. The enemy would withdraw to caves and rabbit holes to fight when their positions were overrun. He would issue forth again to pour out fire as the assault echelon withdrew."

In other words, the Chinese defenders were like prairie dogs with guns, popping up out of hiding holes faster, they hoped, than the Marines could react. Colonel Walt and his fellow planners had not chosen an easy target for Operation Charlie.

Just after 6 a.m. on February 25, the American artillery began bombarding Detroit. At 6:15 , the two Fox 2/5 platoons headed for the hill. The lack of fire from the defenders indicated that the Chinese were surprised. Apparently, they expected the bombardment to last longer and were keeping cover, or they thought it was a feint. In only thirty-three minutes, the Marines were across the ice-blocked paddies and up much of the hill to the first trenches. They gave the defenders a rude greeting of grenades, flamethrowers, and machine guns.

Quickly, though, the Chinese snapped out of their funk. Burp guns responded and hurled potato-masher grenades filled the cold dawn air. The men of Fox 2/5 kept coming, but the losses mounted.

"I was a radioman, so I was always with the lieutenant," recalled Arlen Hensley, who grew up in the coal-mining town of Appalachia, Virginia, and whose father and two of his three brothers served as Marines. "Things were getting pretty bad there on Detroit. We lost the lieutenant. Sometimes I thought I was bad luck because I had three officers killed and one wounded when I was their radioman. But the Chinese had a lot more to do with that."

When PFC Don Johnson reached the main Chinese trench line just ten yards from the top of Detroit, he was one of only five Marines. That number was reduced to four when his platoon leader was killed. The others left were named Goff, Houseman, and Jones.

Johnson had ended up in the Marines because of restlessness and chance. He graduated from Fulton High School in upstate New York the same week the North Korean invasion began the war. He didn't pay much attention until he became bored with his job. Johnson, whose father had served in the Navy in World War I and whose three older brothers had been Navy men in the next war, hitchhiked to Oswego with a friend to join the Navy. They found a Marine recruiter instead and signed up. "We don't know what hit us," Johnson recalled more than sixty years later.

After sufficient training in the States he became a member of the newly formed 3rd Marine Brigade led by Brigadier General Lewis "Chesty" Puller, who was to become the most decorated Marine in the history of the Corps. By the winter of 1953, Johnson was in Korea and in the 5th Regiment. And on that particular February morning, he and three other Marines found themselves in an enemy nest with their CO dead.

A burp gun blast shattered Goff's left arm. Houseman took a bullet in the leg. Johnson caught shrapnel from an exploding grenade in his face. Still, the Marines took care of the Chinese in the trench line. "I don't think there was much thought given to taking prisoners," Johnson said wryly. But when they saw dozens of enemy troops on the reserve side of the hill massing for a counterattack, Goff, the squad leader, told the men it was time to get out.

"We were four, who should have been forty," Johnson recalled. "We fought our way back out, carrying Lieutenant Russell's body with us."

Goff was awarded the Silver Star for bravery, but he never did regain the use of his left arm.

As the attack continued, the Communist defenders were hit hard. During a three-hour stretch, the 11th Marines and Royal Canadian Horse Artillery launched close to twelve thousand rounds at Hill 15. Tanks threw more than seven hundred rounds of 90-mm shells. And there was the contribution of the recoilless rifles.

On this day of intense fighting the 2nd Battalion Marines realized the full value of Reckless, and how remarkable a horse she was. They also saw how the operation tested the mare to her limits. The gun crews under Sergeant John Lisenby on Hill 120 had to provide steady fire from their recoilless rifles, especially when Captain Kurth's men had to cross those three hundred yards of exposed rice paddies to reach Outpost Detroit.

Reckless made trip after trip from the ammunition depot, trotting across the even, hard-packed ground and then launching herself up the incline, appearing atop the hill and having the men there eagerly remove the fresh shells. Morning gave way to afternoon and Reckless didn't quit. Rope kept the six shells secure on her saddle when she left the ammo dump. She kept giving herself a running start, then up the slope of the hill. Marines unloaded her there, then it was back down and to the dump once more.

No matter how intense the firing became and how close the explosions were, Reckless never deviated from her path. Sergeant Latham and Corporal Coleman, who took turns accompanying her, were getting pretty bushed trying to keep up with her, each carrying two 24-pound shells, so they could easily imagine the day's toll on Reckless.

By late afternoon the running starts were considerably slower, as was her progress up the slope, requiring more of her ebbing strength to keep going. Her last trip was the twenty-fourth of the day, and she barely made it to the ridgeline. After not succeeding the first time, she had to actually back up and attempt another wrenching running start to get up the incline. When she came back down and Operation Charlie was wrapping up, Lieutenant Pedersen did the math: Reckless had to have run and walked and hiked close to twenty miles during that one day, and twenty-four trips hauling six shells per trip on her packsaddle meant she had carried at least 3,500 pounds. No wonder the tough little horse was completely spent as darkness covered the battlefield.

Back "home" with the platoon, Reckless was given a bucket of food. As she ate, Marines rubbed her down. She was too tired to be interested in a candy dessert. Only seconds after the platoon CO draped a blanket over her, Reckless was fast asleep.

The assault on Detroit was considered a success. The planners' intent was never to hold the hill—it was not as strategically important as some other outposts, such as the Nevada Cities—but to take it to show the Chinese that the Marines could, and to inflict as much damage as possible while they were at it. That they did.

CHAPTER TWELVE

★ ★

Guarding the Door

Korea was not a country where there was a swift transition into spring. Still, in March, the wind out of the north, which could normally freeze spit on a Marine's moustache, didn't feel quite so harsh, and there was the promise of it shifting soon. Snow fell less frequently and there wasn't as much of it left on the ground when the dark clouds passed. And the Marines felt like they caught a break when during the middle of the month there were days of brilliant sunshine and temperatures in the forties and fifties, and at night it stayed above freezing. However, Reckless still poked her head in a few favorite tents and was invited in to sleep by the stove.

Even if one of the Marines had tried to keep her out, Reckless would have simply shouldered him aside. As one officer, Lieutenant William Riley, who would soon become well acquainted with the recoilless rifle platoon, reflected, "Sometimes she forgot she was a horse."

Indeed, she expected to be treated like any other Marine, which included not being ignored. When she wanted more to drink or to eat and the service wasn't fast enough, she would pinch the arms of the nearest Marine.

There was a surge of hope for a quick end to the war when word spread throughout the diplomatic community and then the 1st Division that Josef Stalin had died, on March 5. If the Soviet dictator were to be replaced by someone less inclined to support the Chinese and North Korean governments, the truce talks would become more serious. However, the absence of a strong central leader meant mixed signals.

"The West could only speculate last week on the significance of the pattern of hardness and softness in the Communists' moves," reported the *New York Times*. "The speculation revolves around the question: Do the Communists intend to deal? One theory is that the Communists want to deal [because] the new Soviet regime needs time to consolidate and fill the vacuum of leadership left by Stalin's death."

While Moscow fiddled, the Chinese military leaders made a decision that saved some 1st Division lives. They kept the U.S. Army and other U.N. units to the east busy by orchestrating attacks there. One that especially stung was the retaking of the Hook, which had cost a lot of Marine blood six months earlier. There was nothing for the leathernecks to do about that now but enjoy the uncharacteristic lack of attention from the enemy in western Korea. The Chinese artillery lobbed about fifty shells a day on the 1st Division's MLR position, but compared to the downpours of the more active months, this was barely a drizzle.

Probably to prevent any further feelings of complacency, Lieutenant Colonel Jonas Platt, the commanding officer of the 1st Battalion, 5th Marines, concocted a plan for another raid. This one was called Operation Item. He figured the Chinese would be unpleasantly surprised to have Ungok hit again. General Pollock agreed.

It was Baker 1/5's turn to lead the dawn attack. It was a relatively easy one. The defenders were indeed surprised—so much so that after offering some token resistance with machine guns and grenades, they hightailed it out of the trenches. The men of the two Baker platoons destroyed what they found and left. The most difficult part of the raid was the withdrawal, as the Marines had to dodge mortar and artillery shells sent by the awakened enemy.

In the fourth week in March, right about the time the calendar says so, spring arrived in western Korea along the Main Line of Resistance. It was an odd sight to see flowers and fresh grass growing out of the ground in the valleys and on hillsides and ridgelines that had been torn up by a wide range of guns as well as being subjected to snow, ice, and single-digit temperatures. But it was kind of a happy sight too, to witness the resilience of the landscape and to see that beauty could be stronger than war and destruction. There was encouragement in endurance.

Warm weather also made the horrors of war even more evident. In winter, the Marines were so muffled in clothes, layers and layers, swaddled against the cold, that a man could be shot to pieces but only a corpsman had to look at the broken bones and the torn flesh and see blood pulsing from cut arteries and veins. The bodies were just as broken, but the evidence was buried under a couple of pairs of pants and an oversized parka.

"Men died more neatly in winter, modestly covered instead of naked and obscenely ripped apart," the Marine rifle platoon lieutenant James Brady would write. "Those heavy clothes gave death a certain muffled discretion. A man could die in decency."

No more. With the spring thaw and clothes being peeled off, the season of indecent death was beginning.

Reckless had endured the winter and now began to thrive as she had when she first was welcomed by Lieutenant Pedersen's platoon. The pasture was replenished with grass, to the relief of Marines who no longer had to forage for the mare's dinner before having their own. Though there were too many aggravating times when they got stuck on the muddy roads, trucks arrived regularly from division supply centers, offering some variety beyond the C rations to the Marines, and to Reckless as well.

More food gave her even more energy . . . and a beauty like what nature was bestowing on both sides of the MLR. After the first few times she did it, Marines kept their eyes peeled for when Reckless would suddenly begin galloping in her pasture. The speed and power the copper-colored horse displayed told the story of the champion racehorse she could have been if war had not intervened. Who knew? Maybe there was a chance that if the war ended soon enough and the Korean economy could recover, Reckless could race once again.

Robust health, exercise, and improved diet turned her coat a deep, distinctive red. The Marines of the 5th Regiment marveled at her. When first encountering Reckless, most of them had recognized or at least sensed her intelligence, humor, and even charisma. They had observed her courage under fire and her refusal to quit when tested to her limits. But now they saw a fully grown mare who was lovely to look at as well. They envisioned being back home finally, and telling family and friends how remarkable this horse named Reckless was.

They still did not know the full extent of it.

They soon would, though. In war, increasingly mild weather led to preparations for larger, longer, more deadly fighting. No doubt the enemy was reinforcing its positions and plotting the directions and details of its spring offensive. They weren't being coy about it either, as every day the Chinese artillery and mortar squads were more active. Nature's display of beauty was going to be short-lived.

General Pollock, Colonel Walt, and the commanding officers of other units right down to platoon level knew that the 1st Division would bear the brunt of new attacks by the Communists because it stood between them and Panmunjom and Seoul. Whether the folks back home cared or not, the Marines had a job to do.

The last week in March, the biggest job was to stay alive. That went for Reckless too. There had been Belleau Wood in World War I and Iwo Jima in World War II, but the Korean War veteran Lieutenant Colonel Andrew Geer would later write, "The savagery of the battle for the so-called Nevada Complex has never been equaled in Marine Corps history." Reckless would be right in the middle of the five-day fight that cost the Marines dearly.

The Nevada Cities complex had increased in importance strategically the longer the war had continued, and thus was of critical importance in the early spring of 1953. The Reno, Carson, and Vegas outposts were northeast of the Ungok hills—the object of those recent Marine raids—overlooking a road that passed between the hills and Carson. This road was important because it led to Seoul and was viewed as an enemy invasion route.

The outposts were the key to keeping the Jamestown Line intact. If the Marines were forced to withdraw to the other side of the Imjin River, that would expose the Army units on the right and they would have to retreat across the Samichon River. The door would be open to Seoul.

The Communists would have weighty leverage at the Panmunjom truce talks—pretty much game over for the allies. Refusing to accept whatever crumbs the Communists offered meant, at best, an indefinitely extended war requiring many more men and much more matériel to recapture lost territory. Even if President Eisenhower was willing to authorize that, fewer Americans would stomach it. A truce would equal defeat for the United Nations and their forces, and essentially the lives lost during the previous three-plus years would have been wasted.

The Nevada Cities complex of outposts had to be held, whatever it took. And it would take a lot.

There was more to the geographical importance of those outposts. They provided something like observation decks for the Marines to see the enemy side of the Main Line of Resistance and at the same time blocked from enemy eyeballs some of the American side. Though they were viewed together as a complex, each hill had its own geographic characteristics that had to be considered when deciding how best to defend it, which was mostly the responsibility of Colonel Lew Walt's 5th Marines.

Carson was on the left. A mostly barren hilltop, it contained a cave housing Marines who manned an oval-shaped perimeter festooned with barbed wire. Behind it were bunkers, tunnels, and a five-foot-deep trench with twenty-eight fighting holes. Vegas was the tallest of the three outposts, at 575 feet. It had an egg-shaped perimeter and behind the barbed wire was a trench five or six feet deep. There were three bunkers—two were living quarters, and the third was a warming station.

In the middle was Reno. It had the most precarious position within the complex. In addition to Reno being closest to the enemy lines, the ridge to be defended required a perimeter that had its open end on the north, facing the Chinese troops. The cave was connected to the trench—this one was as much as seven feet deep in spots—by a tunnel. But on Reno there were no bunkers; thus the Marines had to rely on only their fighting holes. It was especially stressful to be assigned to Reno because every Marine figured that would be the outpost hit first when the anticipated major assault came.

One of the most effective ways of being warned was a decidedly low-tech one. When the Marines were finished eating C rations, they threw the tin cans in the gullies. Hearing them rattle at night alerted the defenders to probing enemy troops, and the carbines and machine guns were unleashed. Many mornings, Korean laborers were called to the gullies to drag off and bury the Chinese dead.

"Rotation was one week on an outpost, then two weeks on the MLR," Corporal James Pruitt of the 2nd Battalion, who was stationed on Reno, recalled. "The outposts stank. Flies, rats, garbage, fecal wastes all contributed to the effluvium. The worst job was covering the Chinese bodies that lay on the side of the hill. Korean laborers were hired to go down and bury the dead, but it took armed Marines to 'escort' them. It was part protection, part compulsion. Then a few mortar rounds would fall and the buried bodies would turn up again, smelling worse than before."

South of this outpost was the L-shaped trench known as Reno Block. It contained a small bunker and a machine-gun position. It existed as a listening post and a jumping-off point for reinforcements if Reno itself was under attack. Reno Block could be seen by Chinese snipers, so the Marines had to keep their heads down during the day and at night cup the glow of cigarettes.

Lighting cigarettes had to be especially tough in late March. "During the spring thaw it rained steadily," remembered Corporal Robert Hall, who at that time was a machine gunner attached to Fox Company of the 2nd Battalion, 5th Marines. "Trenches and bunkers flooded and turned into mudholes that required constant attention. Chiggies did much of the work needed to clean them out. The name 'Chiggie' for the Korean laborers came from our inability to pronounce the Japanese and Korean word for 'move' or 'hurry.' The Koreans were willing and cheerful. They liked it when we would get into the mud and dig alongside them, and they loved American cigarettes."

As important as the three Nevada Cities outposts were, each could be manned by only forty to four dozen Marines—representing a composite platoon culled from the companies in the 1st Battalion—and two Navy corpsmen. There wasn't room atop the hills and in the caves and bunkers for more than that. The defenders had their M-1s, carbines, pistols, BARs, light machine guns, and even a couple of flamethrowers. The outposts were supported by 60-mm and 81-mm mortars. At any given time all three outposts were manned by fewer than 150 men in total, but those Marines packed quite a wallop. Commanders also wanted fresh eyes and reflexes up there, so the defenders were rotated regularly. This also helped keep the stress at a tolerable level. Every Marine who came away from Carson, Vegas, or Reno felt like he had literally dodged a bullet.

Many of the Marines on the Main Line of Resistance knew or at least sensed that something big was about to happen. One payoff from the February raids was a handful of Chinese troops taken prisoner, and during interrogations they revealed that there was a buildup of men, equipment, and other resources on their side of the MLR. Allied observers had noted fewer enemy patrols, and the Marines had not been springing into action to confront probes of the MLR as much as had been routine.

It also made sense that the Chinese would take advantage of the spring thaw . . . or, rather, that the allies would be at a disadvantage with the year's first improvement of weather. They depended much more than the enemy did on tanks, trucks, and other mechanized vehicles to move men, munitions, and supplies from the rear to the MLR as well as to specific positions that were under attack. With early spring offering rain alternating with snow-melting sunshine, roads and trails up and around the hilltop outposts were turning into mudslides, reducing the agility of the allies, thus taking away the benefits they needed to compensate for the enemy's advantage in number of fighting men.

If indeed the Communists were up to something, Colonel Lew Walt and his men would be smack in the middle of it. The 7th Marines were in reserve while the 1st Marines were on the far left side of the Main Line of Resistance. The 5th Marines had six miles of front line to defend. And they had to be prepared for whatever happened, wherever it was.

CHAPTER THIRTEEN

★ ★

"We'll Give 'Em Hell Anyway"

March 26, 1953, was a Thursday, and an unusually mild day. Some of the Marines removed a couple of layers of clothes and turned their stubbled faces to the teasingly warm early-spring sun.

It was a pleasant day, but also a confusing one in some ways. Through the ranks the sense of foreboding was stronger than ever. PFC Don Johnson, who had survived the assault on Outpost Detroit, and the rest of Fox 2/5 had been placed in reserve two days earlier, then sent back to the front lines, and on that Thursday they were again in reserve . . . to be told in the afternoon to get back to the front. "We were introduced to our new platoon leader," Johnson recalled. "He was replacing Lieutenant 'Truck' Cullom, who had replaced Lieutenant Russell, whose body we carried off Detroit."

He continued: "Cullom was something else, completely fearless. I served as his point on a couple of patrols, and he never mailed it in.

Some officers might go a few yards into the paddy, rest, then return. Not Cullom. I think that is what caused him to trip a mine and suffer those terrible injuries. But that mine saved his life. Had he still been in charge of the 1st Platoon on March 26, he would have been out in front, totally unafraid, an easy target. As it was, Cullom's replacement, the new officer, whose name I never remembered, was twelve hours away from being killed."

According to Colonel Walt, "The day of March 26 was normal during daylight working hours with no indication of what was to come except for a large amount of incoming, which had been occurring for several days previous. However, at precisely 1900 the enemy launched a coordinated attack by fire all along our regimental front."

The battle had at last begun.

Because of the sense of foreboding in the days leading up to March 26, the Marines were more protective of Reckless than usual. An incident that had taken place a few nights earlier made them even more concerned.

The only way to explain it is to say that sometimes Reckless became bored. She was such a familiar presence in Lieutenant Pedersen's platoon that the men no longer made much of a fuss over her. She was used to attention—it could perhaps be said that she had become something of a prima donna. Maybe she was as vain as a movie star. Every so often, because of ennui and to be noticed, at night she strolled out of her pasture and headed toward the front lines. Corporal Coleman or one of the others in the platoon would spot her and lead her back to her bunker and bed her down for the night.

Later in March, though, on an especially moonless and dark night, Reckless managed to mosey all the way to Charlie 1/5's position at the front. She was certainly noticed there. A few of the men risked sniper fire by going over to greet her with pats on the head and offered treats.

The Marines had to figure that the men of what was now known as the Reckless Rifle platoon had realized she was missing, but they were in no hurry to designate someone to lead her back.

They regretted that only a few minutes later. Reckless was working on the contents of a C ration can when the Chinese suddenly launched an artillery assault. The abruptness of the attack was surprising, as was the severity of it. The Marines jumped into bunkers and firing holes, but none of them could accommodate a nine-hundred-pound horse.

The men of Charlie Company hurried her into a trench and prodded her into the deepest part of it. Flak jackets were removed and placed on Reckless. She tolerated every one of them except the one that covered her head, which she shook off. The men implored her to keep it on, pointing out that her head and neck were exposed. Apparently understanding them, and surprising the Marines who hadn't witnessed the talent before, Reckless demonstrated that she knew how to kneel.

The enemy barrage did not last long, but it was nerve-racking. Several times a shell landed close enough to shower the red-haired horse with rocks and dirt. She was unperturbed, snorting as if to say she had been in combat before. When the dark night was quiet again, a runner was sent to Lieutenant Pedersen. Reckless did not appear the worse for wear after her adventure, but the men of Charlie Company felt pretty stupid for allowing the horse to remain in harm's way.

Reckless was nowhere near the front on March 26. She enjoyed the mild afternoon in her pasture, which was displaying shoots of fresh grass reaching for the sun. She ate dinner with the others in the Reckless Rifle platoon, and her routine was to roam for a bit in the pasture before watching some of the men play poker or checkers until it was time for dessert.

But this would not be a routine night.

Soon after 7 p.m., when the artillery bombardment had begun,

Sergeant Latham took a risk by running to the pasture to see how Reckless was doing. She had been exposed to enemy fire before, as recently as those few nights earlier, but nothing like this. The sky was repeatedly lit up as though there were hundreds of lightning flashes, and there was the thunder of a thousand storms as the Chinese big guns exploded, soon to be echoed by the responses of the 11th Marines. Previously, the pasture had been considered safe, but now the enemy was letting it all out. Most of the men of the 5th Regiment understood that on this night there wasn't a safe place anywhere in western Korea.

Wisely, Reckless had sought safety in her bunker. But her usual confidence was obviously fragile. She was restless, trembling slightly, and Joe Latham could feel that her coat was slick with sweat. The sorrel mare's trembling increased as the flashes of light and pounding thunder intensified. Latham tried to reassure her with food treats, but she wasn't interested.

Reluctantly, the sergeant left the bunker and made his way back to the platoon. He wanted to stay with Reckless, but he knew he and the other Marines had to be ready for whatever else the Communists were about to throw at them.

When the major assault began, there was nothing subtle about it. Unfortunately, the attack was so massive that Colonel Walt and General Pollock and their staffs could not tell which were feints and which were real targets . . . or indeed, were the Chinese capable and bent on overwhelming a large swath of territory containing up to a dozen outposts. Perhaps this was the Communist version of the Battle of the Bulge, when every German gun and fighting man available was thrown at the Allies.

The early-evening darkness was shattered when at approximately 7 p.m. an intense shower of 60-mm and 82-mm mortar rounds and

76-mm artillery shells fell on Outposts Reno and Carson. It was estimated that in the first twenty minutes close to twelve hundred rounds hit the second outpost. Even when the shelling slowed, it was later estimated that until 8 p.m. a mortar round fell on Carson every forty seconds. During the worst of it, there was nothing for the Marines on Carson to do but burrow down as much as they could and eat dirt.

Within ten minutes of the beginning of the assault by air, it was Vegas's turn for similar treatment. Suddenly, the bunkers and other forms of shelter seemed transparent. As each Marine on Vegas scrunched himself deep into the ground, he felt like there was a huge bull's-eye on his back.

While all this was going on, the Chinese opened up on the entire sector manned by the 1st Battalion with machine guns, small arms, and more mortars. And their artillery sent shells at the positions of the 11th Marines, delaying the American artillery's response. Individual Chinese troops were sent crawling toward Marine positions to cut telephone lines. By this time, every commanding officer in the 5th Marines believed this was finally the enemy offensive they had been anticipating. And dreading.

But the Chinese were making that realization a difficult one. Confusion, they knew, would weaken the defense. They also fired mortars and other weapons at the 3rd Battalion positions at the Berlin and East Berlin outposts to the right of the 1st Battalion. They hit the 1st Regiment positions to the left too, bombarding Outposts Hedy, Esther, Dagmar, and blood-soaked Bunker Hill. Berlin and East Berlin, still manned by units of the 5th Regiment, came under attack as well.

Soon, though, there was no doubt that the Nevada Cities complex was the main target. A total of 3,500 Chinese from the 120th Division of the 46th Army were in the first wave. They streamed out of the Ungok and Arrowhead hills and Hills 190 and 25A to hit Carson while others veered off and vaulted up toward Vegas, and whistling and blowing bugles they came at Reno too.

Some people called it the Korean "conflict," but this was all-out war.

The Communists slugged Outpost Reno hard. A company of them ran across the Seoul road and attacked it from the northwest. More enemy troops attacked the left flank. Within minutes, the outpost was under assault from three sides and the forty Marines there, facing a combined force that was equivalent to a battalion, were threatened with being cut off and surrounded.

Things got bad fast for the Reno defenders. No matter how many Chinese they killed, there were more running uphill right behind them. They overwhelmed the outer works and the Marines had to fall back. On more of them came, and the defenders had to fall back from the trenches too. But they made the Chinese pay for every inch they gained, killing as many as they could before being killed, buying time for the reinforcements they hoped were on the way.

Not soon enough. There were so many enemy troops streaming onto the Reno hilltop from three sides that by 8 p.m. the last resort for the Marines was to drag wounded into the cave and seal it off. The enemy couldn't get in . . . but the men inside were confronted with a dwindling supply of oxygen. Even if they wanted to break out of what had become a tomb, there was little hope of that—a head count revealed only seven Marines still able to fight. The simple facts of their dire situation were radioed to 5th Regiment headquarters.

Because the enemy had pretty much cut Outpost Reno off from the MLR, reinforcements from the regiment were having a tough time getting to it. For the most part, they were pinned down. Colonel Walt and other officers knew that every second counted to save those seven men and the wounded with them. The situation was even worse than they thought. Mortars continued to pound the hilltop, threatening the closed-off cave with collapse. The Marines inside faced suffocation one way or the other—either their air would run out or they would be buried alive when the cave ceiling gave way.

The best that Colonel Walt could do to buy time was to have the gunners of the 11th Marines send shells that burst above the swarming Chinese troops, shredding them with hot metal, and have tanks lobbing 90-mm rounds where the highest concentrations of enemy were. Reinforcements were still pinned down when HQ lost radio contact with those Marines left on Reno.

But Fox Company of the 2/5, commanded by Captain Ralph Walz, was on its way. It had been ambushed near Hill 47 short of Reno Block and pinned down for a time, but with sheer determination and small arms blazing the Marines fought their way out and continued on toward Reno. Every step forward, though, seemed to take too long.

Also hoping to rescue the trapped Marines were the 1st and 3rd Platoons of Charlie 1/5, whose commanding officer was Captain Robert "Big Dog" Young. A few minutes after 8:30 a.m., the 3rd Platoon's CO, Second Lieutenant Warren Ruthazer, received orders to get up to Outpost Reno right away, drive the enemy out, and either defend the position or at least bring back the Marines who were still alive. The combined force of the Charlie Company platoons set off on the 1,800-yard trail that went past Reno Block and ended at the hilltop outpost. One of the guides along the way was Sergeant William Janzen, a member of the Charlie's 3rd Platoon.

His first assignment that evening had been to go down to the "cut"—Charlie's gate through the MLR into no-man's-land—and make sure the troops in the trench line were well dispersed because of the heavy incoming fire. "The Chinese were also firing long-range machine-gun fire on the MLR, something I had never witnessed before," Janzen recalled. "After arriving at the MLR, I accomplished my mission by running like a scared rabbit from one bunker to another. I would talk to the men inside for a while, briefing them on what I knew and giving instructions to be ready for anything. Then, I'd listen for incoming, take a deep breath and run like hell."

There was no running on the trail. It would not have been too tough to navigate even in the middle of the night, but it was very rough going with a seemingly endless supply of enemy shells landing left and right, in front and behind. Drills during boot camp were cakewalks compared to the number of times now that Marines had to drop to the ground, pray not to be in a shell's landing zone, then jump back up and double-time it up the hill. Deviating from the trail was not an option because of minefields and the risk of falling prey to an enemy ambush.

Sergeant Janzen lost count of how many times he hit the ground, recited the Lord's Prayer, felt the earth shake under him, was covered in a shower of dirt and mud, and jumped up again. He felt lucky not to be hit. PFC Bobby Hatcher next to him felt luckier. Seconds after he hit the ground a shell landed next to his head . . . and didn't explode.

"The noise was unbelievable," Sergeant Jansen reported. "Constant explosions. Friendly and enemy mortars especially, mixing it up often in the same locations. And hand grenades. The almost constant rattle of small arms—rifles, BARs, machine guns, and enemy burp guns. Also, flares were up in the sky almost constantly from aircraft, artillery, and mortars. The mortars were the most frightening. From the sound you couldn't tell if they were going to be close or far away."

The Marines reached the point when they had to trudge up a steep incline called the "ladder" to reach Reno Block. Previously, a thick rope extended down so that each man had help hoisting himself up. But at least one Chinese shell had landed at that spot and the rope was in muddy shreds, leaving the Marines to climb the slope on their hands and knees, clawing at the ground. They reached the top to discover that Reno Block had already been taken and was occupied by Chinese troops.

Sergeant Janzen: "By now, the head of the column was heavily engaged with the Chinese at close quarters. We would move forward, then move back, then move forward, then move back. We were packed in like sardines and crawled in the mud on our hands and knees."

Good news was the arrival of Captain Walz with two platoons from his Fox 2/5. Immediately sizing up the situation—despite a barrage of white phosphorus that singed some of his men—and with every second precious, the captain told the Marines to fix bayonets. The ensuing assault, Sergeant Janzen remembered, was both "magnificent" and "ghastly." The Chinese were taken by surprise, turning to find angry and shouting Marines charging, thrusting their bayonets into the first bodies they encountered. Whatever initial resistance there was broke swiftly. The brutal battle was over within minutes, with wounded and terrified enemy troops crawling and running down the opposite slope.

What the Marines did not know—just as well, probably—was that Outpost Reno up ahead was completely in Communist hands. There was a radio transmission at 9:44 p.m. that told listeners the remaining men were using their hands to try to dig their way out of the cave on the side opposite from where the Chinese were trying to dig in and that reinforcements better hurry up. After being told that those reinforcements were stalled at Reno Block, the Marine on the radio said, "Well, we'll give 'em hell anyway."

When the Chinese rushed through the cave opening they had carved, they captured five Marines, including Second Lieutenant Rufus Seymour, the outpost commander, and a Navy corpsman. With thirty-eight dead, those five were the only ones left.

CHAPTER FOURTEEN

★ ★

"Hold at All Costs"

Reno Block, at least, had been retaken. But the cost had been high. For example, just in the 3rd Platoon of Charlie Company alone, only ten men had escaped being killed or wounded. That was where the two corpsmen Lieutenant Ruthazer had brought with him proved valuable—more valuable than anyone would have asked for. One was Hospitalman Third Class Paul Polley, and the other was Hospitalman Francis Hammond.

"As our casualties mounted, our corpsmen performed heroically," Janzen said. "Polley was wounded twice. Hit badly in the shoulder, he was also blinded, but he refused to leave. He continued to treat wounded Marines by having them place his hands on their wounds, and then he'd patch them up."

Polley, from Kentucky, was twenty-three years old. Though he couldn't see, he kept refusing to be carried or at least led back down to the MLR. Finally, though, the time came when weakness from loss of blood combined with exhaustion to persuade him to leave. On his way, however, he encountered a group of wounded Marines. Once more he was led to one man after another, blindly treating them by touch. Polley did this until he collapsed and was carried to a treatment tent behind the MLR. He would receive the Navy Cross for his actions.

Hammond, who hailed from Virginia, was twenty-one years old. He had been hit earlier in the evening but, like Polley, refused evacuation and kept ministering to other Marines who had been wounded. Even when some of Ruthazer's platoon was ordered to pull out, Hammond remained to help evacuate the men he had just treated. It was a mortar shell that killed him. Hammond was awarded the Medal of Honor and was buried in Arlington National Cemetery, next to where he grew up, in Alexandria.

The job of holding Reno Block would have been difficult enough for Captain Walz and his composite company, but the overriding mission was to rescue whoever was left on Outpost Reno. They tried. But every time the Marines prepared to head for higher ground, the Chinese attacked first. Time after time, wave after wave of enemy troops rushed Reno Block, and the defenders barely clung to it. The Marines refused to be forced backward, but they couldn't go forward either. Even when there were lulls between assaults, the Chinese artillery shells gouged the ground between Reno Block and the outpost.

When the Chinese troops came at Carson a little after 7 p.m., it wasn't just the ferocity of the attack that set the Marines back on their heels, it was the sheer number of enemy soldiers. It was estimated that the leathernecks were outnumbered by as much as twenty to one. Being in a strongly fortified position with reinforcements nearby counted for a lot, but the rest was up to the defenders standing their ground.

For more than half an hour the screaming and bugle-blowing Chinese came on, wave after wave of them. As with Reno, they were able to take the outer trenches, but that was as far as they got. The Marines, led by Lieutenant Jack Ingalls of Charlie 1/5, the outpost CO that night, fired carbines and pistols, eventually at point-blank range, and still the enemy kept coming.

An hour after the onset of the attack, at 8 p.m., the Marines were throwing back Chinese forces with bayonets, knives, rifles, and bare fists in the close, heavy fighting at Carson. The hilltop was piled with enemy bodies.

Telephone communication with Lieutenant Ingalls's company commander was gone, but the Outpost Carson radio worked for the first hour. Ingalls could hear the radio operator on Reno calling for help. When that man's voice was replaced by Chinese voices, the lieutenant feared the worst. The Chinese assaults on his position continued, and he radioed for instructions, hoping what he would hear was that reinforcements were on the way. Instead, the message back was: "Hold at all costs."

The Chinese broke off the assault at 8:10—an intercepted Chinese message said that the charge "has completely collapsed"—and they melted off the side of the hill. This gave the Outpost Carson defenders an opportunity to separate the dead from the wounded and move the latter into the protection of the cave where they could be treated by the two Navy corpsmen. The Marines in the fighting holes along the main trench kept busy by firing down at the retreating Chinese. Meanwhile, squads from Charlie and Dog Companies of the 1st and 2nd Battalions of the 5th Regiment arrived to reinforce the outpost. Enemy gunners greeted them with a steady rain of artillery and mortar shells.

The attack on Outpost Vegas had also been launched at 7 p.m. Private James Larkin, a native of New York City, would have been a casualty if it had commenced a little earlier.

He was an artillery forward observer with Able Battery, 1st Battalion of the 11th Regiment. Born in the Bronx, he was only seventeen when he joined the Marines in 1950.

On the 26th, he had spent much of the day on Vegas. Like many other Marines that day, Larkin had a feeling something was about to happen. Who knew how big, but something. He figured it would be when night fell. That was the Chinese way of doing things. Maybe he would be off Vegas by then.

He was. Shortly before 6 that evening, Steve Drummond arrived atop the hill and told Larkin he was there to relieve him. The two men shook hands, then Larkin began to half run, half crawl down past the outpost to the bottom of the hill and across the mud-slick rice paddies to the MLR. It turned out he was in more danger leaving Vegas than being on it because once the Chinese mortar gunners caught sight of him, they began launching shells. The enemy's long-range artillery was getting warmed up too, so Larkin was in double jeopardy. He was quick and fast, though—and lucky—so he arrived safely at a listening post about fifty yards in front of the first Marine trench. There he joined the others at the post who were trying to burrow into the ground because, Larkin recalled, the artillery shells "were lighting up the landscape and sending up huge spouts of water and mud."

The artillery fire seemed to be intensifying. Still, when there was a slight lull, Larkin dashed the rest of the way to make a report to his commanding officer attached to the 1st Battalion, 5th Regiment. It was then that the Chinese attack began in full force. Larkin said sixty years later, "I had the blessings of the man upstairs to walk away alive." However, he was far from finished with Vegas.

As with the men defending Outpost Reno, the Marines of How Company were in trouble quickly. Most if not all of them had never experienced an artillery barrage like the one the Chinese threw at

Vegas during the middle of that dark and noisy night, and it seemed like whatever square foot one of those shells didn't land in, a mortar round did.

As the hordes of Communist troops rushed the outpost, the Marines could tell immediately that they were grossly outnumbered. As the enemy overran the front trench, it was impossible to mount any credible defense. The Marines pulled back from the outer positions. They would make a stand where they could.

Thanks to Chinese infiltrators as well as artillery and mortar shells, most of the communication wire that Reckless and other Marines had painstakingly strung was cut. From the time the attack began, staying in touch with First Lieutenant Kenneth Taft Jr., the outpost commander, and his men on Vegas was difficult. Requests by Colonel Walt for updates usually ended in frustration, especially as the attacks intensified, and even radio transmissions were spotty.

Vegas was being overwhelmed. A desperate Lieutenant Taft requested a "VT"—variable time fuse—artillery bombardment on his own position. "VT fuses could be set to explode shells fifteen to twenty feet above the Chinese troops," recalled Colonel Anthony Caputo, whose 2nd Battalion, 7th Regiment was waiting for orders from his CO. "The Marines on Vegas were magnificent in holding the Chinese off as long as they could, but with such overwhelming numbers, there was no choice to put artillery right on top of them."

The Marines moved into a cave on their side of the hill and prayed while the 11th Marines launched the VT bombardment.

Colonel Walt wasn't giving up on Outpost Vegas yet. At 10:05, a platoon from Dog 2/5 was sent out to reinforce the men on it. They got as close as they could, which was about four hundred yards from the bottom of the hill, where mortar shells rained down on them. There was nothing for the men to do but flatten out and cling to the ground and hope not to be instantly turned into a crater. When they did lift their heads, they saw only Chinese troops on the hill.

A platoon from Easy 2/5 was ordered to reinforce the reinforcements. When the two units linked up they pushed forward, covering about half the distance to Vegas. But once again the Marines were pinned down, with incessant small-arms fire joining the mortar barrage.

On the hill, Outpost Vegas was being overrun, and its loss was inevitable. "We started out with maybe forty guys, and it seemed like there were a thousand Chinese coming up from three sides," recalled Bernard Hollinger, a twenty-three-year-old private with How Company, 3rd Battalion, 5th Marines. "We were firing like mad out of the trenches but they kept coming. Too many of them got close enough that they could toss grenades right into the trenches."

One of those grenades hit Hollinger, and the subsequent explosion ripped the rifle out of his hands and he lost consciousness. After what was probably only a few seconds he came to a bit. His first thought was that he was dead, he said, but "I felt a little ping, and realized here was one of them jabbing me with a bayonet to see if I was still alive."

Fortunately, he was, with the only apparent injury being a sharp pain in one of his ears. Unfortunately, he was taken prisoner by the Chinese, who now controlled the outpost.

Communication with the Marines on Vegas came to a complete halt just before midnight. That and what appeared to be much less firing at the outpost told Colonel Walt that the Marines there were dead or taken prisoner. The combined reinforcements were told to return to the MLR.

Not all the Americans at Outpost Vegas were dead, though. One who was still alive was Billy Rivers Penn. A corpsman from McComb, Mississippi, he was twenty years old and had been in Korea only six weeks, having arrived, inauspiciously, on Friday the 13th. Soon after the Battle of the Nevada Cities began on the evening of March 26,

Penn, while attached to How Company of the 5th Marines, heard that corpsmen were needed on Vegas. He arrived just as the Chinese were beginning to penetrate the defensive perimeter.

He went straight to the command bunker. The artillery barrage was intensifying, but above the roar and thunder he heard a voice calling for a corpsman. He was taking care of the wounded Marine in a trench when two Chinese soldiers jumped him. One stuck a bayonet through his left leg above the ankle, and Penn couldn't move. The soldier couldn't get the bayonet back out, and Penn watched as the soldier's finger tightened on the trigger, knowing he was about to fire the rifle. He could only hope the recoil would help dislodge the bayonet, though it would probably take what was left of the corpsman's foot with it. The gun clicked. The enemy soldier began to cock his rifle with the bolt action when Penn produced his .45 and shot him in the head. The impact lifted the soldier three feet down the trench.

"The Chinese were so small, they just looked like ants with a ten-inch waist," Penn recalled. "They were more of them on us. They had run up the hill with their own artillery still firing."

He was able to remove the bayonet and rifle from his leg and started pulling the wounded Marine into the command bunker with Chinese troops all around him. He was hit in the left knee by shrapnel, then took a shot from a burp gun in the right shoulder, a through-and-through wound. A bayonet in the right lower back glanced off his flak jacket. As Penn turned, his elbow caught an enemy soldier in the throat. The man fell, and Penn jumped on him, adrenaline and anger combining into fury. Penn pounded him so often that when he finally stood up, the soldier was not moving at all.

According to the beleaguered corpsman, "There were more of them on us. I picked up an entrenchment tool and started swinging. I hit one in the neck, and the way his body was shaking on the ground I thought I had decapitated him. I had a flashback of wringing a chicken's neck back home. Dead Chinese were all over. Everyone was in hand-to-hand combat. I saw my friend Woody standing outside his machine-gun bunker, swinging his gun like a baseball bat. Trying to get another Marine back to the command bunker, I was jumped again by a Chinese and I beat him unconscious with a rock."

As he stooped to get out of the command bunker again—the door was only four feet tall—Penn was hit by a rifle butt in the helmet. Reflexively, he raised his .45 and it went off on the tip of the enemy soldier's nose. "I'll never forget the expression on his face as the .45 went off, or the feeling I had seeing what power the .45 had at point-blank range."

Penn backed into the command bunker, seeing what looked like a thousand Chinese all over Vegas. Just as he squatted behind a twelve-by-twelve support, a satchel charge came in the door. All he saw after that was a big flash of white light. When he regained consciousness, he could see only blurs of light. He was mostly buried under dirt and the support beam. Chinese soldiers were digging him out. He thought he was the only one left alive: "I could feel arms and legs all around but no one was moving or crying out."

Penn was dragged away and hauled up into the back of a truck with four or five wounded Marines. They were all now prisoners of war.

By midnight on the 26th, after five blistering hours of battle, the early efforts of the enemy had been partly successful. Two of the Nevada Hill outposts had fallen, and Marine attempts to strengthen them were initially being thwarted by Chinese troops who had overflowed past Reno Block and southward toward the MLR. Outpost Carson was holding. But the Chinese were in control of Reno and Vegas and were using the Reno position to mass troops and firepower to bolster the continuing assault on Vegas.

By then, it was clear to Colonel Walt that his regiment had suffered staggering losses. Reno and its defenders were gone. The same, most likely, for Vegas. Of the three essential outposts, only Carson remained under the control of the 5th Regiment, and the Marines there were barely clinging to it. The men under Captain Walz at Reno Block had been whittled down to the equivalent of a single reinforced platoon.

In his classic book *This Kind of War*, T. R. Fehrenbach wrote: "Compared to Gettysburg, Bastogne, or Verdun, the outpost battles that erupted across Korea from time to time were skirmishes, pinpricks next to the wounds of the world's great battles. But on the bodies of troops actually engaged the casualties were exceedingly high. When companies are reduced to forty men, and platoons to six or seven, to the men in them it is hardly limited war."

Soon after the sun set on March 26, the Communists had unleashed unlimited war, hurling men and bombs and everything else they had on three outposts whose capture could guarantee a sweeping victory. They had reduced companies to platoons and platoons to squads and left them bruised and bloodied.

There was really only one thing left for the most decorated Marine Corps regiment to do: Attack.

PART III

★ ★

★ ★

CHAPTER FIFTEEN

No Marine Left Behind

I f Colonel Lew Walt could have had his way, elements of the 5th Marines would have regrouped immediately and hit the Communists hard before they could bolster their newly captured positions on the Reno and Vegas hills. However, his commanding officers in the field were reporting that there were still many wounded requiring evacuation and even some men who were missing. Too many units, below strength to begin with, had become shells of their former selves. Any hope of recapturing Reno right away evaporated when Captain Ralph Walz reported at 1:44 a.m. on March 27 that in effect Fox Company of the 2nd Battalion, 5th Marines, had been reduced to the size of a platoon.

He was ordered to lead an attack anyway.

The Marines moved forward out of Reno Block—not once, but three times. "Initially, there were only about forty of us who counterattacked

Reno—one understrength rifle platoon reinforced by one understrength squad from another platoon and one machine gun," recalled Sergeant William Janzen. "Intelligence later said that it was estimated that we ran into about 250 Chinese."

For the men remaining in Fox 2/5, it had already been a very long twenty-four hours. According to PFC Don Johnson, early on the day before, the 26th, the company had been told they would soon be going on a raid on Detroit in an attempt to draw Chinese troops and artillery activity away from two other crucial positions held by the Marines, Pork Chop Hill and Old Baldy. That day's task was to practice for the raid.

"We had a new man attached to us who had served his tour in the rear and had volunteered to stay there and join a line company," Johnson recalled. "His name was Struthers. My buddy Everett Jones and I had him in our bunker and got all over him for doing that. He was a sole surviving son and as such could not serve in combat."

Struthers was no dummy. As soon as it dawned on him that Jones and Johnson were making sense, he applied to be rotated back to the States as a sole surviver. That application was approved on the morning of the 26th. However, Struthers felt either guilty or that he was cheating himself out of seeing some action, because when Fox Company was told about the rehearsal raid to be made, he asked to go along. "Since we felt we would be going back to the reserve area after the practice, it would be okay for him to ride along with us," Johnson said.

But the practice run on Detroit was canceled and Fox 2/5 was ordered to lock and load. "We were told that we were going to retake Reno," said Johnson. "The attack was scheduled for the next morning, and I was not looking forward to it. I had already been to Detroit and I had a good idea what we could expect. Sure enough, we moved out and started drawing artillery fire even before we could get out of the trucks in the assembly area. I received one bandolier of ammunition and two grenades. I knew that would never be enough. It wasn't."

"As soon as we got out of the trucks, mortar fire started coming in," PFC Arlen Hensley remembered. "But we just laid our stuff down and went into the nearest bunkers. When the mortar barrage finally stopped, I went looking for my pack. It was gone. I thought somebody stole it in the middle of a battle. Then a guy said, 'No, over there's your radio.' There were feathers all around and the guy said, 'That's your sleeping bag.'"

Unfortunately, more than radios and sleeping bags were casualties of the barrage. Struthers was among those killed. "I think about him often," Johnson said, "and what that must have done to his mother."

Another casualty was Johnson himself, when a mortar shell took off his right leg. "Everett Jones carried me a thousand yards to an aid station where I received the last rites. My leg was amputated on April 1 aboard the hospital ship *Jutlandia*."

"There was another mortar attack, and me and another Marine had started up the hill," Hensley said. "A shell landed close to him and a big piece of shrapnel hit his helmet. He had a concussion and his eyes were full of dirt and I had a concussion. We didn't want to leave him there so the CO told me to take him back. I did, they checked me out too, said I was okay, so I went up the hill again, and then I got wounded. We lost a lot of men on that hill."

Though down to only platoon strength, at 2 a.m. Captain Walz and his men attacked through a hail of shrieking metal. Shrapnel seemed to be flying everywhere, a merciless and almost inescapable foe. The available corpsmen found themselves hurrying from Marine to Marine, trying to repair shredded skin or at least stop the flow of blood so the wounded men could survive evacuation to the nearest aid station.

One of those working as quickly as he could was Hospitalman Third Class Joseph Keenan, attached to Fox 2/5, from Massachusetts. He was barely twenty years old and, like Billy Rivers Penn, the corpsman who had been captured when Outpost Vegas fell, had first set foot in

Korea in February, on Friday the 13th. Keenan became a shrapnel victim himself, but because he only caught a piece in his hand and the wound wasn't serious, he continued working.

Not for long, though. A nearby blast sent countless shards of shrapnel slicing through the air, and this time Keenan was struck in the head. Dazed and with blood flowing from the gash, he staggered down to the 2nd Battalion aid station. His head was bandaged and he was told to lie down and stay there. However, because he found he could still walk well enough, the young Navy man put fresh supplies in his medical kit and hiked back hundreds of yards of open terrain toward Fox Company's position.

When Keenan found it, he could see that there were many more casualties than before. Ignoring the throbbing in his head, he set to work again. There was another nearby blast, this time sending chunks of dirt into his eyes. Now Keenan could hardly see at all. Undeterred, he made his way to Reno Block, where the fighting continued at a fierce and furious pace. There he found the two Charlie Company corpsmen, Hammond and Polley.

Seeing Keenan working near Polley with his sight problems, a Marine called out, "This is a bad night for corpsmen—they're all blind!"

Somehow, Keenan stumbled to a gulley where half a dozen Marines awaited attention. As he was treating them, two Fox 2/7 Marines found him and begged him to fall back to the MLR because of his head wound as well as his sight problems. An enemy breakthrough could come at any moment, they warned. The corpsman replied, "I'm staying. I got a job to do and I'm going to do it."

Keenan at least allowed the two Marines to pour water from a canteen into his eyes, effectively washing out the dirt. They went back to the fight and the corpsman returned to bandaging his patients. Sometime later another shell exploded near Keenan. This time, the shrapnel that struck him in the head killed him. A letter informing Keenan's family of his death was sent by new senator John F. Kennedy.

Keenan was nominated for the Navy Cross, but the paperwork was subsequently lost. (After decades of unceasing efforts by Joseph's younger brother, Michael, the Navy Cross was awarded in May 1999.)

Captain Walz and Fox Company battled the Chinese troops up the slope of the hill, were beaten back, regrouped, and attacked again. After the third time, Walz and his men stayed put. There were too few of them and they had nothing left. As though to emphasize the advantage they had gained, the Chinese sent artillery and mortar shells in the direction of Reno Block, making sure the Marines there stayed pinned down.

"They could have overrun us easily," Sergeant Janzen said, "but I have always believed that they had no idea how weak, in terms of manpower, that we were. We all cashed our chips that night. Nobody got excited about it. We just said we'll take as many of the sons of bitches with us as we can. That's just the way it was."

Until 3 a.m., when Colonel Walt ordered that all attempts to retake Reno be suspended, the best he could do was send reinforcements and assess and evacuate however many dead and wounded were on that bloody hill. The commanders of the 1st and 3rd Battalions were reporting a total of 150 casualties. This figure did not include those killed and wounded in the units that had been hurried into action from the 2nd Battalion, which had begun the battle in reserve, as well as men taken prisoner at Outpost Reno and elsewhere.

Sergeant Janzen was one of the Marines helping to evacuate the casualties. His long night was about to get longer. He and another Marine placed PFC Albert Hughes on a stretcher. It was obvious that he was a large man, but what they found out later was how Hughes came to be wounded. He had been on point for his platoon when a Chinese grenade bounced off his chest and detonated, blowing Hughes into a trench. He landed flat on his back with his rifle in what is called the "high port" position, or out in front of his chest. An enemy soldier jumped in the trench, grabbed the rifle, and shot Hughes in the chest with it. This was observed by PFC Robert "Ma" Durham. His BAR made short work of the Chinese soldier as well as a few of his comrades who had tried to finish Hughes off. It was a struggle, but Sergeant Janzen and the other Marine managed to get the portly PFC onto a stretcher.

Marines were reassembling nearby and trying to account for those who were missing. One who was unaccounted for was PFC Mario Lombardi, a machine gunner. Someone reported having seen him in a trench, and said he appeared to be wounded. Janzen pulled out his .38-caliber Smith & Wesson Combat Masterpiece revolver and took off up the hill and back into the trench to find him.

The three Marines he first found were dead ones from his own platoon. Janzen recognized one as the radioman PFC William Marshall, but the other two had such horrendous head wounds that the sergeant could not tell who they were. He continued on. Farther uphill, he was suddenly challenged. After identifying himself, the voice said, "Sergeant Janzen, it's me, Lombardi! Don't leave me! My legs are busted, and I'm half buried in the trench."

He was buried for sure, up to his chest in dirt from the collapsed trench. It would be a pretty tough job to get him out, especially with little help from a Marine with two broken legs. Janzen began the job anyway. "Just then, PFC Josephat Levesque, another machine gunner, arrived. He had quietly followed me up the hill. I couldn't have been happier to see him."

Working together, the two men freed Lombardi. As if summoned by radio, two other Marines arrived. With their two rifles and flak jackets, a stretcher was created and they hauled Lombardi out of the trench. What the group didn't need right at that moment was an enemy mortar barrage, but that was what they got. As shells landed and exploded around them, Levesque put his helmet on Lombardi's face and covered his body to shield him. When the onslaught ended,

Janzen discovered that Levesque had been struck unconscious by shrapnel to his helmetless head. He put a battle dressing on the wound, and Levesque later recovered.

Eventually, both Lombardi and Hughes were brought to an aid station, and both would survive. "It was a small, ragged band of survivors that straggled into the MLR around 3 or 3:30 that morning," Sergeant Janzen reported.

Exhausted, he made his way to a bunker from which issued the alluring odor of fresh coffee. Inside, among several Marines were two of his fellow guides from other platoons. Janzen asked for a cup of coffee and lit a cigarette. The others stared at him and asked if he was all right. Mud and blood were smeared on his uniform, and his trousers had a large tear in front of his right hip.

"Yes, I'm all right, and can I please have a cup of coffee?" the sergeant said. The astonished men had told him that the walking wounded, returning at intervals, had told them Janzen had been killed three hours earlier.

In just the Charlie 1/5 aid station alone there were fifty-six wounded Marines being treated. The more seriously injured were taken to the 1st Battalion aid station. The air was punctuated with the pounding of HMR-161 and VMO-6 helicopter rotors, as the copters arrived laden with blood supplies for the aid stations and departed with the most critical cases, hurrying them to the hospital ships *Haven* and *Consolation* at Inchon Harbor.

Even before the attacks on Outpost Reno were abandoned, Colonel Walt had made a decision that would have an impact on the next several days. He requested permission from General Pollock to pull all 5th Regiment units back to behind the Main Line of Resistance. Fighting the Chinese at night with inferior numbers, and after the pounding his Marines had gotten since 7 the previous evening, was close to suicide. It had to grate on the veteran warrior no end to ask his commanding officer to be allowed to withdraw, but he had to think of his men first and the overall outcome of the battle. Walt knew he couldn't win it in the first hours of March 27, but he could lose it.

Pollock agreed: best to withdraw, reorganize, and plan for better results the rest of the day. Walt sent word for his battalion commanders and staff members to gather at his bunker. There would be little or no sleep that night as grim-faced officers, brows furrowed and cigarette smoke hovering above their heads like storm clouds, stitched together a game plan for retaking the two lost outposts.

One part of the plan was to strengthen the fist that would hammer at the Chinese when the counterattacks began. Pollock ordered the 2nd Battalion of the 7th Marines out of reserve and to the front lines. Essentially, Colonel Walt would have four infantry battalions ready to go, complemented by all the artillery and airpower at the 1st Division's disposal.

He would need all of it. As Lee Ballenger explained, "Unlike the common small-unit actions of the past year, the counterattack would be a major operation. The Marines would attack the hills in columns of companies. If anything, the fighting would take on aspects of World War I, where companies and battalions of men, with bayonets fixed, had charged 'over the top' yelling and screaming as they ran across no-man's-land to engage the Hun."

There would also be a reference to World War II, when an officer who survived the battle described Outpost Vegas as the "highest damn beachhead in Korea." The outpost was not a Pacific Ocean island in World War II that the Marines could go around. This hill had to be taken. There was no choice but to go head-on and try to ram through.

Another part of that plan was to give the Communists a taste of their own artillery medicine. The 5th Marines staff estimated that from the time the attack began at 7 p.m. the day before to the lull of

3 a.m., at least five thousand rounds of enemy mixed fire had landed in the "Wild." That was the code name for the area on the Main Line of Resistance occupied by the regiment. As impressive as this total was, it did not include what had poured down on Outposts Reno, Vegas, and Carson. It was a wonder that any piece of real estate in the area had gone undisturbed.

But the Marine gunners had dished it out too. The 1st Battalion of the 11th Regiment was the artillery unit in direct support of the 5th Regiment, and it reported launching more than forty-two hundred rounds northward during the same period. Now, in the hours before dawn on the 27th, it was time to ramp that up. The big difference was that targets would include two outposts that the day before the Marines were defending, not aiming to capture.

General Pollock gave the order for mortars and tanks as well as artillery to turn Reno and Vegas into living hells. But they wouldn't be the only hot spots. By 3:30 a.m., observation planes had scouted behind enemy lines and radioed the locations of Chinese artillery and mortar units as well as troop movements indicating reinforcements to Reno and Vegas. The Marine gunners went to work, firing shells at such a swift and steady pace that some of the weapons may have glowed red in the night. By 6 a.m., it was estimated that since the battle had begun a total of more than ten thousand rounds had been sent on their way.

Meanwhile, the ground troops were getting ready to counterattack in the morning light. The previous day's action hadn't really begun until right after sunset. The 27th would be an all-day affair, and the first few hours had been only a preview of the bloody battles to come.

The 2nd Battalion of the 7th Marines had probably expected to sit this one out. The men were in reserve, and rarely during previous outpost-war battles did the division have to draw upon the reserves. But almost everything was different about this battle, so downtime was over for the battalion when it was ordered to move toward the front lines.

The Chinese were not simply waiting for a counterattack. They were industriously fortifying their positions on Reno and Vegas and trying to take more ground, especially wanting to dislodge the Marines holding on to Reno Block. Private James Larkin, the forward observer with Baker 1/5 who had apparently been the last Marine to get off Outpost Vegas alive, was one of the men who managed to get through to reinforce the position.

"The Chinese were in regimental strength, and the minute we were in Reno Block they came at us," he remembered. "Four times we pushed them back. In one attack they reached our trench line, and the fighting was hand-to-hand. They came at us from all sides. White phosphorus shells from our guns illuminated everything; the whole area was like the Fourth of July. Our artillery was firing, our tanks were firing, machine guns on the MLR were firing. The Chinese were twisting and falling everywhere, but there always seemed to be more of them. It was well after midnight and it was as bright as day from all the pyrotechnics and explosions."

It was almost 5 a.m. before the Chinese fell back and those Marines left in Reno Block could breathe a sigh of relief at having survived.

★ ★

CHAPTER SIXTEEN

Reckless Begins Her Journey

It had been a restless night for the men in Lieutenant Eric Pedersen's recoilless rifle platoon, and for Reckless as well. Though not involved in the initial attacks and then the attempts to counterattack the Communist units, the men could not know if there might be a sudden breakthrough of the MLR or if orders would be given to join the battle for either Reno Block or Vegas. With recoilless rifle platoons in an anti-tank company being something like Gypsies, they could wind up anywhere along the front. Whatever the brass decided, that was where they went. That kind of uncertainty was not a comfort.

Like most of the other 5th Regiment units not directly involved in the fighting, Pedersen's men listened to the chatter on the radio, following the action and trying to visualize it as though listening to the broadcast of a Saturday-afternoon college football game. There was very little sleep for the men because the outcome of this contest was much more important.

The first layers of the gray light that was a harbinger of what Homer called "rosy-fingered dawn" were still an hour away when Sergeant Joe Latham went to check on Reckless. She was not sleeping when he arrived, and he wondered if she had slept at all during the night of explosions, flares, burp and machine guns, and shouts and screams of men fighting to the death. Did horses have better hearing than people? Latham hoped they had worse hearing than humans did so that the little sorrel mare was spared some of the nerve-rattling noise of the night.

He wasn't thinking just of Reckless's feelings, though they were very important to him. In the cold darkness Latham stroked each of her ears in turn. He had known and cared for horses, but he had never felt about one the way he did about Reckless. Sometimes he felt like a kid around her—him, a grown man, at thirty-five practically a middle-aged one, a husband and father, a Marine. He would be devastated if anything happened to her. If anyone in the 5th Regiment said, "Joe, you love that horse," he would not deny it. He was sure that the lieutenant and probably Monroe Coleman wouldn't either.

But the sergeant had to think about his platoon and, by extension, all the Marines who would be fighting today. What if, hearing the sounds of battle, a survival instinct kicked in to the point that Reckless was unwilling to enter the arena if called upon? Latham might even feel relieved, but that wasn't what today would be about. Reckless was, of course, much more than a Marine mascot. She would have a job to do. It was a good sign that she had eaten some of the grain left in her feed box the night before.

When Sergeant Latham arrived back at the platoon's camp, Eric Pedersen was just returning from the 5th Marines command post, where Colonel Walt had conducted a briefing. "The counterattack is set for 0930," Pedersen informed his men. The recoilless rifle platoon's initial responsibility was to cover the advance with smoke shells. It was very bad timing that the 11th Marines were running low on them, which meant that much of the burden would be on the platoon to obscure the Marines moving into position for the counterattack as long as necessary. This would be an even tougher job because the weather report given to Colonel Walt stated that there would be a southern wind blowing as strong as eleven knots, and like an ally of the enemy it would be trying to chase the smoke away and expose the approaching Marines.

Even in the predawn dark, Lieutenant Pedersen saw the questioning looks of his men. Yes, he confirmed, they would need Reckless on this one.

This time it was Corporal Coleman who headed out to the pasture. His hands were trembling a bit from the cold as well as nervous fatigue, making it difficult to strap the hard packsaddle onto Reckless's back. He finally managed to make it secure enough that he could lead her toward the platoon's position.

The first stabs of pink and gold and scarlet struck the eastern-facing hillsides. It might even be a nice day, but Coleman suspected that it would be difficult to tell once the air around those hillsides was saturated with gray, white, and black smoke and the sudden eruptions of orange-red flames and plumes of dirt were gouging holes in the ground. Reckless could not imagine any of this. Maybe that was why she accompanied Coleman so easily. Or she was simply a brave horse.

The men poised on the Main Line of Resistance wound up taking more of a breather than they had anticipated. Word had come down from commanding officers to platoon sergeants to squad leaders that jump-off time was 9:30 a.m., with the expectation that air support would by then have followed up on the shelling to further chew up the Chinese defensive positions. Because of communication snafus, though, by 9:30 the Marines were not an inch closer to Reno and Vegas. Finally, the flyboys arrived and began pummeling the outposts. By 11 a.m., artillery batteries were delivering some of the precious smoke they had on Hills 57A and 190, blinding the Chinese of those two primary observation posts to what was about to happen below.

And then, at the last minute, the plan was changed.

Better late than never, General Pollock and his staff realized that with the Chinese superiority in numbers and the fact that they were now the ones in entrenched defensive positions, the odds were not good that units of the 5th Marines could take two hills at the same time. Pollock ordered the shift to making the recapture of Outpost Vegas the priority. Attention paid to Outpost Reno would mostly come from the 11th Regiment's big guns and Marine Corps pilots flying Grumman F9F Panther jets. The responsibility of these pilots would be to bomb and strafe the hill enough that its occupants could not provide much, if any, support to their Communist comrades on Vegas. Outpost Carson, on the other side of Reno, remained in American hands, and as long as that didn't change it would not be part of Friday's scenario.

Finally, it was time to get going. As the sun inched toward the center of the sky, artillery and air support along with intense mortar fire kept the Chinese defenders' heads down. Tanks were part of the onslaught too, and a gratifying sight for forward observers was when tank fire decimated a Chinese company trying to make its way from Reno to Vegas.

Colonel Walt ordered Eric Pedersen's platoon into position. The gun crews would be firing three recoilless rifles. The colonel would need those weapons to be effective, letting loose with everything they had as fast as they could. It would be the ultimate test for the platoon's Mongolian mare.

It wasn't exactly a lull, but more a combined sense of restraint and anticipation on the American side. The Marines along the MLR were preparing in their individual ways to attack and the inevitable exposure to enemy fire that came with it. The Chinese on the hills were conserving their ammunition for the counterattack as well as further fortifying their defensive positions. Most of the firing now was from mortars as the 5th Marines targeted the pathways and wherever it was likely that the enemy was directing reinforcements and supplies.

This was some comfort to Reckless, the comparative quiet. It made being closer to the front lines easier to tolerate. Still, the sounds of the occasional artillery shell rushing past overhead and the *whump* of explosions on the hillsides were unsettling. When they took a short rest on the trip to the forward ammunition supply depot, where Corporal Coleman had been told to bring her, he observed the mare pawing nervously at the ground and shaking her red mane. Her tail appeared to twitch with every explosion that sounded louder or closer than the others. Patting her, Coleman could feel perspiration on her neck and flanks.

The pause was not doing Reckless any favors. He offered her some barley, but she wasn't interested. There was no more clear sign of how the horse was feeling than her having no appetite. She snorted in an agitated way. Then Coleman tugged on her lead rope and they set off again.

A few minutes later, they encountered Sergeants Elmer Lively, Ralph Sherman, and John Lisenby and their gun crews. They told Coleman that Sergeant Latham was waiting for him and Reckless to arrive so that they could load up her packsaddle. The Marines then continued on up the ridge. Coleman wondered what kind of day it was going to be—how big would this fight get and how long would it last? He was thinking as much about the impact on Reckless as about the effect on the Marines of the 5th Regiment.

It was rough going leading Reckless westward, away from the rising sun, along and then down the ridge toward the forward supply depot. It had been set up just in front of the MLR to provide the 5th Marine units easier and faster access to ammunition and mortar shells and other matériel to hurl at the Communists. It was well enough hidden below the slope that it could not be seen by the enemy.

That did not mean, though, that the area wasn't going to be shelled or that maybe a lucky random round wouldn't fall in and explode the whole depot. Corporal Coleman thought nervously that it might be safer to be out in the open traveling with Reckless where only a direct hit would kill him. At the depot, anything close might destroy everything around it. For now, and in the still-uncertain light, he had to concentrate on navigating the ridge and then the slope along a narrow, slippery trail, with a jittery horse right behind him.

As though to give further credence to Coleman's fretting, artillery shells whizzed overhead, going north and south, emphasizing that all it would take was for one of them to fall short. When they finally arrived at the bottom of the ridge, Reckless was there first with Coleman stumbling behind.

He found Sergeant Latham at the forward supply depot. A bumpy, muddy trail that hardly qualified as a road connected the depot to the main supply route, which in turn led to the 5th Regiment's supply dump behind the MLR. The trail made for an unpleasant and aggravating trip for the Marines riding in the trucks that jumped up and down and from side to side on it. In anticipation of the battle for Outpost Vegas, trucks were arriving every few minutes at the forward depot, their irritable drivers bringing full loads of ammunition.

Coleman reported that Reckless had eaten only a small portion of barley during the night. Latham patted her down. He too wondered if she would survive the day. There was no turning back now. Well, that wasn't completely true. If the small mare suddenly pitched a fit and was clearly too frightened and undependable to do the recoilless rifle platoon any good, then best to keep her out of the way. Better to consider Lieutenant Pedersen's grand experiment a failure than risk Marines in a fight for their lives. But Reckless wasn't close to anything like that. Latham could feel her tremble slightly when a shell whizzed overhead, but otherwise she stood gazing at him like any stalwart Marine awaiting orders.

He even thought he could detect a bit of impatience in her eyes, or maybe that was his imagination after so little sleep. Then the sergeant reasoned that Reckless, after all, had been a terrific young racehorse who could well have been a national champion in Korea if the war hadn't written a different play for her to act in. For the valiant Mongolian mare now, going into battle was the closest she would get to running in a big race.

Gazing back at her, Latham told Coleman, "I'd like to start with six shells. Pretty sure the guys up there are going to need every one we can bring them."

The shells were tied to the packsaddle, three on each side, more than twice what Marines other than that cowboy Coleman could carry. The amount of weight didn't appear to concern Reckless. She simply turned and paused, as though waiting to hear "Forward, march!" Neither man gave in to the temptation to be dramatic. Latham and Coleman led the horse out of the depot and to the thin trail that led to the base of the ridge.

The trip would consist of getting up that first ridge, going down the far side, and picking up the next trail, which cut through open terrain consisting primarily of rice paddies. This would allow Reckless and her fellow Marines to catch their breath, but a big disadvantage was that they would come under enemy observation. The Chinese might not ordinarily waste a mortar shell or any other ammo on a horse, but most likely over time and enough trips, observation would reveal that Reckless was at the very least ferrying supplies to the Marines on the hills. The copper-colored mare could then be viewed as a combatant and fair game for firing upon. Latham wondered if somehow Reckless would understand that and act accordingly.

The goal was to arrive at where Lieutenant Pedersen's platoon had established firing sites on Hill 120. Outposts Vegas and Reno were to the southeast. Also within firing range were the enemy-held Hills 190, 153, and 150 and the areas in between. It would be the responsibility of the recoilless rifle crews to support counterattacks on Vegas as well as disrupt efforts to shift troops and matériel from Reno and the other nearby hills to bolster the defense.

At the bottom of the ridge Reckless paused again, took a deep breath, pricked her ears forward, and off she went. As she had in the practice runs and previous actions, she charged the hill. The thunder of explosions and the chatter of small arms did not matter—she was on a mission. That she was carrying over one hundred and fifty pounds on her back didn't appear to matter either. Latham and Coleman had to climb like mountain lions to keep up with her, and for their trouble were showered with dirt and stones that the horse's flying hooves left in their wake.

Full sunrise, with light washing across the sky and the dark sliding away, made that first trip easier for Latham and Coleman. Reckless seemed to instinctively know the way, as though following a homing signal that only she could hear or sense. When she was confronted by the edge of the open terrain and the beginnings of the slope of Hill 120, Reckless increased her pace to a trot, and after only a few seconds she galloped. This ground was nothing like the racetrack back in Seoul, but she treated the incline like it was a straightaway, attacking the slope at a run. Her two companions were easily left behind, listening to the rattling of the shells on the horse's saddle and praying they didn't tear free and go scattering downhill, maybe ending up in their laps.

The final climb to the firing positions of the recoilless rifles was an incline that was close to forty-five degrees. One last burst of energy, and Reckless would conquer that and arrive atop the ridge with her load of precious shells . . . for the first few times, maybe even a dozen, at least. How many times after that the weighed-down young mare would find that well of energy within her was something they would all find out if today's action lasted as long as everyone expected it to.

According to a 5th Regiment officer's account, "Vegas and Reno and the enemy-held hills were coming clear in the growing light. Marine artillery and heavy mortars were mushrooming the ridgelines with black HE [heavy explosives] and white phosphorous, called 'Willie Peter' by the troops. On Vegas there was no sign of life, friendly or enemy. The only sign of war or that men had fought and died on this hill a few hours before were the hollow-eyed holes left by shells and mortars, the jagged, caved-in trench line and the tactical wire ground to a thorny pulp."

On her first trip up, Reckless continued to dig her hooves into the damp ground. She probably knew that Lieutenant Pedersen awaited her above along with her friends in the recoilless gun crews.

With rays of sunlight now illuminating the hills, ridges, and valleys in between, the platoon CO scanned the area intently. Soon it felt like the binoculars were extensions of his eyes. He hoped to observe enemy troop movements—to find out not only when they were happening but where they came from and how many Chinese troops were on the move.

The highest concentrations of Communists and the closest ones to Vegas and Reno would be his platoon's primary targets. Pedersen knew the enemy had many more soldiers to support the defense of both captured hills than the 5th Regiment had—or the entire 1st Division, for that matter—to take the hills back. His platoon would be an important part of severely damaging that support or at least convincing some Chinese units that they should stay on the sidelines. Either way, that tactic went toward evening the odds for the Marines. Would it be enough? Whenever good targets were discovered, the firing had to be fast and furious.

As usual, when Lieutenant Pedersen's men had gone up to their firing position on Hill 120, they had taken a supply of shells with them. The early-morning sunlight was beginning to glint on the noses of the shells that peeked out of their cardboard containers on the neatly stacked piles beside each position. If the day went according to plan, each crew would go through that supply first. By the time they needed more of the 24-pound projectiles, Reckless would have completed a few trips to replenish the piles. The plan did not include what would happen if the horse was wounded, or worse, or if the day's fighting reached a level of intensity that even Reckless could not tolerate. Other Marines were being sent up to the hill as well, but they could carry only two rounds per trip, and quite possibly, at some point during the day some of the men on Hill 120 would be sent directly into the battle.

The sun was up. The Marines of the 5th Regiment waited for orders for the counterattacks to begin. And Reckless was close to completing her first trek uphill to join her pals in Eric Pedersen's platoon.

CHAPTER SEVENTEEN

★ ★

An Angel on Her Back

The Marines waiting in the trenches along the Jamestown Line were of mixed feelings as the tank and long-range artillery shelling occupied much of the morning. Few were yearning to be exposed to enemy fire when the order to advance was given. But they weren't there to enjoy the show; the job was to get Outpost Vegas back. It was agony that it seemed that job kept being postponed.

Finally, at 11:20, the order was given. Leading the way to the battered outpost was Dog Company of the 5th Marines, commanded by Captain John Melvin, who had grown up in the proud shadow of the U.S. Naval Academy in Annapolis, Maryland. He led his men toward the rain-soaked southern slope of Vegas through flooded rice paddies. Only moments after they emerged from the relative safety of the MLR, Chinese artillery targeted them. Crossing hundreds of yards with shells landing front and back, left and right made for a slow, bloody slog.

"Driving for the hill's southwest slope, Dog Company was met by a hurricane of fire barely after crossing the line of departure," went one account. "There were casualties immediately. Forward progress was slowed to a crawl. Marines battled forward into the teeth of the storm like swimmers struggling against a riptide, clawing for every foot of ground as shells rained down on them."

Despite the highly destructive weather, the men of Dog 2/5 managed to run, jump, and indeed crawl to within four hundred yards of Vegas before being bogged down, as even more furious fire came down from the hilltop. Worse for them, Chinese troops issued out of the fortifications to launch an attack downhill that was at least company strength, probably more. (Later, American intelligence would learn that thirty-five hundred Chinese troops had been committed to resist the attempt by the vastly outnumbered Marines to recapture Vegas.) With the addition of enemy artillery continuing to home in on them and intensifying small-arms fire, at 11:50, only a half hour after leaving the confines of the MLR, Captain Melvin's men were pinned down.

There was no better time for reinforcements. Colonel Walt ordered into battle a cobbled-together company consisting of men from Weapons 2/5 and H&S Company. But they too could go no farther than the pinned-down Dog Company.

Not for long, though. Led by Captain Melvin, those men from all three companies who were able to get up did so and surged forward. Then 82-mm and 60-mm shells rained down on them and it was time to eat dirt once more. Melvin tried to rally his men again . . . but he had less than half a company of unscathed Marines left.

In one platoon, for example, the commanding officer, Second Lieutenant Thomas Evans, could count only seven effectives left. That didn't quite include him, as he had been severely wounded. He refused treatment by a corpsman and with it the offer to be evacuated, and instead took the most forward and exposed position to try to provide some cover for his men. Fortunately, after the battle, the Silver Star that Lieutenant Evans received was not awarded posthumously.

Colonel Walt had Fox 2/5 move up from its behind-the-lines position. It had been reconstituted with replacements and Marines who had been only lightly wounded in the previous action and rejoined their company. Elements of Easy 2/5 also saddled up and headed out. Their arrival not only forced the Chinese to retreat but gave new momentum to a surge forward by the Marines. They fought and clawed their way to within two hundred yards of the outpost.

By this time, though, the Chinese had grasped that the focus was fully on Outpost Vegas. It was now their turn to hold it at all costs, and they were going to make it even more difficult for the Marines to dislodge them. By 3 p.m., four enemy units from Hill 153 had arrived on Vegas. A group that was anywhere from platoon to company strength arrived from Hill 21B. American jets tried to slice them up, but the fact was that the battered outpost was now even more strongly defended.

As destructive as the enemy fire was, Captain Melvin's men were managing to inch closer to where the Vegas fortifications began. They were also responding with everything they had. M-1s, carbines, and BARs sent hundreds of rounds into the Chinese positions, each Marine taking a break only to hurl grenades. As the courageous captain, by now wounded himself, later recalled, "It was so intense at times that you couldn't move forward or backward. The Chinese 60-mm mortars began to bother us about as much as firecrackers. It was the 120-mm mortars and 122 artillery that hurt the most. The noise was deafening. They would start walking the mortars toward us from every direction possible. You could only hope that the next round wouldn't be on target."

By this time, Melvin could count only twelve Marines left under his command. Incredibly, despite all this, four of them managed to claw their way to just below the summit of the hill.

It was a good moment to move more Marines into the battle. Captain Herbert Lorence and the rest of his Easy 2/5 had been brought up from reserve, and were ordered to advance, join up with what was left of Melvin's men, get casualties off that slope, and then it would be their turn to climb uphill toward the summit. They were able to accomplish the first and second tasks, but the third was literally stuck in the mud. Chinese artillery and mortar fire was a torrent of exploding metal landing on the slope, and the men of Easy and what was left of Melvin's men had to practically bury themselves in mud to have any chance at survival.

Another company was brought up from reserve—Fox 2/7, the unit that had in its proud memory the holding of Toktong Pass against ten thousand enemy troops in November 1950. Fox was now led by Captain Ralph Estey, who was ordered to join up with Melvin and Lorence and try to revive the assault.

As one account described the advance of Estey's men: "The Marines of Fox Company, no less than those who had gone before, were equal to the challenge. Leaning forward like men fighting their way into a winter blizzard, the Fox Company Marines drove relentlessly toward the blazing hill."

Out in front of this new assault was the 3rd Platoon, led by Lieutenant Theodore Chenoweth. It was not explained to him or anyone else in Fox Company how these Marines would fare any better than the ones ahead who were pinned down and had thus far suffered severe casualties. These Marines knew what waited for them. Nevertheless, continue the attack they did.

Chenoweth led his men across the open ground and then to the path leading up to Outpost Vegas, even though he tried to ignore "the valley of horror we had entered." Scattered about were bodies of dead Marines, "fallen like jack straws over the valley floor," as he described the scene. "Beside the trail, the lacerated, decapitated body of a Marine lay on his back. His flesh showed through the shredded dungarees.

The sadness I felt, to see him so, was intense and twisted my stomach. He had taken a fatal wound through the line of his mouth. His lower jaw and chin were still attached to the stump of his neck on his body. His helmet, the strap still fastened, with the entire head, face and upper teeth in it, lay ten feet away, upside down, the eyes staring at us with the teeth gnawing the sky."

Chenoweth knew that this poor soul, like most of the corporals and privates in his platoon, was only nineteen years old.

There were other gruesome sights to see as Fox Company kept pushing forward, especially the fallen Marines of the three companies that had been part of the previous counterattacks on Vegas. Some had been mutilated beyond recognition by artillery and mortar shells. The closer Fox 2/7 got to the hill, the more enemy fire was tossed at them. Their own dead and wounded joined those of Dog, Easy, and the patchwork companies.

Such carnage placed a heavy burden on the Navy corpsmen who were with the Marines. No one represented them better than Hospitalman 3rd Class William R. Charette, who had accompanied Fox Company. Ignoring the risks of incoming fire and the threat of a Chinese counterattack breaking through at any moment, he hurried from one wounded Marine to another, stanching the flow of blood and injecting morphine and preparing the men for evacuation to the 3rd Battalion's aid station directly behind the MLR.

Suddenly, as Charette knelt next to a Marine, a Chinese potato-masher grenade landed next to them. Without hesitating, the corpsman threw himself on it, smothering the blast and saving his patient. The explosion blew away his medical kit and helmet, but he survived because of his armored vest.

Charette continued to treat wounded Marines without his medical kit, tearing strips from his own clothing to use as bandages. When he found a wounded man whose vest had been blown off, Charette took off his own and put it on the Marine. Though hurt himself and reeling from covering the exploding grenade and without a vest and nearly naked from tearing away his own clothes, Charette stayed with Fox 2/7 as the fighting continued, treating and evacuating others.

A sad but proud testament to the courage of Navy corpsmen is that HM3 William Charette was the only one of them to earn the Medal of Honor in the Korean War and live to receive it.

By 1 p.m. on that blood-filled Friday, Reckless had made ten trips from the forward supply depot to the top of Hill 120. Because the gun crews were following the standard procedure of firing several rounds, then moving before the Chinese observers could register them, many times when Reckless scaled Hill 120 she would find the crews in different positions. She was never confused, though. After all, she had been with the recoilless rifle platoon in combat before, so she knew the procedure as well as her fellow Marines did.

As they began to unload the shells she carried, the Marines noted that Reckless was breathing hard and they could feel the sweat on her. But once her saddle was unpacked, the little mare recuperated. She rested for a few minutes, appearing to be intrigued by what she could see of the battle below, and then with a word from Joe Latham or Monroe Coleman, she began the return trip. Already, Reckless's two companions were taking turns making the trips because carrying shells and keeping up with Reckless was simply too exhausting.

Lieutenant Pedersen too was intrigued by what he saw below. To some of the Marines it might seem that Vegas was the main battleground for now, and soon enough it would be Reno's turn. But Pedersen was one of the few commanding officers who understood why Reno might have to wait indefinitely—not enough smoke. Exploding smoke shells were a very effective way to mask the advance of Marines on enemy positions. With some of the Chinese troops firing blindly, there were fewer American casualties.

In the summer of 1950, outnumbered American troops made a costly but ultimately successful attempt to hold the Pusan Perimeter against North Korean invaders.

The streets of Seoul were a battleground for troops trying to recapture the capital city of Korea, which was taken twice by the North Koreans.

A mule patiently demonstrates a recoilless rifle, which was close to seven feet long and weighed more than one hundred pounds. *Courtesy of the National Archives*

Reckless became accustomed to getting in and out of her two-wheel trailer, though her Marine companions were always ready to provide assistance.

Lieutenant Eric Pedersen leads his four-legged recruit on one of her first training sessions, carrying recoilless rifle shells in the hills behind the Main Line of Resistance.

Courtesy of the General Randolph Pate Collection,
Archives and Special Collections, Library of the Marine Corps

General Edwin Pollock was the commanding officer of the 1st Marine Division when Reckless was undergoing "hoof camp" in 1952.

The much-decorated Colonel Lew Walt (shown here as a general) led the 5th Marines during the Battle of the Nevada Cities.

Though not a big horse, Reckless could easily haul a recoilless rifle up the steep
Korean hills to the firing positions chosen by Lieutenant Eric Pedersen.

After a hard day of work, Reckless liked to get together with her fellow Marines for a cold beer or two.

Marines organize the defense of the Outpost Vegas hilltop, which would see some of the fiercest fighting of the Korean War.

The Battle of the Nevada Cities began on March 26, 1953, when Chinese troops attacked Outposts Carson, Reno, and Vegas.

Courtesy of the General Randolph Pate Collection,
Archives and Special Collections, Library of the Marine Corps

At first, Reckless was frightened by the sounds of battle, but she quickly calmed down and went to work hauling ammunition.

Sergeant Joe Latham, Reckless's chief handler, wasn't being shy. He just knew that there could be only one star of the show when there was a camera around.

After the Battle of the Nevada Cities was over, proud Marines invited the U.S. champion horse Native Dancer to come to Korea and race Reckless in the Paddy Derby.

When General Randolph Pate became the CO of the 1st Marine Division, he was impressed by Reckless. The two would form a special friendship.

Reckless turned out to be a good football coach too. Her team of Marines defeated the Army in a game in the fall of 1954.

The rotation ceremony for Reckless, when she was finally allowed to sail to the United States and meet a public eager to greet her.

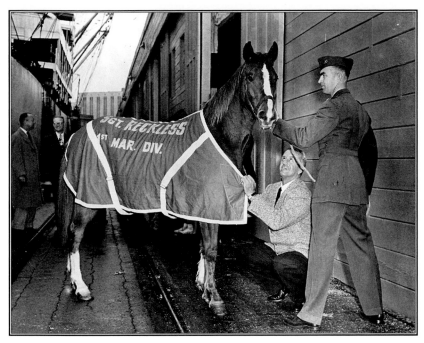

After leaving the ship in San Francisco, Reckless is finally reunited with Eric Pedersen (*standing, right*), who as the leader of the recoilless rifle platoon had recruited the sorrel mare.

Whoa, Reckless! Bored by the speeches, she dives right into the cake that was part of the celebration of the Marine Corps anniversary on November 10, 1954. Not everyone was amused.

General John Selden, commandant of Camp Pendleton, and his wife welcome Reckless and Captain Pedersen. Reckless would live the rest of her life there.

Reckless did not have to haul any more ammo, but she was kept busy making public appearances, like this one at the Carlsbad Spring Holiday celebration in May 1955.

Fearless, shown here at only two days old in August 1957, was the first of four foals Reckless would have during her Camp Pendleton years.

Colonel Richard Rothwell does the honors of promoting Reckless to staff sergeant at a Camp Pendleton ceremony, as her son looks on.

Reckless gives the camera a coy look as she enjoys a hay break.

Together again: Sergeant Reckless does not have to salute General Pate, even though by 1959 he was the commandant of the Marine Corps. The two old friends would soon retire.

The Marines of the 5th Regiment, Reckless's old outfit, pass in review during the retirement ceremony for the valiant warhorse.

The heroism of Reckless was recognized with this monument created by Jocelyn Russell and Robin Hutton and dedicated at the National Museum of the Marine Corps in July 2013.

Courtesy of the National Museum of the Marine Corps

One has to pass by the headstone dedicated to Reckless in 1971 to enter the Stepp Stables at Camp Pendleton, her home for the last contented years of her life.

Courtesy of Leslie Reingold

But Pedersen knew there was a shortage of such shells, which meant that even if enough men could be scraped together—such as pretty much emptying the reserve units behind the MLR—attacking two hills simultaneously would bring more exposure to enemy guns. As it was, there appeared to be enough death and destruction on the slopes leading up to Outpost Vegas.

Pedersen lowered the binoculars and turned when Reckless arrived with the next shipment of shells. She bounded up that last forty-five-degree incline and into view and stood patiently, breathing hard, as her burden was removed. Though she must by now have been feeling tired from bearing the heavy shells tied to her saddle trip after trip, there were no outward visible signs other than the sun's rays highlighting the perspiration on her and the labored breathing, and even that lasted only a couple of minutes. More than ever, the lieutenant admired the horse's resilience. He certainly had not expected so much of it when he'd first seen her, as Flame the racehorse, more than five months ago.

Despite the grim surroundings, Pedersen almost laughed when Sergeant Latham appeared a full three minutes behind Reckless. He couldn't put the two shells he carried down fast enough. Dirt-streaked sweat poured from under his helmet and he gasped for air. Pedersen thought of ordering him to stay there atop the hill, and maybe Coleman too the next time he arrived: He was down to two shells too, instead of three per trip. That would be doing them a favor, to not have to alternate treks up the slope.

But the other reason was he was receiving increasingly urgent requests from the 5th Regiment's command posts to send any men he could spare. If Pedersen did, Latham and Coleman could be replacements. It would be expecting a lot, though, for a horse to continue making the arduous trips by herself. The lieutenant figured he would wait to make that decision until he was ordered to do so.

Suddenly, there was a shout. Pedersen whipped around and saw that one of his men was staggering toward him; then he collapsed. His helmet was a few feet away. There was blood on one side of his head. Immediately, one of the platoon members was beside him with a field dressing. "He's out cold, Lieutenant, but looks like more of a scrape," the Marine said.

"Better get him to a corpsman anyway."

Another dilemma: This was a bad time to spare two men to bear the wounded man on a stretcher down the hill to the nearest triage tent. Then he had an idea. "You take him down, Joe, on Reckless," Pedersen said. "Just watch his head, if the bleeding starts up again. If so, get him off her and wait for help."

The sergeant nodded and two Marines gently laid the wounded man, still unconscious, across the saddle. Reckless turned her head and gave Pedersen a curious look, as though she were saying, "Okay, this is different. Thought I only had to carry weight on the way up!"

She now had close to two hundred pounds on her, so there would be no breaks between resupply trips. At least this one was downhill. Pedersen massaged her head and neck. He saw that her face was rubbed raw where the bridle pressed into it. If this was the only injury Reckless suffered today, that would be fine indeed.

"Go on, girl," he whispered, and Reckless set off, bearing cargo that was even more precious than usual.

One of the Marines in the fray who spotted her was Sergeant Harold Wadley. As she made her way down from the top ridge, "the ground under her had been shelled and was torn up. She really had to scramble to keep her feet under her."

On her next trip, he reported, "Going up the ridge, in and out of view, was this little mare. I tell you, her silhouette in all the smoke, I couldn't believe what I was seeing. I thought, 'Good grief, it's Reckless!' I thought for sure there had to be an angel riding that mare."

With the unconscious Marine on her back, Reckless doggedly picked her way down the rest of the ridge and across the rice paddies with artillery and mortar shells landing all around her. Nothing but a direct hit would stop her. When she got to the supply depot, the men there gently took the Marine off her saddle and replaced him with a fresh load of recoilless rifle shells. Barely pausing to rest and totally on her own, Reckless turned and set off on the next stage of her journey into Marine Corps legend.

CHAPTER EIGHTEEN

★ ★

Wounded in Action

The men of Fox 2/7 who had managed to survive all that the Communists had thrown at them thus far had to continue climbing up the slope to reach the outpost. There was no respite from the Chinese mortar shells and grenades pouring down on them. They passed more Marines along the way. Most of them were alive but were wounded or too exhausted to join Fox Company for the next stage of the assault.

Lieutenant Chenoweth reported seeing a captain (he does not identify him) who stood on the southern slope with a sergeant behind an outcrop of rock: "The captain had that same stupefied stare that I had seen before. He was talking into the handset of his radio, but the wire was not connected to anything. The radio was not to be seen. He never stopped talking. The sergeant had his arm around the captain's shoulder and gave us a long, sad look before turning back to his companion."

Despite the terrible punishment the men of Easy Company had endured, as Fox had still been on the way across the crater-filled ground toward Vegas, they had found the resolve to press farther forward and reach the right finger of the outpost. They had to pause, though, as fire from the Chinese defenders grew even heavier.

When the Fox Marines reached Captain Melvin, Estey told him the orders were for him to make his way back to Colonel Walt and take with him whoever was left of Dog 2/5. There weren't many.

Captain John Melvin would be awarded the Silver Star. He "repeatedly exposed himself to devastating hostile mortar, artillery and small-arms fire to direct and encourage his men in their gallant attack," his citation stated. "As the number of casualties mounted, he courageously moved his depleted forces up the fire-swept slopes until, at the furthest point of advance, his effective fighting strength was reduced to twelve men. Although painfully wounded, he tenaciously directed his shattered garrison of Marines in holding the bitterly contested position until the next company could pass through his valiant line of defense and continue the assault on the final heights."

At that point, the exhausted Melvin had somehow managed to reorganize the remnants of his company. Under heavy enemy fire and despite repeated efforts to outflank or overrun his unit, Captain Melvin "inspired his men to heroic endeavor in defending their vulnerable positions. After an enemy mortar fragment shattered the radio in his hands and ended communications with the battalion command post, Melvin forged ahead alone, braving heavy enemy mortar and artillery fire across eight hundred yards of terrain, somehow avoiding enemy suicide patrols attempting to cut the line of supply to the company holding the outpost. Finally arriving at the trench line, he grabbed fresh radios and returned—traveling the same hazardous route—to his embattled company."

———

One of his men being shot at told Eric Pedersen that his crews had to move sooner than after firing five shells. As far as he could tell in the early afternoon, with the battle for Outpost Vegas in full fury, the recoilless rifles were effective. He and his crews were working as fast as they could.

That meant, though, the gunners were using the recoilless shells at a faster rate. It was furnace-hot work—setting up the positions, fixing on the targets observed by Pedersen, firing, and now after launching, changing positions more frequently. After a sniper had wounded one of his men, Pedersen had instructed the crews to change positions—making sure to stay low—after three firings instead of the usual four or five. The effectiveness of the platoon was indicated by the Chinese sharpshooters' paying extra attention to the Marines on Hill 120 who were doing the damage.

The enemy knew that the recoilless rifle platoon had a distinct advantage: They could actually see their targets and often the result of their firing at them. This was true to some extent of tanks too, but many times they were at some distance and were given coordinates and fired without knowing exactly what they were firing at, and they had to rely on the reports of forward observers for the results. The heavy mortars and other big guns behind the lines and the 11th Marines artillery were totally dependent on forward observers.

The forward observer for the gun crews atop Hill 120, however, was right next to them. Lieutenant Pedersen found and decided and ordered the targets, and if he could spare the time before hunting the next target, he could report the damage of each shell. He was pleased that his experienced gunners were doing a heck of a lot of damage. Praise, though, would have to wait until later.

The lieutenant knew that his men must be tiring. But there would be no relief that afternoon with the battle for Outpost Vegas reaching new heights with every passing hour. Those Marines on the slopes had to be a lot more tired than everyone else. Pedersen knew that even when a unit was relieved, it didn't provide much of a reprieve. The commanding officer of that unit—and Pedersen suspected that with this level of fighting, many times the CO wasn't the same man who had gone up the hill—had to see to his dead and especially his wounded, make sure his men gulped water and shoved some food down, hope they had time for a short rest, learn from his company or battalion CO what his next orders were (if *they* even knew), accept replacements and integrate them on the fly, and get himself ready to lead the unit back into battle.

With another incredible burst of energy, Reckless suddenly appeared, winded and, Pedersen could feel when he stroked her, quivering slightly. The horse must be very weary. The lieutenant badly wanted to say to Latham or Coleman—he had lost track of which one would arrive a few minutes after the little sorrel mare did—to take Reckless aside the next time she was back at the supply depot and feed and water her well and let her rest far from the fighting and all its ugly noise. But Pedersen had no one to take her place. And since she carried six shells to any man's two, and also made the trips in almost half the time, Reckless was the best at keeping the platoon supplied.

It was not a stretch at all to believe that without Reckless, Pedersen's platoon would have periods of several minutes or longer when they couldn't fire at enemy positions. The Marines clawing their way up the Vegas slopes would pay the price for that. No, Reckless would have to keep going . . . die in her tracks, if necessary. And Pedersen was about to make her situation worse.

The horse's payload of shells had been removed. Corporal Coleman arrived, and immediately after handing off his shells he sprawled on the ground, his chest heaving as he hungrily gasped for air. It was obvious that even the big, strapping man from Utah didn't have too many trips left in him. What would happen when it was the same for Joe Latham? What would happen when the time came that neither of Reckless's handlers could get up the hill? By then, exhausted herself, she might feel she'd had enough too.

Pedersen could give Coleman another couple of minutes, but then he and the horse had to get back to work. So did the lieutenant, seeking out targets for his gun crews. The only thing that made the mare's ordeal a little easier was that the shifting of the firing positions sometimes brought the platoon a couple of hundred yards closer to the supply depot.

He gazed at her face as he stroked her wet neck. Reckless was no longer quivering and she was breathing easily. A swift wind rustled her red mane. She probably enjoyed the cool air, but that same strong breeze was causing a problem down below, scattering the smoke just seconds after one of those precious shells landed, and thus not providing the advancing Marines with as much cover as they needed.

Reckless's three white socks were hard to see because they were covered with dirt and looked the same as her right foreleg. Her ears flicked back and forth as she listened to the explosions and the whine of flying missiles and the roar of fighter jets, but she wasn't frightened, just paying attention to the progress of the battle. Her eyes, though, were fixed on Pedersen, a steady brown gaze to match his own.

It was like they were acknowledging something—probably that what Reckless was doing this day was what she was recruited by him and the 5th Marines to do. Not born to it at all, though. She was born to be a champion racehorse, like her mother could have been. But here, on this battleground in Korea in March 1953, Reckless was doing what was needed of her, and maybe what she felt she had to do.

A somewhat recovered Corporal Coleman stood beside Reckless. "When you two get back to the depot, see if she'll take eight shells," Pedersen said.

"But, Lieutenant, that's easily way over two hundred pounds on her, with the saddle."

"I know, Coleman. And maybe she can't do it. But we have to have more shells and I can't spare any more guys to get them."

The corporal nodded. He latched onto the mare's bridle and they began the return trip. Watching them go before raising the binoculars, Pedersen wasn't sure if Coleman was leading Reckless or it was the other way around.

Reckless left the forward supply depot to begin her fifth trip that afternoon bearing eight recoilless rifle shells. Coleman had done the arithmetic fast, but he was correct. Each shell was 24 pounds, and with the weight of the packsaddle added to that, it meant the small mare was hauling close to 250 pounds now on every trip. That was an eighth of a ton, on a horse barely fourteen hands high who had a talent for speed. What no one could have anticipated was a kind of stubborn strength that wouldn't let her quit. Like the thousands of other Marines in combat that day, Reckless had her orders and a job to do.

For the second time that afternoon, she made the trip alone. Both Latham and Coleman, after their respective treks with her, had remained on top of Hill 120. Well, technically Reckless had made every trip after the first few alone, since she easily outdistanced her favorite noncom companions, whose tongues were hanging out of their mouths. Latham and Coleman had joined a couple of gun crews, taking the place of two men hit by Chinese sharpshooters. Lieutenant Pedersen had to hope that the platoon's main supply vehicle didn't break down or go off course. It appeared, though, that in Reckless he had the sturdiest vehicle on the field of battle.

Every trek to the top of Hill 120 was more difficult. Reckless no longer trotted, but she still moved briskly enough. It was now several hours since the counterattack had been launched and the sounds of battle coming from Vegas—but also from Reno, with the artillery pounding it was taking—were unceasing. Reckless heard them become louder as she crossed the rice paddies.

It wasn't the noise that made that area the most dangerous for her. As Coleman had noted, this was when Reckless was the most exposed. And the time had come, with enough resupply trips having been made, that Communist observers had pointed her out as a worthy target.

She wasn't the only one, though. Hustling through the paddies were Marines in groups of four or five or larger being sent as replacements or as human supply vehicles, carrying ammunition or water. Heading in the opposite direction, at a much slower pace, were wounded Marines. Some had heads, arms, other parts of their bodies bandaged up but could at least walk. Others were borne on stretchers, not every one of them still alive. For the stretcher bearers, their immediate mission was accomplished. For those who had already been part of the murderous maelstrom that was the battle for Vegas, it took an extraordinary amount of courage to return to it. That they were hurrying toward it—well, that was either special courage or an effort to give the Chinese sharpshooters less time to target them in the open terrain.

On this trip, the firing was the worst so far. There was some small-arms fire, but that was pretty much a waste of ammunition. Efforts to deter Reckless by scaring her off never had a chance, and not just because the Chinese burp guns were too far away to do any damage. Those were close-combat weapons. The sharpshooters and mortars told a different story. As Reckless loped along the path through the paddies, the snipers stared at her through their telescopic sights and pressed their triggers. How disappointed they had to be when their next look showed Reckless forging ahead, straining under the weight but ignoring the bullets making the mud around her percolate.

Then the mortars began peppering the rice paddies. Either the enemy officers had finally grasped that sniper fire was not being ef-fective or some fresh mortar crews had taken up a more useful position. Any Marine who saw combat in Korea would say the damn Chinese never lacked for mortar shells and the enthusiasm to fire them. A direct hit would tear a man apart. One landing nearby could shred him with shrapnel. Just getting nicked could put a man out of action if a searing metal shard struck a particularly vulnerable piece of flesh.

Reckless found this out. Every so often a grenade or some other shell landed close enough that she could hear the shrapnel skittering off nearby rocks and penetrating the sludge of the rice paddies. She was nearing the end of the open terrain, closing in on when the incline of the slope began, when she was hit.

She may have just decided she was close enough to enter the running start—or as much as she could run with the extra weight and having already hauled herself uphill on two dozen trips—when the mortar shell landed and exploded an instant later. Shrapnel sliced the flesh above her left eye.

She would be okay . . . for a while. She was wounded—there was no getting around that—but the blood that emerged from the wound was a trickle, not a flow. Still, while she might be fortunate enough not to lose more blood, that wound would only hurt more as she kept climbing up and then gingerly made her way back down to level ground. Combine that with mounting exhaustion, and Reckless might not have too many trips left in her.

And there was plenty of fighting left that day.

It was still only midafternoon when the gun crews of the recoilless rifle platoon were targeted by Communist gunners, but instead of shifting positions they stood their ground for what became an uncommon firefight.

As weary as Eric Pedersen's eyes already were, they were sharp enough to catch sight of a major enemy troop movement. His binoculars were roaming past Hill 139 when his back and neck stiffened. What he saw was not groups of a dozen or even fifty Chinese soldiers, but hundreds of them, bursting into view and running for Vegas. The enemy must have needed a fast and large transfusion of troops, which was sort of good news because it implied that the battle for the beleaguered hill was not going their way. What the sudden appearance of a large number of Chinese double-timing it implied was that their commanders expected that quite a few wouldn't get through. They had two hundred yards to get across before finding shelter from Vegas.

It was the recoilless rifle platoon's job to make sure that that expectation became reality. Pedersen's radioed message to regimental headquarters echoed those sent in by forward observers, and all had the same objective—unleash hell on those making the two-hundred-yard dash.

The lieutenant gave his gun crews their instructions and they began firing. Only seconds afterward Marine mortars and artillery joined in. The ground shook and churned under the Chinese soldiers and geysers of dirt and dust spewed into the air with every shell that landed. For the madly running Communists, the carnage was inescapable.

And for Pedersen's platoon, so was the enemy fire that was fixed on them. The back blasts gave their positions away. But the lieutenant did not give his crews orders to move to new ones. That would take valuable time, and every second without firing possibly would allow some of those reinforcements to reach the defensive positions on Vegas and make things a lot tougher for the Marines dragging themselves up the slopes.

While mortar rounds landed dangerously close and small-arms fire sprayed the rocks around them, the recoilless rifles continued to spew shells, adding more death and destruction to the enemy side of the ledger. Pedersen half expected the barrels to glow red like barbecue coals. Even so, they would blister the hand of a man foolish enough to touch them.

Only when there wasn't a single Chinese soldier left to be seen still staggering toward Vegas did the gun crews move. They had a few wounded men to drag to safety. They had fewer shells to bring with them. The rapid firing of a few minutes earlier had sacked much of the supply. Fortunately, only a minute after the gun crews set up in their new positions, Reckless arrived, again knowing exactly where to find her Marines.

A couple of them had witnessed her final lurch to reach the top of the ridge. For a moment it appeared that she wasn't going to make it, and that she might even topple over backward. But she got all the way up, that seemingly infinite reservoir of strength coupled with stubbornness assisting her once again. Pedersen wondered which trip this was—the twenty-second, twenty-fifth? Who could keep a certain count on a day of such chaos and uncertainty?

Reckless looked like she had just completed her hundredth trip up the ridge. She was covered with perspiration that was interspersed with curls of white lather. Her flanks were heaving and her breathing was a rapid series of snorting gasps. The Marines hurried to take the eight shells off her packsaddle and distribute them. One of them overturned his helmet and poured a canteen of water into it. Reckless drank it down as fast as she could. With all the trips the valiant horse had made, this day near the end of March felt more like one in the middle of July.

Suddenly, the ground shuddered. Either eagle-eyed Chinese gunners had found the platoon again or it was just a lucky strike—explosions rocked the ridgeline all around the Marines. The blasts and the dirt and shards of rocks they kicked up were bad enough, but what frightened the men—and Reckless—most were the fiery clouds of white smoke. The enemy mortar rounds had included Willie Peter, or white phosphorus. A hit close enough could burn a man alive, and a small horse wouldn't fare much better.

A couple of Marines grabbed Reckless's bridle and hauled her away, finding some shelter in a tall grouping of rocks that formed something like a bunker. The roar of the explosions continued for only a few more seconds, but after the sound faded the air still held fast to smoke and a foul, burning stench. The horse's eyes were wide, and to the Marines it looked like any moment she would make a panicked getaway down the dangerous decline of the ridge.

Sergeant Joe Latham appeared. Sizing up the situation immediately, he put down the two recoilless rifle shells he had just hauled up and shook off his flak jacket. He placed it over the horse's head. "Easy, take it easy, girl, it's okay now," he murmured over and over. Gradually, Reckless calmed. Not seeing the poisonous cloud helped, as did the wind from the south that was dissipating it.

"See now, see?" Latham whispered, removing the flak jacket.

Reckless cautiously checked her surroundings, and then seemed satisfied. She emerged from the rocks and shook her head. She peered at Latham and the other Marines watching her as if to say, "Okay, then. Sorry about that. Let's go back to work."

Lieutenant Pedersen had not been paying much attention to Reckless because one of his men had caught some shrapnel during the brief bombardment. The field dressing he applied had stopped the bleeding in the Marine's neck—fortunately, the carotid artery hadn't been cut—but the man needed that wound looked at in one of the hospital tents. There would be no relief from bearing weight for Reckless on this trip down to the supply depot.

When she left the top of the ridge, the wounded Marine was strapped to her back. Even the dreaded Willie Peter wasn't about to stop her.

CHAPTER NINETEEN

★ ★

"A Symphony of Death"

By 5:30 of that seemingly endless afternoon, Fox 2/7 was in position for its first full assault. Many of the men had to think they would be moving into certain death. Dropping all around them were 76-mm and 122-mm artillery shells and 60-mm and 82-mm mortar shells, and bullets filled the air from Chinese fixed machine guns and burp guns.

The leathernecks listened anxiously to grenades exploding, tanks bellowing, BARs and other small arms chattering incessantly, and all the other sounds of battle at its most intense, punctuated by the shrill whistles of the Chinese commanders urging their troops on. As the Marine veteran Lee Ballenger put it, what the waiting men heard was "a symphony of death."

Still, when told to advance, Fox 2/7 did so. They inched ahead slowly, crawling like crabs, eyes filling with dirt whenever a shell landed nearby, a few men screaming when hit—but at least screaming meant that they were only wounded and not destroyed. Overhead, American jets hurtled through the air to attack enemy positions, which were also being battered by tanks firing from along the Jamestown Line.

By shouting "Execute! Execute!" Captain Estey called upon his men to attack. From behind them, tanks specifically targeted the Chinese trenches and bunkers above and fired round after round into them. In lines of five men each, the 1st and 2nd Platoons zigzagged up the slope toward the summit.

That was when the fight to retake Outpost Vegas reached its peak.

Reckless had made at least thirty trips from the forward supply depot to the top of the ridge by five p.m., when the fighting was soon to be at its fiercest. It was more difficult for the little mare to keep her head up, even when traversing relatively undamaged ground, what little there was of it. The wound above her left eye throbbed. The noise and smoke and shuddering of intense battle were incessant.

She had taken on additional duties and was no longer just an ammunition hauler. Reckless was now an ambulance on every downward trek. Even when there was not a wounded Marine to transport at the top of her trip, there was always one to be found on the way down who needed help. A man struggling to reach a medical tent would haul himself up onto her empty saddle, or a corpsman would push a man up across it. At the depot, the wounded man was removed and taken away for treatment. He was replaced by the next cargo of eight recoilless rifle shells. Reckless turned and set off, very little trot left in her steps, heading closer to the noise and smoke and shuddering— going toward danger, alone.

She was not alone for long. As soon as Colonel Lew Walt and other commanding officers could scrape together replacements, they were being sent to join what had become the epic ordeal of Vegas.

Also hurrying to the front lines were Marines who had already been there, been wounded but not too badly, and after getting patched up were returning to join their brothers in harm's way. A few of them wanted to minimize the chances of getting hit again on the way, so Reckless had a third job—as a shield. As she progressed in her determined way through the crater-strewn rice paddies, she was joined by Marines who in groups of twos and threes scampered along on the side of her that offered some protection from snipers. Reckless didn't seem to mind the company.

Every step uphill was more difficult. Gone was any lingering appearance of a graceful racehorse. Reckless was purely a pack animal now. And like her fellow Marines, she was following orders, doing her job, and "fighting" for them the way Marines fought for each other. Every trip up and every trip down was a grind. Every muscle ached, with her forehead where the shrapnel got her being the worst. Each time she hauled herself and her precious cargo up the last few feet to the top of the ridge was a triumph.

When Sergeant Latham or Corporal Coleman was there at the time Reckless arrived, one of them persuaded her to linger a few extra minutes. If left to her own devices, after greeting Eric Pedersen and the rest of his men and catching her breath, Reckless would wait for a wounded Marine to be tied to her back, then immediately begin the journey of however many hundreds of yards down to the depot. Latham or Coleman would lead her aside to a more protected spot, away from the back blasts of the recoilless rifles. Reckless didn't appear to even notice those explosions of air and smoke and dirt anymore, but of course the enemy did.

Once her breathing slowed and she cooled off a bit, Latham or Coleman would drag the packsaddle off of her, place a helmet full of water on the ground, and offer her whatever food was left over from what had last been carried up from the supply depot. She ate only a small portion of grain, but she always drank the water. While she was occupied, Reckless received a rubdown, which was especially welcome on her legs. Sometimes they trembled slightly, an indication of the weariness creeping through every part of the little sorrel mare.

After she'd had a few more minutes of rest, her caregivers reluctantly hoisted the packsaddle up on her back once again and tied it tight. If a wounded man needed to be evacuated, he also was tied to her. But there was no complaint from Reckless. To her, it was time to get back to work. Her Marines needed her. She gingerly stepped down onto the long trail that led to the depot, the wound above her eye not throbbing as much as it did before . . . but would be again in a few minutes.

The men of Fox Company had gotten within four hundred yards of the summit. According to Lieutenant Chenoweth, "What a sorry sight Vegas is. Smashed white rock." With what was left of Easy Company, Captains Estey and Lorence had the strength of close to three platoons. Desperate Chinese soldiers, becoming aware that they were about to either repulse the assault or lose the hill, threw all they could at the attackers. Naturally, in such a cauldron of death, that was when the Marines surged forward in a final charge.

Chenoweth and his 3rd Platoon were ordered into the fight. Within minutes they had joined the other Fox Company units, and together they gained the lower trenches. For the next hour or more the Chinese wouldn't quit and neither would the advance forces of the Marines. All the combat was close, so close that mortars and heavy weapons were no longer any good. The fighting was with small arms, knives, and bare hands.

Feeling something hit his chest, Chenoweth looked down to see a grenade with a lit fuse that had bounced off him and landed on his right foot. Fearing that if he bent down to grab and toss it the grenade would blow his head off, the lieutenant didn't react at all. And he was lucky. The grenade did explode but it didn't pack much of a wallop because even though "my right foot and lower leg began to burn," they "still worked," so he continued to help take the outpost. He would not find out until later that the leg he continued to walk on was fractured.

The company commander, Estey, was everywhere, disdaining any consideration of his own safety. According to one witness's description, he was "always in the thick of the fight, he was a bulwark in the face of a firestorm, setting an example of courage and leadership that inspired his Marines to the heights of valor." And as for his fellow CO on that hellish hill: "Captain Lorence, at the head of only 12 men left in Easy 2/5, was a burning flame of inspiration, always at the point of greatest danger."

His courage, leadership, and utter disregard for his own safety would be recognized by the award of the Navy Cross. Captain Estey would also be awarded the Navy Cross.

And a Navy Cross would go to the Chicago-born Chenoweth too. Struck during a salvo of mortar and artillery fire, he refused medical attention. After seeing to the evacuation of the wounded, he went back to the head of his platoon and led the charge against the Chinese position. There was fierce hand-to-hand fighting in the trenches until finally the enemy, preferring to face the wrath of their Communist commissars, fled.

This was no time for a breather, though. Chenoweth, as weak as he was, had to make sure the hard-won trenches could be defended. Even from a prone position he issued orders, which included the care and evacuation of the newly wounded. Only then did Chenoweth allow a corpsman to treat his own injuries.

The next time Eric Pedersen saw Reckless, as she gave one last surge up and joined the platoon atop the ridge, he immediately noticed the blood on her left flank. The little mare had been hit by shrapnel again. And again, it had to have hurt when that hot sliver of metal sliced open her flesh. Obviously, though, it hadn't stopped Reckless from completing what may have been her fortieth trip.

"What's keeping this heroic horse going?" the platoon leader wondered. It had to be more than strength, more than simple stubbornness too. There was something in Reckless that was also in the best Marines, that quality that urged them onward beyond their natural strength and spirit.

Once more, Pedersen went into his field medical kit. He wiped the wound and her flank clean. The shrapnel had indeed only sliced her; none of it was embedded. He dabbed iodine on it. Reckless was still and patient during the treatment . . . or, more likely, she was too tired to move.

He hadn't really been able to keep track, but it did seem to Pedersen that more time had passed between her appearances atop the ridge on her last few trips. No mystery there, though. Reckless had to be making stops along the way, gulping in air, shaking her head as though clearing her exhausted mind, and maybe leaning to take a little of the weight off her wounded flank. To Pedersen, by this time of day, in the late afternoon, it was astonishing that she was still getting up the ridge at all.

The wound above her eye was closed; no more blood seeped from it. The relentless Reckless was being given another wounded Marine to carry. She glanced at her commanding officer, who thought of the Shakespeare line "Once more into the breach." He patted the side of her face and then she turned away. It was time for the next trip down the hill.

★ ★

CHAPTER TWENTY

Bravery Beyond Exhaustion

The daylight was waning as Reckless began her forty-fifth trip, leaving the supply depot behind step by hoof-dragging step. As had become the norm, she was not alone. Five Marines walked beside her. They weren't crouching or glancing nervously toward the enemy positions. Maybe these men didn't care about Reckless as a shield; maybe they simply wanted to keep the gallant horse company. Maybe like what those Virginia students thought about General Robert E. Lee's horse, Traveller, they considered Reckless a lucky charm. Fortunately for the weary Reckless, though, no Marine tried to pluck any hairs out of her.

If they had tried, by this point Reckless would not have been able to run fast enough to escape them. She was drained down to the last drops of her endurance. She was dehydrated too. Despite the efforts of Sergeant Latham and Corporal Coleman to provide her with water at the top of the ridge or at the supply depot, there had been few breaks from perspiring, and cool sweat soaked every inch of her coat. Her left flank ached more than any other part of her, thanks to the second shrapnel wound. Yet still she moved forward and upward, carrying out her mission.

There were no more running starts when the ground began to incline. Now Reckless began the meandering trail upward by simply digging her hooves into the ground one grinding step after another, sometimes stumbling and then righting herself. If she had been a human and a corpsman had found her like this, wounded and weak and seemingly wandering, he would have had her lie down on a stretcher to be carried to the nearest aid station. But the overwhelmed corpsmen, many of them also wounded and weakened by exhaustion, couldn't be distracted by a horse, even if she was their Reckless.

And it wasn't like she was looking for help, or even to be noticed. Like all the other Marines around her, Reckless was bent on fighting and winning this battle, one torturous trip at a time.

Latham was waiting the next time she returned to the forward ammunition depot. He gave her grain and water and pieces of chocolate. Maybe it was his imagination and knowing how weary she must be, but it sure appeared that she yawed a bit from side to side. She might not even be able to make one more trip. But he and another Marine loaded her up anyway. He put his arms around her neck just for a moment, feeling the quivering in her. Then she turned and began her next trip.

Obviously, what Reckless meant to the effort of the Marines to take Vegas back from the Communists was the very practical matter of the resilient little mare keeping the recoilless rifles supplied with shells so they could do the most damage possible. That Reckless would make trip after trip, piling up miles of travel on wearying legs, without needing to be prompted or guided, was not what anyone, even her close companions in the platoon, could have foreseen. This one lone horse was helping to tilt the scales.

But Reckless meant something even more than that. She was an inspiration to the Marines. "I saw her three or four times that day and night, and I figured she'd end up dead. I never thought she'd survive, but she kept going," remembered Sergeant Harold Wadley. "She knew exactly what her job was. And the impression she made on us, to look up and see that little Mongolian mare making another trip up or down that hill, alone, explosions all around her—we thought there's not another horse in war history that could even touch Reckless."

Indeed, she seemed more than a horse. Reckless was viewed as . . . well, a Marine. "The instinctive nature of horses is to flee from danger, whereas the nature of Marines is to run toward it," added Wadley, who after returning to the States would settle in Idaho and become a noted expert on horses and an author.

He recalled one interval that day when his unit was pinned down in a dry creek bed: "The noise was just a roar. Five hundred rounds per minute were coming in, and our artillery and mortars were firing in return. Rounds would collide in the sky, and I can still see the white-hot shrapnel fading to red as it fell on us. But we'd look up, and there was Reckless trotting by."

"I remember seeing her in action through my binoculars," recalled Sergeant William Janzen. "The path she followed—all by herself!— was about a mile from my location on the MLR. She was trotting through the abandoned rice paddy at the base of the hill mass leading up to Vegas. Every time we saw her, we gave a cheer."

"Reckless was responsible for what happened that day and the next," asserted Private James Larkin, who after barely escaping off Vegas with his life the night before had joined How Company of the 3rd Battalion. "Of course, the Marines themselves were mainly responsible, but Reckless did a hell of a job. When we kept seeing that little horse hauling that heavy ammo, how could any of us think of quitting?"

The setting sun illuminated smoke and flames and even the sweat on the bloodied and bruised faces of the Marines clinging to the Vegas hillsides. The air reeked of burned metal and flesh and Willie Peter. It was also filled with the chatter of burp guns, machine guns, and BARs, as well as the shouts of men battling to the death.

Inch by bloody inch, the Marines fought their way to within fifty yards of the summit of the hill. The enemy fell back, leaving room for their comrades at the top to toss grenades and pour down machine-gun fire. Not only were more reinforcements arriving from Reno, but Chinese troops stationed there were directing machine-gun and mortar fire at the attacking Americans.

Fox Company and the remnants of Easy had gained enough ground that by 7:15 p.m., with light scarce, they could organize the men still able to fight for what they hoped would be the final assault on the remaining Chinese position. Half an hour later, artillery fire was concentrated on the summit. At 8 p.m., the shelling stopped, replaced by flares. That was the signal to charge the top of the hill.

The end for Reckless came as full darkness descended on the field of battle—the end of her mission, anyway. Somehow, after making one more straining and struggling trip up the ridge, she was still standing with other members of Eric Pedersen's platoon, who were very wrung out themselves.

As long as there had been light, the platoon's gun crews had been relentless, hammering away with their 24-pound shells at targets identified by their commanding officer and whoever could be spared to back him up with another pair of binoculars. Pedersen found himself praying for the sun to set before his burning eyeballs turned to cinders and drifted out of their sockets. There was a lot of satisfaction in knowing that the pinpoint precision of the recoilless rifles had heaved a lot of destruction on the Communists. He had been able to observe a series of assaults that had the Marines threatening to recapture Vegas. The men of the platoon had surely played their part in what was hoped to be a complete victory.

After Reckless had completed her last trip and had been unloaded—she was quaking with exhaustion and barely able to keep her head up—Pedersen ordered her to remain with them. Just in case Reckless tried to refuse the order or was too tired to comprehend it, he had Corporal Coleman hold fast to her bridle, being careful not to rub the raw spots on her face and of course the wound above her left eye.

By that time, the sun had, at last, set, which meant it would be fully dark by the time Reckless made another trek down the hill to the depot. While mortar crews and the artillery of the 11th Marines would continue to pound enemy positions behind Vegas, darkness removed the advantage of the recoilless rifles in meticulous shooting. The long day was done for the platoon, and for Reckless too.

Though his brain felt almost as fried as his eyes, Lieutenant Pedersen did some quick calculations. Allowing that he could be off by one or two, he figured that Reckless had made fifty-one trips up to the various firing positions on the ridgeline and back to the supply depot. With some of her loads consisting of six shells and others of eight shells, the lieutenant allowed that the little mare had hauled three hundred eighty rounds. Easily, that totaled more than nine thousand pounds—four and a half tons, and ten times her body weight. The calculations also told Pedersen that she may have traveled as much as thirty-five miles that day while carrying all that ammunition, and added to that was the burden of however many Marines she had carried back down the hill. The enormity of the achievement by the gutsy and stubborn Reckless made his head spin almost as much as sheer exhaustion did.

The sky was dark and the early-spring night air was cool when Reckless made her last descent of the hill and trudged slowly through the muddy rice paddies, by luck or a last bit of willpower managing to avoid the craters created by exploding mortar and artillery shells. Well, she had some help too. Several of the platoon's Marines, seeing that her head hung so low that she couldn't really watch out for obstructions, gently changed her course when necessary with either a tug on her worn bridle or a few whispered words. Reckless was another weary, battle-scarred Marine plodding toward someplace where there might be some chow and a few hours of sleep.

The battle for Vegas still raged, but Reckless was oblivious to the sounds of the shouting, machine guns, and explosions. She left what remained of the trail and turned into the pasture.

Even after thirty minutes of intense and close combat, Chinese troops were still on the summit. The more advanced Marines thought they could almost reach out and touch the enemy from where they were clinging to the slope immediately below. Corpsmen, again braving enemy fire, tried to keep up with those advancing units, treating Marines as they fell.

On the side facing the MLR, the Marines could consolidate behind a perimeter defense at the base of the outpost. As full darkness took hold on the second day of the Battle of the Nevada Cities, that was where they would stay . . . unless the battered Chinese had other thoughts.

They did. The forward units of the 5th Marines had barely caught their breath when the Chinese came pouring across the summit and down to the Marine positions. The fighting was no less brutal than it had been earlier, with guns blazing and knives and bayonets slicing through the air and attackers. The assault failed. Before midnight there would be two more, and the Marines withstood both of them. The men of Fox 2/7 and Easy 2/5 still occupied the outer trenches and the slope and simply were not about to let go.

And they had some serious assistance. Allied fighters ruled the night sky, as they had during the day. They made one sortie after another, lashing the top of Vegas and nearby enemy positions with a destructive barrage of explosives. It was later estimated that more than twenty-four tons of bombs were dropped that night and into the early hours of March 28.

That day's *New York Times* would report accusations by the Communists that U.S. forces were using germ warfare in the battle. The article also included a peculiar summary about how March 27 drew to a close: "Leathernecks mopping up during the night on the northern slopes of the rocky ridge known as 'Vegas' ran into strong bodies of the Chinese Reds." As the second day of the battle ground toward midnight, no leathernecks were viewing the action as "mopping up."

Sergeant Joe Latham had been waiting for Reckless when she staggered into the pasture. She was filthy, covered with dust and mud and even some blood—though Latham noted that both her wounds had remained closed; Doc Mitchell, assuming he had survived the day, could check her over in the morning.

Perspiration had dried and caked in her coat, and her eyelids drooped along with her head. Latham was accustomed to seeing the little mare's tail whisking from side to side, but now it moved listlessly, or maybe it moved only because of the wind gusting a bit.

The sergeant removed her empty packsaddle. The hand-me-down from California as well as the hand-me-down horse had survived a lot of wear and tear. He offered Reckless a can of water and some grain. Latham was glad to see she was not too weary to gulp both down. When Corporal Coleman arrived, the two men gave her a thorough rubdown. She sure needed it, though a few times she glanced at them as if to say, "Enough already. I have to sleep."

Finally, it was time for sleeping. After a few last laps of water, Reckless stepped into her bunker. Latham had spread piles of fresh straw on the floor. He was surprised when she was reluctant to lie down. He'd thought she would be anxious to take the load off her aching legs. Then he realized that she had willed herself to stay upright and complete her mission for so many hours on end, a part of her couldn't give in. She did, eventually, lie down, with the gentle persuasion of her two handlers.

When Latham covered her with a blanket, Reckless's eyes closed and she breathed a loud sigh.

CHAPTER TWENTY-ONE

★ ★

Taking the Rest of Vegas

T hat night, Reckless lost her commanding officer. Thankfully, it was not because Eric Pedersen was wounded again.

In one of those quirks of military bureaucracy, when he had returned to camp that night, the spent lieutenant learned that orders had come through relieving him of command of the platoon. Those orders had originated well before the battle began, but didn't reach him until that night. Of course, he hated the prospect of leaving his command in the middle of a big fight. However, this time when he went to see his friend at division headquarters to protest the timing of the orders, Pedersen was essentially told, "Don't even think about it."

He wasn't too upset, though. It wasn't like he was being shipped home and leaving his men high and dry. In fact, Pedersen was being given command of the entire anti-tank company, which would put him in line for a promotion. It helped too that he was being replaced by a first-rate lieutenant, Bill Riley.

He had an answer when he returned to his men and was asked the obvious question: Reckless would stay with the platoon.

"She belongs here with the rest of the men, not with me, Joe," he told Latham. With Lieutenant Riley expected to arrive in the morning, Pedersen gave his last order as the unit's CO: "Be in position to start firing at first light."

The sergeant was glad to know that the gallant sorrel mare would remain where she belonged. He just didn't know if she had another day in her like this one had been.

As much of an achievement as it was to gain and cling to that foothold near the summit of Outpost Vegas, it was not enough. The stalemate was only a few hours old, but every minute that it lasted favored the Chinese because the summit and its complex of trenches and bunkers remained in their hands, and no doubt the Communist negotiators in Panmunjom had already been made aware of the allies' loss of Vegas. And there was still the ongoing numbers dilemma—the enemy had more reinforcements to move into position than the 1st Marine Division had.

There was no way around it—the enemy had to be dislodged and that hill retaken completely. The numbers advantage could be neutralized by having a high-ground defensive position . . . though more than a few of the Marines recognized that hadn't prevented Vegas and Reno from being overtaken a little more than twenty-four hours ago.

At 3:55 a.m. on March 28, the third day of the battle, the 105-mm and 155-mm howitzers of the 11th Marines opened up. This was no routine soften-them-up assault—the American artillery would send twenty-three hundred rounds soaring at the Chinese position on Outpost Vegas and what were believed to be surrounding assembly areas. After a half-hour bombardment, Captain Estey's Fox 2/7 was called upon again to advance.

The artillery had done a good job. If room had allowed for it, the Chinese troops would have been staggering in their trenches. They were still digging the dirt out of their eyes as Estey and his men approached. The Marines clawed their way to within grenade-tossing range and let fly. They also cut loose with their machine guns and BARs. The Chinese countered with burp guns and potato mashers. The exchange of lead and grenades was so intense that Fox Company had to stay where it was—rising even a few inches off the ground or slipping around the protection of a mound of rocks was suicide.

With the company depleted by KIAs and wounded Marines, there was no need to turn this into a slaughter. Captain Estey was ordered to pull back to where he could send his wounded to the aid stations and absorb replacements for what would no doubt be a very long day.

Knowing that he would be assuming his new command at first light, and though also knowing he really should be trying to grab some shut-eye, during that night Eric Pedersen went to see Reckless. He couldn't go to the company command post without a last visit. Sure, he wasn't going far, but Reckless would no longer be *his* horse. And who knew what could happen to either of them during another day full of fighting?

Reckless was sound asleep. Maybe she hadn't heard him approach, or maybe the exhaustion had so overwhelmed her that rising up from unconsciousness was more than she could manage. The lieutenant knelt to adjust the blanket so that it covered his little wounded mare again.

It was a poignant few moments for Eric Pedersen. He remembered the lightning-quick racehorse with the apparent ability to run circles around her competitors. If the war hadn't intervened, Flame could well have been the most famous horse in Korea by now. She would have been a champion in her prime. She could have gone on tour, racing in Japan and possibly even the United States. He didn't know how international racing worked—maybe it was something like boxing, where a heavyweight fighter in whatever country wasn't a true world champion until he came to America and defeated Rocky Marciano.

Reckless would not get that opportunity to come to America and be a champion, to hear those cheers. Being part of the 5th Marines, especially after today, had taken too much out of her. Perhaps when the war was over . . . but who knew when that would be? Heck, she might not even survive the next twenty-four hours.

Reckless breathed deeply, snorted slightly, and one leg gave a twitch. Pedersen felt some guilt about what the little horse had experienced. Not a lot, though. Many of the Marines had come to love Reckless, and she had been treated like the royalty she apparently thought she was. Pedersen admired her more than he ever had any animal. He would do whatever he could to make sure she was taken care of down the road.

The lieutenant's own legs were creaky and sore when he stood up. Reckless slept on. He bent over to softly pat her neck, then turned and quietly walked away. The new company CO hoped he could get some sleep before being sent back into battle . . . but he doubted it.

As Lieutenant Pedersen had ordered, the recoilless rifle platoon prepared before dawn to scale the ridge to the gun crews' firing positions. Bill Riley would be the one with the binoculars this new day, searching out enemy targets. He was no rookie when it came to combat, but still, Sergeants Lisenby and Lively and the others wanted to be really on the ball and make the new command a little easier for him.

And they wanted to help kick the Communists off Vegas.

Corporal Coleman hauled a bucket of barley and fresh water out to the pasture. Reckless's ears pricked up at his approach. It was something of a struggle for her to stand. The soreness in her legs must have been almost crippling. But she did get up and steady herself. She gazed at the Marine, though it was hard for Coleman to read any expression in her eyes in the predawn dark.

He could see immediately that there wasn't as much of Reckless as there had been twenty-four hours earlier. Without a doubt, she had lost weight. All the effort and strain of the hiking up and down the ridge and hills more than four dozen times, carrying thousands of pounds of shells—along with wounded Marines on the return trips— had shrunken a Mongolian mare who had not been that big to begin with. How could she get through another day like that?

The corporal gave her the barley and water, and while she had her breakfast he gave her a rubdown. She began to warm up a bit, and the morning chill seemed less biting. However, Coleman noticed right away that as they started off for the forward ammunition depot, the stiffness in her legs prevented her from walking in her usual graceful way.

When Sergeant Latham met them at the ammunition depot, he wasn't worried. Stating the obvious, he told Coleman, "She's gimpy from overwork," then added, "She'll work it out when she gets more warmed up."

The sergeant was right. They loaded Reckless up with six shells and both men accompanied her across the shredded rice paddies and up the ridge to the position that the new CO had staked out. Reckless moved well. Her strength had been renewed by the rest, water, and food. As she loped along, the way her slender head bobbed up and down made it look like she was nodding and acknowledging the Marines she encountered on her way. "Royal" Reckless had returned.

The next attempt to retake Vegas came just before sunrise, at 6 a.m. Once more Fox 2/7 attacked, pulling themselves up the side of the hill.

The Chinese defenders were more alert and ready for them this time. They poured down small-arms and mortar fire and an apparently inexhaustible supply of potato-masher grenades. The second assault of the day was stopped more than three hundred yards south of the crest.

For a second time, Fox Company rested and regrouped and welcomed replacements from reserve units. Captain Estey received orders to attack once more following a series of air strikes. The first rays of sunlight glinted off the cockpits and wings of the Marine and Air Force jet fighters as they swooped down out of the safety of the sky toward the battered Outpost Vegas. The flyboys, most of them in Grumman F9F Panthers, administered more punishment on the defenders, turning some of the remaining fortifications into matchsticks.

When the roaring and screaming receded, Fox Company was on the move again. Step after bloody step they climbed the hill, this time managing to get within fifteen yards of the forward trenches. The Chinese knew there was no going back. Their commissars and commanding officers would not welcome them with praise for having given all they had and almost holding the hill. It was defend or die for the Communists. By the same token, the Marines who had gotten this far were not giving up.

The close-range, pistol-hot exchange of fire lasted five minutes, then ten, fifteen, twenty minutes. At one point in the firefight a Chinese machine-gun position at the base of a rock formation was keeping the company pinned down, and especially vulnerable was a corpsman trying to drag a wounded Marine to safety. A squad leader, Sergeant Daniel Matthews, only twenty-one years old, crawled under the steady stream of bullets to the formation, scrambled onto the rocks, then leaped up to charge the enemy position, firing his rifle as fast as he could.

The Chinese soldiers manning the machine gun never saw him coming. Unfortunately, enemy soldiers in a nearby position did and they let loose with bursts of automatic weapons. Bullets ripped through the sergeant's body, but that didn't stop him. As the corpsman pulled his patient out of harm's way and other members of the company jumped to their feet, Matthews was hit at least once more, but that was no satisfaction for the enemy gun crew who were cut to pieces by the sergeant's fusillade.

When his squad mates reached him, Matthews was taking his last gasping breaths, and he died on the muddy rocks. He was one more brave Marine whose family received a posthumous Medal of Honor. His body would be escorted home to Van Nuys, California, by his twin brother, who was in the Navy.

Despite this stirring advance, Fox 2/7 was stuck. Captain Estey reported to regimental headquarters that his company could now boast only forty-three able-bodied men. In response, Colonel Lew Walt ordered Easy Company of the 2nd Battalion in his 5th Marines to relieve Fox and take Vegas.

Staff Sergeant John Williams, who sported the nickname "Trigger Jack," exemplified the never-quit mentality of most of the men of the 5th Marines. He had been a mortarman with Easy Company, but was taken out of action when notification of his transfer to Japan came through. However, during the fighting, Second Lieutenant Edward Franz, who led the 1st Platoon, was wounded and evacuated. Williams joined Easy Company on the battlefield.

"Take over the 1st Platoon," Captain Lorence told him. "We're going to take Vegas. Your platoon is over to the right. Let's go."

When he found it, Trigger Jack was more than a little surprised at how badly the platoon had been mauled, and that there were only a handful of Marines left in it.

Among the men sent up the hill to evacuate dead and wounded Marines was Corporal Robert Hall, a member of the weapons company attached to the 2nd Battalion of the 5th Regiment. He had given up studying advertising art and design in college to join the

Marine Corps. He had arrived in January, yet since he was coming from Schenectady in upstate New York, the Korean cold hadn't bothered him too much. Still, he was a long way from home and in the middle of a desperate fight.

"Most of what I did was carry bodies out, then go back up the Vegas hill to get more," Hall recalled six decades later. "It was pretty disheartening how many more there still were after every trip."

In groups of three, four, and five, the men of Fox 2/7 who could still walk—though most of them were wounded—were coming down off the hill. There were fewer of them for Hall to see in the smoke and dust-filled air the closer he got to the outpost. One of the last to emerge from the cloud-like air of the slope was a lieutenant with a pistol in one hand and a stick in the other that supported him as he walked. Hall would find out later that this was Lieutenant Theodore Chenoweth, somehow still alive and upright, who had not left Vegas until the rest of his platoon had walked or been taken off. At the time of being relieved, his platoon had only eight men left who had escaped being killed or wounded.

Corporal Hall, after he and a corpsman had placed a Marine with a badly mangled foot on a stretcher, paused to observe the lieutenant, who was obviously in pain, as he hobbled toward them. Hall's most vivid memory was of Chenoweth's "total lack of concern for himself, and his concern for the men who had fought with him." When the lieutenant arrived at the stretcher and saw that the man on it was crying from the pain, he knelt down, grimacing but suppressing a groan, to comfort the Marine. Then Chenoweth lurched to his feet and turned to stare up the slope, hoping one more survivor from his platoon would appear out of the mist.

"It was his platoon and he was the last man down," Hall recalled. He remembered hoping that the lieutenant was decorated for his courage and dedication to his men. He would learn the following year of Lieutenant Chenoweth's Navy Cross.

As Captain Lorence's men were working their way uphill, air and artillery assaults were renewed. This time the gunners and pilots targeted not only Vegas but Outpost Reno too and other enemy-held hills nearby to disrupt supplies to Vegas and to reduce the amount of small-arms and mortar fire coming from those positions. The American jets were particularly active—it was estimated that during the twenty-three-minute aerial attack, more than a ton of bombs per minute landed on the stunned Chinese.

Their gunners were not idle, however. "The enemy started clobbering us and I only had ten men left," Trigger Jack Williams later reported. "But we stayed. We started digging, but fast, and hung on."

Reckless needed no time on this second full day of battle to become accustomed to the earsplitting and terrifying sounds of battle. Right from her first trip, she was ready for them. And the sorrel mare seemed totally oblivious to any personal danger. The two wounds suffered the day before had not left much of an impression. In fact, during one of her morning treks a shell landed about twenty yards away and a plume of white phosphorus erupted from it. Reckless barely glanced in that direction, continuing on her mission.

The tough little horse did on that Saturday what she had done the day before. This included at times carrying eight shells instead of six. She set off from the forward ammunition depot at almost an eager trot, then wound her way through the pockmarked paddies, and again she had the energy to give herself a running start up the ridge. Climbing uphill was still a struggle, though, and Reckless was breathing hard when she arrived at the gun crews' position. Lieutenant Riley let her rest for as long as she needed, and the men of the platoon offered her water and snacks.

She didn't dally, though. As the battle for ownership of the Vegas hill increased in intensity, Reckless seemed to know it was reaching its peak. Everything rode on what happened in the next couple of hours. This was no time for a Marine, even a four-legged one, to shirk her duties. Reckless took one last big breath, gave her mane a shake, and began the descent. And again along the way, if a wounded Marine needed a lift, he climbed or was placed aboard.

Lieutenant Riley's recoilless rifle platoon did not participate directly in the last surge up to the Vegas summit. It did, however, contribute in a big way. The pinpoint accuracy and unceasing efforts of Sergeants Lisenby, Lively, Sherman, and the other men put the 24-pound shells into the trenches and right on top of the heads of the Chinese troops desperately trying to defend the outpost. At the very least they reduced the number of defenders, but just as likely the onslaught of shells being fired deliberately at them had to lower the morale of those enemy soldiers. That made the job of taking Vegas a bit more doable.

As the rifles practically glowed red with repeated use, Reckless trudged up and down, bringing shells to her Marines. By that point in the day she was exhausted again, but the little mare couldn't give in to it. Every time she mounted the crest of the ridge, the eight shells were snatched from her packsaddle and distributed. Minutes later, they were landing on the disheartened and soon-to-be-defeated Chinese.

Reckless and her regiment were about to win the day.

At precisely one minute after 1 p.m., the final effort to recapture Outpost Vegas had begun. Led by Trigger Jack Williams, the 1st Platoon of Easy Company, 2nd Battalion, 5th Marines attacked what remained of the enemy position: Within a few minutes, all the defenders were either dead or had fled in the face of the determined assault.

The three platoons of Easy Company converged on the nearly destroyed outpost, and a head count was taken. The 2nd Platoon had seven men left, the 3rd had fifteen, and Sergeant Williams had eight, meaning a grand total of thirty Marines had taken Vegas, the lone survivors of Easy Company.

Finally, at 2:55 p.m. on March 28, Outpost Vegas was once more in American hands. There were a few enemy soldiers just on the other side of the summit, probably snipers, but for now, the exhausted Marines let them be.

CHAPTER TWENTY-TWO

★ ★

It Can't Be Given Back

The immediate challenge, of course, was to keep the freshly re-acquired outpost. Only minutes after the last enemy soldiers left it, the Chinese attacked. This was a smart move, to throw whatever they had available at the weary and wounded Marines before they could dig into defensive positions. Unfortunately for the attackers, after it had taken so long to capture Vegas, the Marines were not about to go anywhere. They beat back the assault.

Colonel Lew Walt did not believe for a moment that the Chinese would be willing to accept defeat. Vegas had to be prepared for more enemy attacks through the rest of the afternoon and into the night, and it simply could not be lost again. The man who would be chiefly responsible for that was Major Benjamin Lee.

The forty-two-year-old operations officer of the 2nd Battalion in the 5th Marines was born and raised in Kansas City and had been a

Marine for nineteen years. Despite his Midwest origins, Major Lee liked to carry a walking stick and was described by one Marine in the 5th Regiment who observed him under fire as "like a British officer on his way to a picnic, calm as you please." Lee had seen plenty of action in the Pacific Theater in World War II as a noncommissioned officer, including on Guadalcanal, and had received a Silver Star and a Purple Heart.

As soon as he knew that Outpost Vegas had been retaken, he approached his commanding officer and volunteered to lead the defense of Vegas. Colonel Walt agreed, and Lee left immediately.

It wasn't a given that he would even reach the hill. To get to Vegas, Lee had to cross a thousand yards of craggy ground that was swept by mortar and artillery fire. According to an after-action report, he "reached the hard-pressed unit and, moving among the men to encourage them and assure the integrity of the position, succeeded in reorganizing the forces and in launching a series of attacks upon the enemy who were attempting to overrun the position."

Despite having turned back the first counterattack, Major Lee's new command was in a precarious position. Most of the fortifications had been destroyed, forcing the Marines to hurriedly dig holes and use mounds of dirt, fortified by little more than sandbags, for protection. Moving around was dangerous because of the enemy machine gunners and snipers on other hills as well as the few diehards somewhere on the summit.

But the biggest challenge was, once again, numbers. Even with the sturdy job done by the 11th Marines and the jets to hit supply and assembly points, Major Lee knew the Chinese had many more soldiers to throw at Vegas. This became even more of a grim reality when a count revealed there were only sixty-six Marines left at the outpost, including seven men from Fox 2/7 who had chosen not to return to the MLR when their wounded comrades had been evacuated.

The recapture and control of Outpost Vegas meant a reprieve for Reckless. There would be no need for her to make fifty-one trips from the forward ammunition depot to the crest of Hill 120. With Marines occupying Vegas, orders came from the command post of the 5th Marines for Lieutenant Riley and his men to stand down. Their role was not completely over, though, because there would be opportunities to disrupt Communist troops massing for the almost certain counterattacks. But the seemingly endless repetition of locate a target, load the shell, and fire had, in fact, ended.

The always reliable Joe Latham was waiting for Reckless when she returned from her last trip of the day. He estimated that she had made at least two dozen that Saturday, March 28. He calculated the same way Pedersen had done the night before and figured that the little mare had carried close to two tons of shells, and thus between six and seven tons in the two days of unrelieved battle. Most of those trips, as had been true the day before, had been done on her own, and with Marines on her back as she negotiated the path down and across the rice paddies, with artillery and mortar shells falling nearby. At any moment one of them could have blown Reckless to bits, but fear for her own life was obviously not part of her nature.

Reinforcements were a very welcome sight when Easy 2/7, commanded by Captain Thomas Connolly, arrived on Vegas. Units of a reconstituted Fox 2/5 were on their way too, Major Lee was told. With fewer than two hundred men, the garrison was still significantly understrength, but even with some of Captain Lorence's Easy 2/5 being relieved, Lee had more men and firepower to resist the next attack.

He did not have to wait long. Any thought that the Communists might hold off until later that night, perhaps hoping to lull the Vegas defenders to sleep, was dispelled at 7:55 p.m. when an artillery barrage signaled the beginning of a new assault. Major Lee and his two hundred or so Marines found themselves having to face an entire Chinese battalion that was hurrying from the captured Outpost Reno and beginning to throw themselves against the dug-in Marines.

But Lee and Connolly had help. Forward observers fed the 11th Marines the information the gunners needed to target the moving enemy and the artillery shattered the dark night with sound and flame. Joining in was a 4.5-inch 1st Division rocket battery. Much of the Chinese battalion was caught between the two hills and cut to ribbons. Apparently not enough men made it to Vegas to give adequate support to the attackers because before long the assault ended.

The Communists had not forgotten Outpost Carson. Ever since the early-morning hours of March 27 there had been probes and feints and some artillery action. On the evening of the 28th, about the time of the enemy battalion attack on Vegas, the Carson contingent of Marines came under heavy fire from mortars and automatic weapons. The return fire from the defenders was so swift and strong that if the Chinese leaders were planning an attack, they thought better of it, perhaps reasoning that it could wait until Vegas changed hands again.

General Pollock and Colonel Walt had not forgotten about Outpost Reno. Marines still occupied Reno Block and had beaten back the occasional probe. The officers didn't know if such forays by the enemy were part of preparations for a full assault or were designed merely to distract the 5th Marines and the supporting 7th Regiment units. As long as the Chinese held Reno, they could do both.

A second problem about the enemy occupying Reno was that it was used as a staging area, a discreet position where Chinese troops could gather and get organized and then light out for the next attack on Vegas. And one more problem was that Reno provided a perch for Chinese sharpshooters and fixed machine guns. There was even a fourth problem: With the battle for Outpost Vegas being so ferocious and lasting so long, the 1st Division still couldn't commit Marines to try to retake Reno.

Colonel Walt had the solution: Destroy it. Pulverize the enemy position to such an extent that it would be no good for anyone, especially the Communists. A blistering series of air strikes as well as a barrage of high-powered bombs from the 11th Marines combined to wipe the hill Lieutenant Colonel Caruso had named Reno off the map. It could only be estimated how many Chinese troops were on it when it was destroyed.

The Marines holding Vegas could smell the Chinese, meaning they were quietly approaching for another assault. The odor of garlic was not the only indication. Veteran Marines like Major Lee could just feel it, the attack that the enemy was preparing—possibly, the most powerful one yet. This was a time for the adage "Every Marine a rifleman" to become a reality, with no one shirking while his brothers were on the line waiting for the Communist advance.

Two Marines took this to something of an extreme. One was clad only in long johns when he approached Sergeant Gerald Neal of Dog 2/5. His clothing, he explained, had been sliced off by a corpsman who had been treating his shrapnel wounds. "I may not be in the proper uniform," he told Neal, "but I'm reporting for duty and I want to go back out." Not batting an eye, Dog Company's first sergeant handed him a rifle and a helmet.

The other man wandered into the company's position and also declared that he was reporting for duty. It appeared to Neal that the Marine was in a daze, perhaps from an explosion close by. He asked him where he had been. "I don't know," the Marine replied. The sergeant asked him his name. The Marine responded, "Yeah, it's Vegas." The sergeant directed him to go back down the hill to the nearest aid station.

There is nothing surprising about this to Sergeant William Janzen. "Marines fight for one another," he stated sixty years later. "Far worse than the fear of death is the fear of letting your fellow Marines down. If a Marine unit is in danger of or is being overrun by the enemy, those Marines will fight together as a unit until they either all get out—with their dead and wounded—or none of them get out. It's that simple."

At 11:30, Major Lee radioed Colonel Walt to say that the next assault was, he believed, only minutes away. It came before midnight, with the Chinese pouring over the summit and running and climbing up the hillside. There were two battalions of them this time. At 11:48, Lee reported that the outpost was surrounded.

Fighting alongside his men, the major could see immediately how badly outnumbered his mongrel company was. He ordered his men to give some ground and radioed a request for an artillery strike right on the outpost. The support was provided immediately. Aircraft dropped flares to illuminate the enemy soldiers, and then the 11th Marines got to work. In one of the most intense artillery assaults of the entire war, American gunners launched six thousand rounds.

The earth literally moved for the attacking Communists. Those who weren't smart or fast enough to get down or lucky enough to be knocked down became targets for Major Lee's men as their guns chattered relentlessly. The artillery shells competed with bullets as to what would kill Communist soldiers first. The carnage was horrific, but it was the means to keep Outpost Vegas in American hands. It was a testament to the bravery of those Chinese soldiers or the fear of facing their own commanders at the base on the other side of the hill that allowed the attack to last as long as it did.

Finally, though, it ended, leaving the cold night air filled with the smell of smoke and the cries of horrendously wounded Chinese soldiers.

CHAPTER TWENTY-THREE

★ ★

Snake Eyes

As much as the attacking Chinese had been blown apart on Saturday night, the early-morning hours of March 29—Palm Sunday, 1953—were no time for Colonel Walt and his 5th Marines to rest. In case the Communists had still not had enough, it was best to clear the Vegas summit of snipers and other stragglers and set about building fresh fortifications at the outpost. This meant more work for the men commanded by Major Lee and Captains Lorence and Connolly. By this time, Captain Ralph Walz and the remnants of Fox 2/5, filled out a bit with replacements, had rejoined the Marines on Vegas.

Of course, there was no shortage of casualties on the American side. Many of them were seen during the battle by Dr. William Beaven, who was a medical officer with the 2nd Battalion of the 5th Marines. They had been carried to him and other doctors and corpsmen for at least thirty hours, and the medical workers were hard-pressed to keep up, improvising along the way.

"Stretcher cases in coma, profound shock, or brutally mutilated were placed directly in 'high shock' position," Beaven later wrote, "three abreast in rows on the floor of the tent. Bayoneted M-1 rifles were rammed into the ground, providing poles from which plasma was hung." Hour after hour more casualties arrived. And then Dr. Beaven and others learned that their position was in danger.

At around 2 Saturday morning, the battle-scarred Captain John Melvin strode into the medical tent. He tried to speak, but the roar of the "symphony of death" was so loud he could not be heard. He ripped a flap off a cardboard carton and with a crayon he wrote: "Gooks bypassing Vegas, coming around your side. Close to battalion strength. Laying down smoke screen first. Can't bug out! Load walking wounded with grenades. Send them down far path. Pitch them into smoke screen!" He turned and left the tent to return to where the fighting was most fierce.

There were about a hundred wounded Marines in the tent. The piece of cardboard was passed around and read by each of them. A few moments passed, then all the men got up from their cots, rummaged for hand grenades, and left the tent to limp and hobble the fifty yards down the path to where the hill ended and the unmistakable garlic smell of the advancing Chinese troops began.

"But the end didn't come," wrote Beaven. "The artillery barrage lessened, the smoke screen drifted apart, and the garlic smell wafted away. The wounded Marines had held their ground. Some of the men, overcome by emotion, fell to their knees. These damaged yet proud men would live to fight, perhaps die, another day."

The 11th Marines were at it again on Sunday, lobbing shells on the summit and the hillside behind it. Whatever was left of the enemy resistance after that was broken when the combined Marine force reached the summit and started down the other side. The Chinese either died where they stood or fled. More than forty-eight hours after the hill had been taken away, all of Vegas belonged to the Marines once more.

At 5 a.m., ten minutes after the rest of Vegas was taken, Major Lee and Captain Walz, weary but satisfied, were standing together in the outpost, perhaps planning on how to best defend it against the next attack, if the enemy still had the stomach for it. A 120-mm mortar shell landed between them, killing them both. Lee's second Silver Star was awarded posthumously. As the citation stated, "By his inspiring leadership, outstanding tactical ability and exceptional courage, Major Lee was directly instrumental in the accomplishment of the vital mission. His great personal valor reflects the highest credit upon himself and enhances the finest traditions of the United States Naval Service."

The widow and two young children of Captain Walz, a thirty-one-year-old born in Montana, were given his posthumous Navy Cross. As much as any other Marines in the history of the Corps, these two men had given another demonstration of Semper Fidelis.

It would be left up to Major Joseph Buntin, who served as the executive officer of the 5th Regiment's 3rd Battalion, to oversee the rebuilding of the Outpost Vegas defenses. Along with the sunrise that Palm Sunday morning came supplies—picks and shovels, barbed wire, more communications wire, planks of wood, and other matériel hauled by Korean laborers as well as replacements sent up from the Main Line of Resistance.

But the day conspired against the efforts to create new bunkers, trenches, and fighting holes. The earth of the hilltop consisted of troughs of thick mud containing shell fragments and even body parts. Even once that was navigated, the Marines and workers were plagued by clouds covering the sun and a mixture of snow and rain falling upon them. The risk was heightened because the nasty weather also frustrated forward artillery observers and pilots searching for signs of a new Chinese attack.

Still, by 11 that morning, trenches had been excavated that varied in depth from waist height to shoulder height. The sheer stubborn perseverance of the Marines had produced results. "The guys were like rabbits digging in," observed Corporal George Demars of Fox 2/5. "The fill-ins gotten by the company during the reorganization jumped right in. We didn't know half the people in the fire teams but everybody worked together."

Perhaps helping that feeling of unity was that the men, between grunts, began to hum and sing the "Marines' Hymn": "From the halls of Montezuma to the shores of Tripoli, we will fight our country's battles, in the air, on land, and sea. First to fight for right and freedom, and to keep our honor clean, we are proud to claim the title of United States Marine."

Major Buntin could report to Colonel Walt that "the situation was well in hand." Indeed, a Fox Company second lieutenant, Irvin Maizlish—the only one of the officers originally attached to the company not killed or wounded—stated: "Everybody knew Fox was here to stay. I've never seen men work so hard. We were going to hold this ground and the spirits were unusually high."

Trigger Jack Williams also had an experience he wouldn't forget. A Marine from Able Anti-Tank Company arrived atop Vegas and said, "Kind of hairy up here, isn't it? This is a real adventure." After the sergeant agreed with him, the Marine informed him that he had started out from the MLR a few hours ago with a "Chiggy Train," slang for a group of Korean Service Corps workers. Because of those killed and wounded along the way plus those who had simply fled, of the sixty-five men he had set off leading across the muddy terrain and up the hill, only two were left. Unfazed, however, the Marine said, "I'm new at this game. Should I take the dead away?" Sergeant Williams pointed to two bodies still on the hill. Without hesitation, the Marine and the two remaining Korean workers took the bodies down the hill.

Evidently, the enemy commanders were not inclined to agree with Major Buntin's assessment and saw the weather and the fading light as allies. Spotter planes had observed large groups of Chinese troops moving toward Vegas, and a few minutes after 6:30 p.m., having congregated at a jump-off point at the base of the battered hill, they commenced a new assault. Enemy troops climbed up the Vegas hill. There had to be thoughts among a few of the Marines atop the hill of being overrun if enough of the Chinese reached them. Fortunately, they had an even better ally than the enemy did.

Despite the reduced sighting abilities of the forward observers, the American artillery was ready. Its bombardment of the attacking enemy troops and assembly areas actually exceeded the one when the day had begun, with sixty-four hundred rounds landing. They were joined by mortar shells and small-arms fire from the outpost Marines. It was all too much for the Communists, who retreated rapidly and in disarray, ready to do anything to get away from the brutal thunderstorm of metal and lead.

"Incoming fire on Vegas was a withering rain of steel as the enemy again surrounded the hill on three sides, left, right, and forward," wrote Lee Ballenger. "But the artillery onslaught was devastating. . . . Even the Chinese, with their vast numbers, could not sustain casualties of this magnitude and continue the attack."

Incredibly, despite staggering losses, the Chinese stubbornly tried twice more, but it was obvious that the attackers were low-level officers and troops who had no choice but to follow the orders of desperate commanders who in turn were following the orders of Communist commissars and senior officers seeing Outpost Vegas slipping away for good.

The last attacks came at 8:45 p.m. on the 29th and shortly after midnight of the next day, Monday. Again, the enemy attacked on two sides. Again, they did not get too far before artillery fire tore them part. There had to be some realization, too, that with every hour that went by and every attack that was repulsed, the Marines bolstered the fortifications of the outpost, meaning even if Chinese troops got that far they faced a second source of destruction.

Most likely, it was that, combined with the enormous casualties and the physical and psychological depletion of the remaining troops, that finally persuaded the Communist commanders to leave Outpost Vegas—and Outpost Carson, which was no longer threatened—to the Marines.

That is, except for one peculiar incident. At 11 that Monday morning, with replacement units sent by Colonel Walt on their way from the MLR, five Chinese soldiers appeared, walking up toward the outpost. The Marines expected that they would raise their hands and surrender at any moment. But as if on a prearranged signal, they hurled grenades and opened up with burp guns. Four were killed, cut down by Marines who had to be shaking their heads over the waste of life, and the fifth was taken prisoner.

With that last act of defiance, desperation, or madness, the Battle for the Nevada Cities was over. Colonel Anthony Caputo had called the defense of the Nevada outposts a gamble. At age ninety-four, sixty years after leading his battalion into battle, he summed it up: "The Chinese were tough and relentless and they fought without regard for their lives. We faced our most critical minutes when the Chinese attacked with heavy numbers. Still, our Marines performed magnificently and we did not doubt that we would prevail."

And as one post-battle account concluded, "The Chinese roll of the dice at Vegas had come up snake eyes."

PART IV

★ ★

CHAPTER TWENTY-FOUR

★ ★

Victory at Great Cost

The men of the 5th Regiment as well as the rest of the 1st Marine Division had given all they had to defeat the enemy in a battle that stretched across five days. And so had a horse. To say that the little sorrel mare had offered everything and had nothing left would probably be an exaggeration, given the way she had surprised and even awed her commanding officers and noncommissioned handlers those few days. But even Reckless must have been grateful on that last day of the fight, Monday, when Joe Latham brought her to the pasture, where she would stay put.

The 5th Marines would have preferred to begin the week with an order to go into reserve. Certainly they had earned a rest. But General Edwin Pollock and Colonel Lew Walt believed that any sudden shift of troops could weaken the Main Line of Resistance. The Communists had not gone anywhere; they had only ceased their assaults on

Outpost Vegas. They could be quick to exploit any indication of vulnerability on the American side. For this reason too, on that Monday air units and the artillery of the 11th Regiment remained persistent in their pounding of enemy positions, slowing enemy attempts to reinforce and reorganize shattered units.

With the Chinese unable or at least refraining from mounting new attacks, on the allied side the rest of Monday and into Tuesday were devoted to retrieving bodies. Most of the fallen Marines were, of course, found on Vegas. What made this an especially grim job was that because of the almost incessant barrage of artillery and mortar fire for days, some of the bodies were not intact. Locating, collecting, and removing body parts was a chore that would give Marines nightmares. For a few, even when they were back in the States, those nightmares would never end.

For the Marines who had been taken prisoner, every day after the fighting ended was a waking nightmare. One of them was the corpsman Billy Rivers Penn. He hadn't stayed long on the Vegas hill after his capture that first full night of battle. He could not see because the Chinese troops had put either a blindfold or, more compassionately, a bandage over his damaged eye. Penn was hurried through a tunnel that he realized the enemy must have dug to get under the layers of barbed wire in front of the trenches. When they emerged, he was put into a truck. He did not know what to expect, but more than forty years later, he wrote, "I think maybe the Vietnam POWs were a little more prepared than we were then. As you know, the Chinese and North Koreans had never heard of the Geneva Convention."

Penn and other prisoners were taken to a small area with several huts, where they remained for three days, shivering in the chilly early-April air, without food or water. One Marine had an arm wound, and when Penn checked him, the corpsman could smell gangrene. Penn called to the guards and they hit him, but at least "they took [the wounded man] off, and when I saw him during the exchange of prisoners of war, he was absent an arm but otherwise in good shape."

Eventually, with guards prodding them, the prisoners walked north into the mountains and arrived at an abandoned gold mine that had been converted into a POW camp. With ten men to a leaky shack, the quarters were very cramped. The situation would get even worse.

"For me, the brainwashing really started then," Penn reported. "After a few rifle butts to the head and body, I told them I was from Mississippi, had a mother, father, and two brothers. I was accused of germ warfare. I didn't know what on earth they were talking about. After about four days of no sleep, being kicked and hit with rifles and so forth, you learn to fake unconsciousness after the first rifle butt to your head or ribs. Then I had fifteen to sixteen straight days of fake firing squads. They would go through 'Ready, aim, fire,' then click. At that time, I was hoping that they would kill me. One time after a firing squad, [an interrogator] told me that the International Red Cross had informed him that my mother, father, and brothers were killed in a car wreck. I asked him about my sister. He said that she was also killed. By that time I was pretty mad. I informed him that he was lying . . . I had no sister. He hit me and called in some guards. They held me down and pulled the nail of my right ring finger out with pliers. It never grew back. It is a constant, daily reminder to me of my captivity."

Captivity was more endurable for PFC Bernard Hollinger, who had been taken prisoner by the Chinese when Outpost Vegas was overrun the first night of the battle. He and the handful of other Marines who had survived were held captive that night in their trenches. The next day they were put on a pickup truck and driven north to a temporary camp, then moved farther north, to a POW camp in North Korea. Hollinger's situation would have been more miserable but for the expertise of an enemy physician.

"I still had that piece of shrapnel in my ear," Hollinger recalled.

"But soon after we got to the POW camp I told them I was bleeding off and on. When I asked, 'Do you have a doctor?' they didn't answer me. Then eventually they did take a bunch of us to one of their doctors and he examined us. He stuck a long pin in one of my ears and pulled the shrapnel out. At first I thought, 'Oh, that's going to hurt,' but I didn't feel it. He was an amazing doctor. I couldn't believe he knew what he was doing but he pulled that shrapnel out. I could hear again and get some sleep at night."

Even those who had avoided capture or being killed were scarred by the intensity of the furious fighting. Sergeant William Janzen found that of the forty Marines he had started toward Reno Block with that first night, he was one of only eight who had not become casualties . . . although, in some ways, he indeed was a casualty.

"After it was all over and in the days and first couple of weeks or so, I lost my appetite and lost a lot of weight," Janzen recalled six decades later. "I just couldn't believe I was still alive and not even scratched. I don't know if I was feeling guilty for having survived or what. I don't recall having any of those feelings, but I just couldn't eat."

Was all the pain and suffering of the living as well as the carnage that took hundreds of lives worth it for just a handful of hills? Yes. Because of this clash of two determined forces, the war was irrevocably changed, and not in favor of the Communists. That the Marines had bent but not broken and then stubbornly stormed back robbed the enemy of what would have been enormous leverage at the negotiating table in nearby Panmunjom.

The five days of action would be given several names, with the one used most often in subsequent reports being the Battle of the Nevada Cities. One only had to look at the landscape north of the MLR that Monday to see the consequences of more than eighty hours of continuous fighting: Outpost Carson, bruised but unbowed, was still held by units of the 1st Division. Outpost Vegas, barely resembling what it had looked like a week earlier, was back in American hands after an epic struggle. And Outpost Reno essentially was no more, pulverized into a smoking mound of dirt and rocks and mangled bodies, of no use to either side.

The battle was the bloodiest one for the Marines since they had taken up positions on the western front. The pain of that reality was tempered a bit by the fact that it had resulted in a victory for the Americans and their allies along the MLR. The Communists had indeed thrown everything they had at them, but by thwarting the vicious attempt to capture all three outposts, they had, as Colonel Caputo coined it, prevailed. The position of the Communist negotiators was now weaker. Brass on both sides of the MLR recognized that it was a disturbing defeat for the Communists to invest so much in the Battle of the Nevada Cities and have only thousands of their own casualties to show for it.

Clearly, it was no coincidence that the Communist negotiators informed their United Nations counterparts that they were now willing to discuss the long-standing proposal for at least the return of sick and wounded prisoners. True, this was not a huge concession. However, it was a concession . . . and it would turn out to be the first in a series of moves on both sides that would lead to a truce four months later. The victory by the 1st Division, spearheaded by the 5th Marine Regiment, turned the tide of the war by busting through the diplomatic logjam.

The price of victory for one adversary and defeat for the other was high. On the American side, the five-day ordeal had involved more than four thousand ground and air Marines. They suffered 1,015 casualties—this stunning total meant that close to one out of every four Marines who participated was a casualty. Of that total, 116 Marines were killed, 801 were wounded—more than half of them severely enough that they had to be evacuated to hospitals in Seoul and

Japan—and 98 were missing, a combination of being taken as prisoners by the Chinese, like Penn and Hollinger, and being buried so deep in the rubble of Vegas and Reno that they might never be found. The total also represented almost three-quarters of the casualties the 1st Marine Division recorded for all of March 1953.

Given the Chinese method of attacking with what they hoped would be overwhelming numbers and the soldiers' fear of retreat, it was no surprise that enemy losses were significantly higher. The total of 2,221 enemy casualties was considered conservative by General Pollock and his staff. Close to twelve hundred were killed and there were a thousand wounded, with a handful of prisoners taken. The biggest blow, one that had to damage the enemy's morale, was that the 358th CCF Regiment had virtually been destroyed as an effective fighting force because of the extent of its casualties. Its officers' and soldiers' reward for admirable courage—as well as fear of the Communist commissars—was to have an entire regiment cease to exist as a field unit.

Anyone who would compare unfavorably the intensity and destructive nature of the Korean War to World War II need only contemplate the onslaught of exploding metal that the Marines withstood. During the five-day battle forty-five thousand rounds of artillery, mortar, and mixed fire rained down on positions occupied by the 1st Division and the 11th Regiment. To put this deluge in perspective, during the first two weeks of March, only 3,289 rounds landed on and behind the allied side of the MLR. There was even less escape from a firestorm for the Communists. Records show that all the artillery, tank, and mortar units combined, as well as Reckless's recoilless rifle platoon, launched almost 105,000 rounds at the enemy. It was something of a miracle that anything was left undamaged.

And there was no shortage of courage on the American side. There were three Medals of Honor awarded because of actions in the Battle of the Nevada Cities, and ten Marines and Navy corpsmen received the Navy Cross. No doubt there were many instances of bravery and selflessness that did not receive recognition. This epic battle further illustrated that while Marines fight for their country and follow the orders given to them to the best of their ability, ultimately they fight for each other, their brothers in arms, and Semper Fidelis.

This was recognized by Lieutenant General Lemuel C. Shepherd Jr., the commandant of the Marine Corps, who pointed to the Battle of the Nevada Cities as demonstrating the best that leathernecks could offer. "Have followed the reports of intensive combat in the First Marine Division sector during the past week with greatest sense of pride and confidence," he wrote in a dispatch to General Pollock. "The stubborn and heroic defense of Vegas, Reno, and Carson Hills coupled with the superb offensive spirit which characterized the several counterattacks are a source of reassurance and satisfaction to your fellow Marines everywhere. On their behalf please accept for yourself and pass on to every officer and man of your command my sincere congratulations on a task accomplished in true Marine Corps fashion."

The battle gave birth to a new outpost. To compensate for the loss of Reno, another hill was christened as a Nevada city. On April 1, thanks to Korean laborers and their Marine overseers, Outpost Elko was established on Hill 47, southeast of Carson and just under eight hundred yards from the MLR. It was occupied by a platoon-strength unit. And to fortify Outpost Vegas, it was reconstructed to accommodate 135 men. The enemy would have to try even harder to take it next time.

The battle also emphasized to the Chinese more than ever before the superiority of allied airpower. To the Marines on the ground, that airpower was represented by the sound of screaming jets overhead and the eruptions of dirt and rocks and body parts when their rockets had hit the hillsides and trenches. Such support was appreciated, but it was a bigger picture being painted for the Chinese by the bombers and associated war birds.

With U.S. F-86 Sabre jets disposing of forays by Chinese MiGs, bombers from Seoul airfields and even from Japan were free to do damage and reduce the impact of the enemy attacks. On the night of March 29, for example, B-29 Superforts took off from Okinawa and dropped their payloads northeast of the Nevada Cities outposts, blasting bunkers, trenches, and gun emplacements. The bombers also turned supply depots into fireballs. The result was that after days of fighting the Communists were running out of matériel as well as men and could not continue the attacks beyond a fifth day.

Marine brass, though, hoped the Communists knew when they were licked. They did, and they didn't.

There would not be the sort of full-scale assault like those that had begun at 7 p.m. the previous Thursday, but the Chinese would not simply lie low and lick their wounds either. Perhaps thinking the 5th Marines were distracted by cautious expeditions to recover their dead, at 8:21 on the night that Outpost Elko had been constructed, enemy troops were sighted on the forward slope of Vegas. They were hit with mortar fire, but instead of dispersing, a platoon of Chinese attacked the outpost. During a nasty fifty-minute tussle, a reconstituted Easy Company of the 2nd Battalion, 5th Marines, broke up the attempt to gain some traction on the hill. There were two more enemy forays that night, but they were halfhearted efforts.

At long last, it was time for Colonel Lew Walt and his regiment to be relieved. They had served and fought and endured on the front line for a full sixty-eight days in the most trying conditions nature and the enemy could provide. On Thursday, April 2, the switch began. On each of three nights a third of the regiment was relieved, so that by the end of the day on April 4, the 5th Marines had turned all of its MLR positions over to units of the 7th Regiment. Colonel Walt led his command south to Camp Rose. This was a rudimentary reserve base but an oasis compared to life on the front lines. There, finally, the men of the regiment would rest and recuperate. As would Reckless, their gallant, battle-tested warhorse.

A whole new life awaited her . . . which included, for a time, being left behind by her Marine brothers when they went home.

CHAPTER TWENTY-FIVE

★ ★

Pedersen Sells His Horse

Eric Pedersen's tenure as the anti-tank company commander was a surprisingly short one. The 5th Marines were in reserve only a few days before his transfer orders arrived. There was no wiggle room this time—he had to head back to the States. He had served in Korea with distinction long enough, and he would have a total of three Purple Hearts to show for it.

He asked Joe Latham to see him at his tent. The sergeant was truly sorry that his longtime commanding officer was leaving the outfit completely, but he couldn't help voicing a question: "What about Reckless?"

Pedersen replied that it was best if she remained with the regiment. He certainly could not put the horse on a plane or ship with him. And just because the regiment was in reserve, that didn't mean its fighting days were over. Unless something suddenly happened at Panmunjom, the regiment and its recoilless rifle platoon could be back in battle. The lieutenant told Latham that Reckless would stay on here, where she belonged.

"When the fighting is done, Lieutenant, then where does she belong?"

"I'll be working on that," Pedersen replied. "To my mind, Reckless should be going to the States like other Marines who have done their jobs here. I'll try to figure out a way."

Sergeant Latham was back only a few hours later, and he handed the lieutenant a wad of cash. "The men took up a collection," he explained. "Now we have a share in Reckless along with you."

"You didn't have to do that, Joe."

"Yes, sir, we did. Now she truly belongs to all of us."

In the very short time that he had been the platoon's commanding officer, Lieutenant Riley had grown fond of the little sorrel mare. Knowing this, Pedersen had him go along for his last visit with Reckless. She had not necessarily seemed like a sentimental horse—though she was clearly attached to the men and enjoyed their affectionate pats and rubs—but Eric Pedersen and Reckless had known each other for almost seven months. Now the lieutenant was officially turning her over to his successor.

They found Reckless feeding on grass. Thanks to full spring taking hold of the Korean countryside, the early shoots were green and lush and, no doubt, especially tasty. Pedersen immediately remembered the late winter when Marines were on their hands and knees pulling out stems by meager handfuls to keep Reckless fed and healthy.

He realized there wasn't much to say. He didn't want to offer "Good-bye" because he fully intended to see her again—preferably, if it could be worked out, when the sorrel mare was at his ranch in Vista, with Kay and their two kids there to greet her too. Pedersen gently ran his hand along her smooth neck, thinking about how much they had experienced together since that day at the Sinseul-dong track when he had been impressed by a racehorse who could almost fly. He was more impressed now, since she had become a battle-tested Marine.

Reckless whickered softly, her bright brown eyes gazing into his own. She bobbed her head a few times as though agreeing with Pedersen's thoughts—she would see him again, and she expected it to be soon.

As Eric Pedersen walked away, he murmured to Riley, "Take good care of her." That was not only all he had to say—that was all he could say.

Soon after the 5th Marines went into reserve, the regiment received a new commanding officer when Colonel Lew Walt was assigned to the staff of the 1st Division and replaced by Colonel Harvey Tschirgi.

Under Colonel Tschirgi, the 5th Regiment was kept busy even in reserve. Though it was hoped it would never be necessary, behind the Main Line of Resistance was the Kansas Line, the fallback position should the front line be breached. It had suffered some severe structural damage—not so much from enemy artillery but from a steady diet of spring rain and thawing. Doing the repair work was mostly the responsibility of the 3rd Battalion.

This did not mean more grunt work for Reckless because officially Lieutenant Riley's recoilless rifle platoon remained attached to the 2nd Battalion. She and the Marines had quite an experience together, one she and they hoped never to repeat.

It was decided by division brass that the 2nd Battalion would participate in a landing exercise at Tokchok-to. This island was on the west coast, thirty miles southwest of Inchon. The exercise did not go smoothly at all. In fact, it was cut short because of gusting winds and tossing waves . . . but not before Reckless and her companions had a high-seas adventure.

In retrospect, Riley and members of the platoon recognized that it hadn't been wise to so casually include a horse in the exercise. Obviously without much thought, they put her name down on the loading list to ride on an LST (landing ship, tank) that was carrying tanks toward the pretend invasion. First, though, they had to get Reckless to Inchon, where the "armada" would depart. Corporal Coleman and Captain James Schoen, who had replaced Eric Pedersen as CO of the anti-tank company, drove the little mare in her trailer while the rest of the Marines took the train fifty-five miles to the port city. Mercifully, as it turned out, Sergeant Latham was allowed to stay behind.

Reckless and her drivers made it as far as Ascom City, a Marine supply base, before dark and spent the night there. The next morning they arrived in Inchon and presented themselves on the dock, waiting to be invited aboard LST-527. The captain's eyes almost popped out of his head when he saw a nine-hundred-pound horse apparently eager for a new experience.

A witness to what happened next was Lieutenant Colonel Ed Wheeler, who was executive officer of the 5th Regiment. The skipper, he reported, was not keen "on transporting livestock in his clean tank deck. It was obvious his embarrassment was profound when the Marines pulled out a loading plan approved by him, which included in its myriad columns and figures, '1 horse, w/appurtenances.' From that point on, I imagine that this officer is a firm believer in reading 'the small print' in any loading list he signs."

The Navy men had only jeers for Reckless, even though she had braved more combat than all of them combined. "Hi ya, Man o' War!" one shouted. Another said, "No, that's Seabiscuit." A third observed, "Looks like a walking can of dog meat. Where'd you get that nag, Marines?"

Reckless was reluctantly welcomed aboard and Corporal Coleman created a makeshift stall between two armored tanks. He also brought along two days' worth of horse rations. When the last of the loading was done, the LST, its skipper grinding his teeth, left the dock.

The game plan was pretty simple: Land the units of the 5th Marines on Tokchok-to, advance a couple of thousand yards as though penetrating enemy positions, then call it a day, get back on board, and return to Inchon. Reckless would have been excited to disembark and race along the beach, most likely leading the Marines in the "invasion."

Alas, she never had the opportunity. The task force wasn't far from Inchon when it encountered heavy weather. An LST is no place for a horse in a storm, even one with the fortitude of this particular horse. The rolling of the ship and the fumes of sloshing gasoline in the tanks on either side of her were exactly the wrong combination for her constitution. Reckless made quite a mess of the deck. Making the embarrassment that Captain Schoen and Coleman felt worse was that this specific LST was commanded by Captain John Kaufman, who was also the commodore of the entire LST squadron.

"When are you Marines going to get that haybag off my ship?" Kaufman demanded.

It was gently relayed to him that they were out at sea and there was nowhere for Reckless to go. The unhappy captain lamented, "My ship has won the 'E' for being the cleanest vessel in the fleet two years running, but I can assure you Reckless is going to end that tenure."

While the Communist negotiators at Panmunjom seemed somewhat more flexible on issues that could lead to a truce, their troops were apparently not in a conciliatory mood. Unfortunately for all concerned, there would be four more months of fighting before a truce took hold.

The enemy still wasn't done with the Nevada Cities, and the blood of brave men had to be shed to keep them. There was a fresh attack late in the day on April 8, one result being that a Marine patrol that had been out on a scouting mission was pinned down in the no-man's-land in front of the MLR. Second Lieutenant Wallace Butler led men out that night to retrieve them.

They found the patrol—all of them wounded, some severely— and they also encountered Chinese troops who were looking to take wounded Marines prisoner. Butler and his men successfully held the enemy off as the Marines were placed on stretchers and brought back to the MLR.

The next night, after an estimated two thousand rounds of artillery and mortar shells pasted Marine positions, three hundred Chinese soldiers attacked Outpost Carson. They fought as fiercely as they had the previous month, and an hour after the assault began they reached the trench line. Here the units of the 7th Regiment assigned to Carson stood their ground and the battle continued between the adversaries at point-blank range.

The fighting went further than that. At the most intense point of the battle for Carson, Chinese soldiers and Marines stood toe-to-toe, fighting with knives and fists. Leading the defense was twenty-four-year-old First Lieutenant George Yates. He had been wounded soon after the battle began, but he was still able to move about among his men. His encouragement was more than verbal—the Marines saw him personally kill enemy troops. At the height of the battle he organized his men into a new perimeter and called for close artillery and mortar fire. This was effective, but with a last thrust the Chinese poked through one flank. Lieutenant Yates rushed there, and after more hand-to-hand fighting the enemy retreated.

After radio contact was lost, a Dog Company platoon was sent to reinforce the defenders. When they reached the new Outpost Elko, four hundred yards southeast of Carson, they were pinned down by Chinese mortar and machine-gun fire. American tanks put an end to that interference and the platoon set off again. The arrival of fresh troops made a difference, and by 5:30 the Chinese were retreating. The holding of Carson cost George Yates his life, however. Though bleeding from several wounds, he was actively fighting to keep the perimeter intact and attending to his wounded. He was hurrying toward one of the Marines when an exploding shell injured him so severely he would not recover. The family of Lieutenant Yates in Mississippi received his posthumous Navy Cross.

In what could be considered a postscript to the Battle of the Nevada Cities, he was one of fourteen Marines who died that day, and there were sixty-four wounded men to keep the division surgeons busy.

A heartening sign for the allies was the construction of Freedom Village. The day before the Communist surprise assault on Outpost Carson, there had been a breakthrough at Panmunjom. Serious talks were held on what would be called Operation Little Switch, which was an exchange of prisoners that would take place two weeks later, on April 20. To welcome the allied prisoners, the Marines went to work in nearby Munsan-ni. Freedom Village, built in a mere thirty-six hours, was a tent city with running water and electricity, graded roads, medical facilities, accommodations for expected reporters and photographers, furniture, and even a helicopter pad.

Operation Little Switch lasted for seven days. The Communists allowed 684 wounded and sick prisoners representing eleven countries to be transported by Army trucks to Freedom Village, passing under a sign that read "Welcome Gate to Freedom" when the trucks first left Panmunjom. They included fifteen Marines and three Navy corpsmen—two of whom were captured when Outpost Reno had been overrun—and they were greeted at the village by General Edwin Pollock, Lieutenant General Maxwell Taylor, Lieutenant General Mark Clark, and other top officers. In exchange, United Nations officers and officials sent 6,670 Communist prisoners north.

One of the welcomed corpsmen was Billy Rivers Penn: "The first Americans we saw in uniform, we all cheered and cried. The first nurse I saw was a lieutenant in the Army and boy, was she beautiful. She took the bandage from my right eye and she almost passed out. I realized then that it must be pretty bad. A corpsman from Tennessee told me about the high casualty rate on Reno, Vegas, and Carson." Penn was also informed that his unit had believed he was dead and a memorial service had been held for him.

Only three weeks later, Penn was working at a Navy hospital in Pensacola, Florida. Three surgeries managed to save his right eye. He went back to college, and after he graduated he earned a medical degree and became an obstetrician. "I promised myself I would never eat rice again and would never treat a Chinese patient. So what happens? I move to Louisiana, where they put rice in. And during my first year of practice, I delivered ten Chinese babies."

Dr. Penn had a long and distinguished career as a physician, introducing innovations that included using the epidural anesthetic as a pain reliever during labor. He passed away on April 27, 2013, exactly sixty years to the day since his parents received a letter notifying them that he had been released from the POW camp, bound for Freedom Village.

Another encouraging sign was that after that nasty firefight at Outpost Carson on April 9, enemy activity declined as the month wore on. It seemed like both sides had an ear cocked for sounds from Panmunjom that a cease-fire had been agreed upon. There were still skirmishes and shells lobbed by both sides, and men died, but in previous years spring was the time for new offensives and they weren't to be found along the front lines of the 1st Marine Division.

And then, finally, it was time for the division to come off those front lines. General Pollock's force was to be replaced by the 25th Infantry Division, commanded by Major General Samuel Williams. One would think the members of the 1st Marine Division, which had been manning front lines in eastern and western Korea for twenty months, would be eager to leave. However, an Associated Press article reported that the Marines were leaving "under protest from commanders who wanted the Division to remain on the line." This was less a bias against the abilities of the U.S. Army than a desire to finish the job.

But orders were orders. On May 1, the division began to turn over their positions. It took four days and 2,370 truckloads of men and ma-tériel to move everyone and everything to join the already-in-reserve 5th Marines, who shifted from Camp Rose to Camp Casey. Among the outposts in front of the Main Line of Resistance that became the re-sponsibility of other units were the Nevada Cities and the two Berlins, which were to be occupied by two Turkish battalions.

Coming off the front lines meant the countdown began to a change of command. It ended on June 15 when General Pollock turned the 1st Marine Division over to Major General Randolph Pate. The retiring commanding general was presented with the Distinguished Service Medal, with the award citing his "outstanding success in the defense" of Carson and Vegas.

The new leader of the 1st Division already had a long Marine Corps résumé, dating back to 1918. Before the 1920s ended, Randolph Pate had served in Santo Domingo and China, and during World War II he served on Guadalcanal, Peleliu, Iwo Jima, and Okinawa. Another of his achievements, this one still to come: He would become the most powerful and influential friend of a certain sorrel mare.

At Camp Casey, Reckless was treated like a celebrity. In the weeks since the Battle of the Nevada Cities had ended and more units of the 1st Marine Division were placed in reserve, tales of her bravery and resilience in the battle made the rounds. Officers from outside the 5th Regiment paid her visits. So too did General Pollock and then his re-placement, General Pate. Reckless was "interviewed" by reporters and had her photo taken a few times. An article about her was published in *Stars and Stripes* in Japan. An aspiring author and the new commanding officer of the 2nd Battalion, 5th Marines, Lieutenant Colonel Andrew Geer, vowed to write about her for a magazine back in the States. Whenever Marines caught site of the little mare, they called and waved to her. She was a hero Marine who happened to have four legs instead of two.

Reckless began to put those four legs to the use they were intended for. Thanks to plenty of rest and food and risk-free exercise, she was as healthy as she had ever been—and that meant she had a desire to race. There was no other horse to race against, so Reckless ran and jumped just for the fun of it. At times Marines of any rank had to dive out of the way as the fastest horse in Korea never to win a national championship sprinted by, nostrils flared, ears back, red mane trailing like the tail of a comet.

Reckless made a game of terrorizing poor, put-upon Joe Latham. Wherever he was, she would find him and set off at a gallop. The sergeant was smart enough to stay still and let her go past, no matter how close she came. Latham had faith that Reckless knew what she was doing. Others weren't so sure. Lieutenant Riley said, "She's going to make a mistake someday and we'll be looking for a new gunnery sergeant."

There were more than a few Marines who swore that as Reckless ran by, they could hear her laughing.

Her effortless speed gave some members of the 5th Marines an idea. Maybe Reckless could be a champion racehorse after all. Why not see if Native Dancer would accept a challenge? This thought gave birth to the Paddy Derby.

A photo was taken of Reckless with Lieutenant Riley and Sergeants Latham and Lively. It and a letter were sent to Alfred Vanderbilt Jr., owner of the three-year-old that had been Horse of the Year in 1952. The challenge was to bring Native Dancer to Korea for a race at "Upsan Downs." The 1st Division would put up $25,000, to be matched by Vanderbilt. Each riderless horse would carry eight rounds of shells and run 1.5 miles over hills and through rice paddies toward a firing recoilless rifle.

The Marines had complete confidence that Reckless could beat any horse, including the one nicknamed "the Grey Ghost." But a death-blow to the slim chance of a "world championship" was dealt when Native Dancer lost for the first time, at the Kentucky Derby that May. He would go on to win the Preakness and Belmont Stakes that year, but Vanderbilt was not taking any chances. There would be no match race while the 5th Regiment was in Korea.

Reckless received an honor nonetheless. Word came down that General Pate was going to give her a medal. Sergeant Latham insisted that Reckless have new shoes for the ceremony, so he put her in the trailer and made another attempt to find someone who could shoe horses. He thought his chances would be better if he drove all the way to where Eric Pedersen had first found her, the Sinseul-dong racetrack.

As soon as Reckless backed out of the two-wheeled trailer she was surrounded by men who worked at the track. They seemed in awe to be seeing her, as though they were encountering a ghost. A young man appeared and called out "Flame!" Casually, the man put his one arm around her neck. As Reckless nuzzled him, it was obvious to Joe Latham that they were old friends.

The one-armed man turned to the sergeant and said, "My name is Choi, and I have known Flame a long time." He held his one hand high enough above the ground to indicate how big she was when Ah-Chim-Hai had given birth to her.

"We call her Reckless." The sergeant pointed to her hooves. "Can you fix her shoes?"

Choi nodded and tugged at her lead rope. Reckless followed him, happy to be with an old "pony-hood" friend. There was about to be another surprise: As she was taken into a stall, another young Korean man arrived. He had been running hard, and now he stopped abruptly, his breath catching in his chest and both eyes stinging, though he could see out of only one of them.

As Joe Latham walked away to find a cup of coffee with the Army helicopter unit stationed at the racetrack, Kim Huk Moon stared at Flame. He had never expected to see his beloved horse again. His sister, Chung Soon, had been able to walk fine since he had purchased the prosthetic leg and had it fitted correctly at the American military hospital. Kim had never regretted his decision, but that didn't mean he could forget Flame. Hundreds of times he had imagined her injured in battle, or worse, torn to pieces by an explosion. Yet here she was, looking stronger and more beautiful than ever.

Most people believe that horses do not have long-term memories. That evidently was not true of Reckless, if her behavior was any evidence. Seeing Kim, she tugged the lead rope out of Choi's hand and stepped toward him. Her tail swung from side to side, she made a low rumbling sound in her throat, and she bent her head down, though still keeping Kim in her sight. Clearly, she wanted him to stroke her head and neck. Even knowing that meant it would hurt all the more when she left, Kim obliged.

He knew Flame could never be his again. She had belonged to the Marines for too long now, and whatever future the horse had was with them. The dream of riding Flame to the heights of championship racing had died the day he sold her to Pedersen. Taking care of his sister and his nephew and niece, Kim could not afford to keep her, let alone buy her back.

"The American soldier said she needs new shoes," Choi said.

Kim could at least do that—after this one final and miraculous visit, he would send the little sorrel mare, the foal of Flame-of-the-Morning, on her way. Flame's new shoes would be the last reminder of the boy who had fallen in love with two horses and would forever cherish both in his memories.

Gently, willing his hands not to tremble and his eye to stay clear, Kim Huk Moon set to work.

★ ★

CHAPTER TWENTY-SIX

Left Behind in Korea

There were two more significant battles of the Korean War involving the 1st Marine Division. One was for Hill 119. Known as Boulder City because of a large granite outcropping, it overlooked a major route to Seoul, down a valley called "76 Alley" and to a bend in the Imjin River. If the Communists were to take this hill, they could strike at the capital and truce negotiations could become moot. That was exactly what they did, on July 24, 1953.

Defending Boulder City was a single company, George, of the 3rd Battalion, 1st Regiment. Beginning late that morning, artillery and mortar shells rained down on them. With rumors rampant that a Panmunjom agreement was close, the Marines may have hoped that this barrage was just for show, little more than some final saber rattling. As the day went on, that hope held. It dissipated quickly, though, soon after nightfall, when Chinese infantry attacked.

They were repelled, and they attacked again. And again. By 9:30 that night, the enemy was breaking through the line of trenches at the outpost. The Marines fell back and called for help from the 11th Artillery. First Lieutenant Oral Swigart Jr., the senior officer left on the hill, had noted a buildup of Chinese troops on the forward slope, obviously preparing for another assault. The artillery was effective enough that twenty minutes later the Marines counterattacked and took back some of the trenches.

What was left of George 3/1 could not hold them, however. There were too many dead—including two corpsmen—and wounded. And on the forward slope, Chinese soldiers who had been shredded by artillery shells had already been replaced. A new enemy attack was under way. By midnight, the Marines' forward portion and both flanks had been pushed back to the reverse slope of the hill. "Only the Marines' never-say-die resistance was keeping the Chinese from seizing the rest of Boulder City," reported Lee Ballenger.

The battle for Boulder City continued the next day, Saturday, July 25, and on Sunday and into Monday. At one point the Chinese had three thousand troops attacking across the 1st Division's front lines around the disputed hill. The tenacious Marines simply would not give it up. The battle might have continued for the rest of the day and the day after that, eclipsing the Battle of the Nevada Cities in length, but on that Monday, at 10 a.m., the fighting stopped.

Also beginning on July 24 was the Battle of the Samichon River, and this one necessitated the return to action of Reckless. The battle also involved units from New Zealand, Australia, and Great Britain fighting alongside the 1st Marine Division. The location was a familiar one—the Hook. The Communists' intent was to break through to the Imjin River by slicing between the 1st Marine Division and the 1st Commonwealth Division. The attack on Boulder City was initially to be a distraction, but it turned into a full-fledged fight of its own.

While the allies repelled assault after assault launched by the Chinese against the Hook, How Company of the 5th Marines under Colonel Tschirgi was hit at 9:15 p.m. by a reinforced enemy company. The intense firepower of tanks, mortars, machine guns, and artillery fire finally, by dawn the next day, finished off the attack, even though during the night the Chinese had committed almost a full battalion to it.

The battle on several fronts, including the Hook, continued the next day and into July 26. With Lieutenant Riley's platoon supporting the regiment with its recoilless rifles, shells were tied to Reckless's packsaddle and she was on the move once again. Her handlers prayed that after all the sorrel mare had already done she wouldn't be hurt in a battle that most of the Marines knew was taking place only days, if not hours, before a truce. Reckless came through it untouched, and in her way was as glad as the others of the 5th Marines when on that Monday, July 27, at 10 a.m., the truce was declared.

At long last, the negotiators at Panmunjom had come to an agreement. The documents that were signed decreed a cease-fire to begin twelve hours later, at ten p.m. Within seventy-two hours of that time all military forces, supplies, and equipment were to be withdrawn from a newly formed demilitarized zone, which was two thousand yards wide and contained the original Main Line of Resistance.

The war wound down to the last minute. The last offensive action of any kind was at 9:52 that night, when five Chinese mortar rounds landed on an outpost defended by South Korean soldiers. However, elsewhere along the MLR the truce was going into effect even before 10 p.m. Bemused, resigned, and even disgusted Marines observed Communist troops wandering in front of their positions, and some, according to a 1st Division report, "waved lighted candles, flashlights, and banners while others removed their dead and wounded, and apparently looked for souvenirs." Some of the Communist soldiers, who only moments before had been the enemy, called to the Marines, "How are you? Come on over and let's have a party." There were no takers.

Troops on both sides were on the move. The truce required that each side withdraw a thousand yards from its front line. When that maneuver was completed, the Demilitarized Zone was created.

A welcome display marked the beginning of the cease-fire—white-star cluster shells bursting, thousands of them filling the sky, briefly brightening the rocky hills, grass-filled valleys, and cool fresh-water streams all along the front lines from the Sea of Japan west to the Yellow Sea, a total of 155 miles.

The celebration marked what was believed to be the end of the Korean War. Alas, it has never ended. A state of war still exists more than six decades after the "police action" began. Communist and United Nations forces continue to face each other across the Demilitarized Zone, and the fighting can resume at any time. Fifty years after he served and was wounded there, Lieutenant James Brady returned to Korea and wrote about his experiences. The title he chose was *The Scariest Place on Earth*.

The Marines there at the end of July 1953 were glad the fighting in whatever the conflict was called was over. Since they had first landed in Korea in August 1950, they had suffered 4,262 killed, 26,038 wounded, and 221 taken prisoner. It was time for them to go home.

Reckless was ready to join them. But where was home?

The final action for 5th Marines in the Korean War was having fifty-six rounds of artillery and mortar fire aimed at their positions, with the last one landing at 10 p.m., right when the truce went into effect. The explosions did not make an impression on Reckless. By now she was more of a veteran than some of the veteran Marines were. While not welcomed or necessarily expected, shells landing nearby were just part of fighting. Now the fighting was over.

That meant the question of what would become of Reckless could no longer be postponed. Lieutenant Riley's platoon accompanied Lieutenant Colonel Andrew Geer and his 2nd Battalion to its new position between the Panmunjom corridor and the Imjin River. The new camp was in a valley, and at the river was an abandoned ferry crossing station. The shore there consisted of black sand. Reckless enjoyed strolling on it and gazing at the water. It would have been especially remarkable if she remembered a very different experience—that frightening and turbulent night when she had helped the Kim family cross the river.

Joe Latham went to Geer and told him that he wanted to bring Reckless back home when the time came to return to the States. "How many children do you have, Gunny?" the colonel asked him.

"Two girls. The younger was only two months old when I shipped out to Korea."

"What would your wife say?"

"She's all for it," Latham replied. "We like kids, horses, and dogs."

Geer thought for a moment, then said, "This I'll promise you, Joe—I'll get Reckless home."

The colonel was about to be shipped back to the States. He wanted to make the rounds with Reckless before he left. The battalion CO had also arranged for Lieutenant Riley to be assigned to Fox Company.

The next evening, Riley, Latham, Geer, and Reckless visited the various units in the battalion. The little mare, not the CO, was the celebrity. She enjoyed the attention, wandering in and out of tents and deciding which treats she would accept or refuse. The departing colonel was something of an afterthought, but he didn't seem to mind.

When the walkabout was over, the group took advantage of the officers' galley at the battalion command post. Again Reckless was not shy, snacking on bread and peanut butter and coffee. The peanut butter proved to be a problem when it stuck to the roof of her mouth, so a second cup of coffee was required to wash it down.

The next morning, Colonel Geer said good-bye to Reckless. He had grown very fond of her. His expectation was that in just a few weeks he would have arranged for her journey across the Pacific Ocean to a new home in the United States.

He was wrong.

★ ★

CHAPTER TWENTY-SEVEN

Return Reckless, or Destroy Her

General Randolph Pate became even more enamored of Reckless than his predecessor as 1st Marine Division commander, Edwin Pollock, had been. The South Carolina native had joined the Marine Corps during the last year of World War I and was fifty-five years old when he became commander of the 1st Marine Division. With Reckless, General Pate did more than simply visit and rub her muzzle. To signify how much a Marine the sorrel mare was, he made her a corporal.

Reckless now had a blanket that sported two stripes. That did not get her out of basic field chores, though. She was put to work stringing communication wire. As the months passed, the truce between the United Nations and the Communists held, but it was only a truce and could be broken at any moment. The allied units had to remain ready for whatever might happen.

Also in the months after the truce went into effect, Reckless's fellow leathernecks left Korea. In October 1953, both Joe Latham and Monroe Coleman received orders transferring them to the United States. The sergeant was very happy to be going home to his family, but he hated leaving Reckless behind. There was nothing he could do about it, though, other than hope that Colonel Geer could make good on his promise. It was some comfort that General Pate would visit the four-legged Marine whenever he was in the 2nd Battalion, 5th Marines, area. Being under the protection of the 1st Division commander meant that Reckless would continue to receive first-class treatment from the Marines.

Or, as Second Lieutenant William McManus, Riley's replacement as CO of the recoilless rifle platoon, put it to the departing Latham and Coleman: "The surest way I know of getting locked up is to have the general find her bunker dirty and Reckless unhappy."

And then, with Latham and Coleman out of the way and no longer protecting her, Reckless was kidnapped.

The perpetrators were not Communist infiltrators but members of a Marine mortar unit known as the Four Deuces. One night they snuck into her bunker and took her. Enticed by a few tasty treats—and after all, the kidnappers were Marines—Reckless went along willingly enough. They had another bunker prepared for her near their camp, and she spent the rest of the night there.

The next morning, Lieutenant McManus's men awoke to find signs tacked up around the camp: "First Marine Division Marine Corps Memorial Association. Ransom Reckless. Tickets $1." With Sergeant Elmer Lively spearheading the effort, a collection was taken up and the platoon donated $400 to the association. But the Four Deuces did not reveal Reckless's whereabouts right away, because as word of her "predicament" spread, money began pouring in from all over the 1st Division. By the end of the day, more than $28,000 had been given to what was now called the Ransom Reckless Fund.

Reckless was returned none the worse for wear, and seemed to have enjoyed her extended visit with the mortar unit. Still, the Reckless Rifle Platoon put a guard on her bunker at night so that she wouldn't be "borrowed" again, whatever the cause.

Fall gave way to winter, and then the winter of 1954 finally loosened its grip on western Korea. More Marines familiar to Reckless—including the unfortunate "rough rider" Private Arnold Baker—had their tickets punched to return Stateside. However, thus far, efforts by Eric Pedersen, Joe Latham, and even Colonel Geer to send Reckless home as well proved futile. Reckless was indeed viewed as a hero horse by the Marine Corps, but that wasn't enough to have her transferred to America.

Her tenure as a corporal was short-lived. No, she did not do something wrong that got her busted down to private. There was instead a successful effort to give Reckless a third stripe. The ceremony took place on April 10.

This was a much more formal affair than being made a corporal. The 5th Anti-Tank Company was now commanded by Captain Andrew Kovach, and he and the company's senior noncom, Master Sergeant John Strange, arranged the ceremony. The captain designed a special blanket, and a Korean tailor was found to stitch it together. It consisted of red silk with gold trim with a globe and anchor on either side of it and her unit identification. A rapid passing of the helmet in the company produced the $51 to pay for the new "uniform."

Reckless liked the blanket . . . perhaps too much. When she was first fitted with it, she began to nibble a corner of the garment. Sergeant Lively, one of the few holdovers from Eric Pedersen's platoon, informed the horse's handlers of how Reckless had once eaten an Australian hat and advised that she never be left alone with the blanket.

Colonel Elby Martin was now the commanding officer of the 5th Marines, and he gave the go-ahead for the ceremony. Reckless's demeanor that morning indicated that she expected the pomp and circumstance as her due. The preparations included Marines building a reviewing stand. Reckless had received a good rubdown and brushing and looked every bit the lovely sorrel mare who had captured the hearts of her comrades. Wearing her blanket, she arrived on the improvised parade ground where Captain Kovach's company was in formation. The regiment's Marine Corps colors and the American flag fluttered in the gentle breeze, mirroring the motion of the horse's red mane.

To no one's surprise, General Pate was on hand to do the honors. As Reckless waited patiently, Sergeant Strange read a citation that had been composed: "For meritorious achievement in connection with operations against the enemy while serving with a Marine infantry regiment in Korea from October 26, 1952, to July 27, 1953. Corporal Reckless performed the duties of ammunition carrier in a superb manner. Reckless's attention and devotion to duty make her well qualified for promotion to the rank of sergeant. Her absolute dependability while on missions under fire contributed greatly to the success of many battles."

General Pate stepped forward and pinned the sergeant's stripes to the red silk blanket. She was officially Sergeant Reckless.

The week after her promotion saw the beginning of the end of her exile in Korea. Reckless was featured in an article in the *Saturday Evening Post*. Colonel Andrew Geer had fulfilled his promise to write one, and the *Post*'s audience was the perfect one for it, enticed by the author's colorful prose: "Every yard she advanced she was showered with explosives. Fifty-one times she marched through the fiery gantlet of the Red barrage—and she saved the day for the Leathernecks. The true story of the warhorse of Korea." Overnight, the newly minted four-legged sergeant was embraced by everyday Americans from Maine to California.

The piece had the impact that Geer and other Marines who had known Reckless in Korea had hoped for. Readers were unhappily surprised to learn that this horse they had immediately taken to was still in Korea. Worse, that it was military bureaucratic red tape that was keeping her there. It turned out the inaction was because the Marine Corps viewed Reckless as private property—she belonged to Lieutenant Pedersen and the other members of the platoon who had used their own money to purchase her. Since the horse was not government property, federal funds could not be spent to transport her to the United States.

The overwhelming sentiment among taxpayers—especially those who had read the *Saturday Evening Post* article—was that Reckless had fought and literally shed blood for her country and should be home where she belonged. Technically, of course, Reckless was a Korean-born horse, and she was being well taken care of by the Marines there, but her tour of duty was over and she should be in the States, with the other returned heroes who had fought in Korea. With letters and telegrams and phone calls, a campaign began to bring Reckless across the ocean.

Fortunately, one of the readers of Geer's article was Stan Coppel. He was an executive at Pacific Transport Lines. If paying for the horse's passage was the problem, he had the answer: Coppel offered one of his company's ships. It would pick Reckless up in Yokohama and she would ride for free from there to San Francisco. When? As soon as the Marines could get her to Japan . . . and that would involve her first trip in a plane.

Like thousands of Marines before her, Reckless was being "rotated" back to the United States, so a rotation ceremony was arranged for her. It took place during halftime of a football game between a team representing the 1st Marine Division and one representing the 7th Army Division, held on October 17, 1954, almost two years after her first encounter with Eric Pedersen, which had changed both their lives. The boisterous ceremony included a band to serenade her, and all involved enjoyed a few beers, including Reckless. It was a fond farewell to the Marines in Korea, who sent the sorrel mare off with a 23–7 victory over the Army team.

Then it was time to implement what had been named Operation Horse Shift. Reckless was motored to the nearest landing strip. There she was ushered onto an R4Q, also known as the Flying Boxcar, a transport plane provided by the 1st Marine Aircraft Wing. The crew had never airlifted a horse before and may not have been aware of her experience on the water during the abbreviated "invasion" of Tokchok-to, but it did not matter—Reckless was quite content to be in a sort of flying trailer on the way to Japan.

Technically, the 1st Division was using government equipment to transport Reckless out of Korea. However, division staff turned a blind eye to the transgression, and by morning Reckless was in Yokohama.

The oceangoing leg of her journey began on October 22, when Reckless sauntered aboard the SS *Pacific Transport*. The trip was supposed to take two weeks, but the necessity of having to skirt the worst of a typhoon added four days. The ship couldn't avoid the violence of the massive storm completely, however, and Reckless had another unpleasant seagoing experience. She was as happy as her handlers when the *Pacific Transport* finally docked in San Francisco on November 9.

Reckless did not emerge from the ship until the next morning. She still seemed woozy from the typhoon, and PFC John Moore and her other handlers wanted to be sure she would have her legs under her going down the gangplank. That turned out to be the least of the problems, and at first it was a less-than-triumphant arrival. Customs

Bureau inspectors waited for her to leave the *Pacific Transport* and were willing to pass her through. But Department of Agriculture officials were much less welcoming.

They insisted on not only a full medical examination but also tests that required results from a lab before Reckless could disembark. Marines were outraged that such tests were being sought and that waiting for the outcome meant missing the Marine Corps banquet that was to honor her at the Marines' Memorial Association there in San Francisco. Frantic phone calls were made, with the matter being taken higher and higher up the Corps chain of command.

The compromise was almost worse: Agriculture Department officials would waive the delay, but blood would still have to be drawn before Reckless left the ship. If it turned out that the tests showed that she had glanders or dourine, she would be seized and returned to the dock. Glanders was an infection usually caused by contaminated food, and dourine was a sexually transmitted disease. Her handlers were outraged once again that the honor of Reckless was being called into question.

Then the situation became more serious—the Marines were informed that if the horse had either disease, the decision to be made was whether to ship Reckless back to Japan or have her destroyed.

First things first: It was time to officially arrive in America, her new home. It looked like Reckless was wearing her blanket, but few knew it was not the same one. The night before, she had eaten the original! Her handlers frantically made the rounds of San Francisco, and in the nick of time acquired a new red and gold silk blanket. Wearing the replacement garment festooned with the uneaten medals, ribbons, and insignia she had earned, Reckless walked down off the ship.

She was led by her oldest American friend, Eric Pedersen.

Now a captain, he finally was reunited with his hero horse. With Pedersen by her side, Sergeant Reckless first set foot on American soil on November 10—the hundred seventy-ninth birthday of the U.S. Marine Corps.

Few soldiers returning from war had been as famous as Reckless. The *Saturday Evening Post* article and subsequent news reports about the campaign—especially those by the well-known war correspondent Bob Considine in his newspaper columns and radio broadcasts and the San Francisco columnist Herb Caen—to bring Reckless to the States had already made her famous in America. Reporters and photographers waited on the dock, and there was a lot of excitement and camera bulbs flashing as the famous sorrel mare greeted the crowd. Most knew that Ed Sullivan, the popular newspaper columnist in New York City, had offered to pay all transportation costs for Reckless to travel cross-country and appear on his television show, *Talk of the Town*. Sullivan had also offered a $1,000 donation to a fund for Marine families. Unfortunately, the delay caused by the typhoon meant that Reckless arrived too late for her November 7 television debut.

Captain Pedersen had made the trip up from Camp Pendleton, accompanied by Sergeant Elmer Lively, who had finally rotated home from Korea. The two men had hauled a horse trailer with them. Theirs were not the only familiar faces to greet her. Colonel Geer was on hand, as was the stalwart Monroe Coleman, who had driven nine hundred miles west from Utah.

As Geer later reported, "It is said by some who know horses that they have little intelligence and no memory—but these detractors had never met Reckless. When the Marines appeared on the hatch they found her straining over the crossbar of the stall. She nodded to Lively, Coleman and Pedersen in turn. It was apparent to anyone who witnessed the meeting that she knew them and was delighted to see them again. It was a scene to be remembered."

Coleman, who had mustered out of the Marines, had tears in his eyes as he hugged her neck. Reckless allowed this familiarity even though she now outranked the former corporal. Coleman explained to her that another old friend, the Marine lifer Joe Latham, stationed at Camp Lejeune in North Carolina, had been unable to receive permission to travel west, and they would have to try to be reunited later.

The reporters and photographers gathered around. One of them remarked, "She has more cameras and reporters to meet her than Vice President Nixon had a week ago when he came to town." Governor Goodwin Knight of California issued a proclamation welcoming Reckless, an honor that hadn't been bestowed upon the future president.

Finally, after plenty of posing and eating carrots, it was time for Reckless to be off to the Marines' Memorial Association building on Sutter Street. Awaiting her there was another first—an elevator ride. The banquet hall was on the tenth floor and there was no sensible way that a nine-hundred-pound horse was going to walk up to it. No problem— Reckless strolled right into the elevator car as though it was just another stall. As it moved upward, she waited calmly for the doors to reopen.

This was the moment everyone—including, by this time, much of America—had been waiting for. As Reckless entered the banquet hall, the four hundred people at the Marine Corps anniversary ball stood and applauded the hero horse. She was as unfazed by the popping flashbulbs as she had been by explosions on the battlefield. Her tail twitched, she bobbed her head, and some thought she almost smiled. Reckless was home among her people.

She accepted the applause for several seconds, then noticed the 179th anniversary birthday cake on the head table. Before anyone could stop her, Reckless stepped over and began to eat it.

Obviously, organizers had not prepared for this. Nor for what came next. As one politician and official after another stepped to the microphone to give short speeches and have their photos taken,

Reckless sauntered from table to table, munching on each one's flower arrangement. Pedersen, Lively, and Coleman simply glanced at each other and shrugged. That was Reckless, all right.

It was back in the elevator for Reckless. She was taken up one more flight, to the ballroom. Fortunately, a fresh cake was available there. According to tradition, the first slice was cut to be given to the guest of honor. It was presented to an apparently still-hungry Reckless by Kay Pedersen, meeting for the first time the other woman who had captured her husband's heart.

CHAPTER TWENTY-EIGHT

★ ★

A Hero Horse Goes Home

Though Reckless was still a relatively young horse—it was be-lieved that she was six years old in 1954—the end of that Marine Corps birthday bash in San Francisco was the beginning of the hero horse's golden years. The next day, accompanied by Captain and Kay Pedersen and Sergeant Lively, Reckless was on her way south—in a trailer much more accommodating than the two-wheeled one in Korea—with Camp Pendleton being the destination.

It was decided that the pleasant environment of Southern Cali-fornia would be a suitable home for the sorrel mare. Her first stop was the Pedersen family's ranch in Vista. During her few days there, Reckless received the devoted attention of not only the captain and his wife but of their two enraptured children, Eric Jr. and Katy.

For her care and comfort at Camp Pendleton, little would be left to chance. Colonel Geer wrote a letter to the Marine Corps headquarters in Quantico settling the issue of who owned Reckless and detailing how Reckless was to be treated.

She would be owned, Geer wrote, by "the hundreds of Marines, living and dead, who were at the Battle of Vegas, where she won their love by her valiant service." As if this needed to be reiterated, Geer insisted that Reckless was "no ordinary horse and she should have special care and attention. She should have a large and luxurious box stall constructed for living quarters. Her pasture should be commodious and watered to provide the best grass."

Her packhorse days were over—the little mare was never to have to bear any burden again. If she was to be ridden at all, it could not be "by oversized, leaden-seated, heavy-handed cowboy types, nor should she ever be considered one of the post stable horses." Reckless was not fond of dogs, but Geer assured that she "likes children and is gentle in their presence."

Her caretakers would have to really be on the ball because the new rules called for Reckless to "be groomed each day and her mane and tail should be encouraged by daily brushing. The Headquarters Duty Officer should be directed to inspect her and her quarters once in each twenty-four-hour period." Geer, perhaps with tongue in cheek, warned that "under the stress of battle she has been known to drink beer. However, all liquids should be served in a common variety water glass." The Marines at Camp Pendleton would learn that even normal daily life could make Reckless thirsty for some suds.

One might expect that the higher-ups in the Marine Corps on the other side of the country in Quantico might think such requests— which were more like demands—were rather arrogant. But Reckless had a champion there in the form of the new assistant commandant of the Marine Corps, who wrote back that such suggestions would become the rules, no questions asked.

Randolph Pate, now a lieutenant general, concluded: "I am confident that arrangements can be completed at Camp Pendleton which will ensure that Sergeant Reckless may enjoy the care and surroundings which her faithful service in Korea justifies."

When Reckless and her entourage arrived at the camp, waiting to greet her was Major General John Taylor Selden, the former commander of the 1st Marine Division and now Pendleton's commanding general. He found her "every bit as beautiful and well trained as I had been told."

The trailer and accompanying vehicles drove to General Selden's home on the base, where his wife welcomed Reckless. "It was a case of love at first sight for both," the commander reported. The horse was invited to make her mark in the camp guest book "and if it hadn't been for Captain Pedersen, she would have eaten the pen."

Concerning the future for Reckless, General Selden vowed, "I can assure that there are twenty-five thousand Marines on this base who are determined she will want for nothing—ever."

That promise was kept. No horse could have had a more contented life. Her home was in the Stepp Stables on the base, which she shared with other horses—although no dwelling received as much care as hers. Thanks to being not far from San Diego, Reckless never had to experience anything like the bitter cold of Korea again.

Her beloved 5th Marines were now stationed at Camp Pendleton, and the commanding officer was Colonel Richard Rothwell. "My father was glad it worked out like that because he and Lew Walt had been lieutenants together in San Diego," said Richard Rothwell Jr. "When my father was dating my mother, Lew would drive him on a motorcycle. It didn't have a backseat, just a fender over the tire. He would ride on that, and my mother was always surprised he could father children."

It was also fitting, then, that Colonel Rothwell was there to be part of the next promotion ceremony for Reckless. On August 31, 1959, she was elevated to Staff Sergeant Reckless, the rank she would carry proudly for the rest of her life. The ceremony included a nineteen-gun salute and a parade of seventeen hundred Marines. A few familiar friends, like Eric and Kay Pedersen, were there along with the man who personally bestowed the promotion and who was now the commandant of the Marine Corps—General Randolph Pate.

Reckless's red and gold blanket was now full. In addition to her stripes, she had been awarded two Purple Hearts for her wounds during the Battle of the Nevada Cities, the Good Conduct Medal, the Presidential Unit Citation with Bronze Star, the National Defense Service Medal, the Korean Service Medal, the United Nations Korea Medal, the Navy Unit Commendation, and the Republic of Korea Presidential Unit Citation. That was almost enough hardware to make carrying recoilless rifle shells easy in comparison.

As usual, though, there was no burden too great for Reckless. The happy horse was surrounded by friends and family—and not just her Marine Corps family. At her side during the ceremony was Fearless, her first foal, born in 1957, and her second, Dauntless, born earlier that year. Like her mother, Flame-of-the-Morning, Reckless got a late start on having children, but she would manage to give birth to another foal, in 1964, who was named after Lieutenant General Puller, the most decorated Marine ever.

Though the doting mother, Reckless was not about to retire to her stall. Being promoted to staff sergeant was a big deal and she wanted to celebrate—which meant it was time for her and her pals Eric Pedersen and Randolph Pate to go get a beer.

EPILOGUE

★ ★

The ceremony would begin in the lobby of the National Museum of the Marine Corps, shift to the unveiling of the monument in Semper Fidelis Memorial Park, and then conclude with a reception back inside the museum. It was a beautiful day in Northern Virginia: July 26, 2013. The following day would mark the sixtieth anniversary of the truce that halted the Korean War, but on this Friday, the focus was on honoring Staff Sergeant Reckless. People had come from all over the country to attend the long-planned ceremony that was to dedicate a life-size memorial depicting the four-legged hero.

Being enshrined at the museum that commemorates the men and battles that have defined the Marine Corps for well over two centuries was certainly a high honor. The peak of the building is visible from Interstate 95, its tall spire reaching for the sky at a forty-five-degree angle intended to resemble the leaning of the flagpole being raised on Mount Suribachi on Iwo Jima on February 23, 1945. Within the building were 118,000 square feet of exhibits and memorabilia about a branch of the military that had been founded the year before the Declaration of Independence established what would become the United States. On the manicured, tree-filled grounds were dozens of memorials and plaques, each one telling a special story. Sergeant Reckless's memorial was about to become one of them.

The dedication event had been organized by Robin Hutton of Moorpark, California, who had also spearheaded the fund-raising for the creation of the memorial itself. On this day she was seemingly everywhere, dashing about inside and outside the museum, greeting guests, giving instructions to reporters and camera crews and assorted technicians, hopping in a golf cart to take a final look at the memorial—about a seven-minute walk from the museum's front door—before the unveiling, and then she was back, resuming conversations as though they had not been interrupted by her abrupt absence.

Volunteers had set up chairs in the rotunda. They had done a good job of it, too, but this was a Marine Corps–related facility after all, and a good job was not enough. One Marine knelt at the end of one row as another moved along it, meticulously adjusting the position of a chair until the first Marine said, "Okay," then stepped to the next one. There were eighteen rows of chairs, nine on the left side of the podium, nine on the other. The first three rows on each side were for specially invited guests and had twelve seats; the other six rows had fifteen seats each. The first Marine said "Okay" precisely 252 times before the task was deemed complete.

Some of the guests were veterans of the Korean War. A few, like Sergeant William Janzen and Sergeant Harold Wadley, were still able to fit into their Marine dress uniforms. Others wore black or red caps with "Korea" stitched on them. They paid particular attention to the Korean War section of the museum. Quotes lined the wall. One was from President Harry Truman right after North Korea's invasion on

June 25, 1950: "If this were allowed to go unchallenged, it would mean a third world war." Another, from the July 31 edition of the *New York Times*, was about the desperate fight to hold on to the Pusan Perimeter: "For five weeks we have been trading space for time. The space is running out."

The ceremony began when Lieutenant General James F. Amos, commandant of the Marine Corps, and his wife arrived. As many as three hundred people took seats or stood in the back of the museum's rotunda. The Marine Corps Band, which had unobtrusively gathered at the side of the rotunda away from the main entrance, played a patriotic overture that included an abbreviated "America the Beautiful." A color guard made its way from the entrance to the band, crossing in front of the Amoses sitting in one of the two front rows. Chaplain Charles E. Hodges, a commander in the U.S. Navy, gave an invocation, the band played the National Anthem, remarks were made, then it was Hutton's turn at the podium, and finally Sergeant Wadley stood up to speak. When he concluded his affectionate remarks about Reckless, the band struck up "Anchors Aweigh" and, eliciting more than a few tears, the "Marines' Hymn." Many in the audience were humming along by the last lines: "If the Army and the Navy/Ever look on Heaven's scenes/ They will find the streets are guarded/By United States Marines."

It was time to visit the Reckless memorial itself. Many in the crowd were pleased to find a dozen trolleys resembling golf carts waiting right outside the entrance for them. A few, though, walked past the vehicles, preferring to wander along the winding path that ran through Semper Fidelis Memorial Park. They were accompanied by the steady thrumming buzz of cicadas. The first glimpse of Staff Sergeant Reckless was through a stand of tall, slender trees. Then the path straightened and the entire clearing could be seen, surrounded by maturing trees bursting with summer foliage. The bronze monument at the center of the clearing is not a large one intended to impress with size and the implication of power. The power of Reckless was evident in the strength of her will and courage and persistence. The inscription on the monument was from Sergeant Wadley: "The spirit of her loneliness and her loyalty, in spite of the danger, was something else to behold. Hurting. Determined. And alone. That's the image I have imprinted in my head and heart forever."

The monument gleamed bright in the midsummer sun. Reckless stands on an incline of rock that represents the sides of the hills that she climbed repeatedly to bring the next batch of recoilless rifle shells to the Marines above. The saddle on her back carries four of the 24-pound shells, two on each side. Her right front leg is raised as she prepares to take the next step upward. Her back hooves are planted and pushing, and her left front leg is like a piston just thrust into the barely yielding hillside. Her tail, lifted by a slight breeze, is spread to the left. The muscles in her powerful chest are taut as the horse gives every ounce of her strength to haul her burden. Her ears are up, nostrils are flaring, and there is indeed sheer determination in her slender face.

The monument is a fitting tribute. However, there is another one that is more intimate and, these days, a lot more difficult to find. It is at the Stepp Stables on the grounds of Camp Pendleton, where a contented Reckless lived out the remainder of her life.

A week after her promotion ceremony presided over by General Pate at Camp Pendleton in 1959, Reckless, harking back to her original destiny, was the star at a racetrack. "Top Del Mar Fillies Share Stage with Korean Plater" was the headline of Jack Murphy's column in the September 6, 1959, edition of the *San Diego Union*. "Reckless, winner of two Purple Hearts, was paraded on the track before the Reckless Handicap here yesterday and the jockeys on the premises were warned to keep a discreet distance. It seemed likely that that she might fluff out her skirts and curtsy when the crowd gave her a noisy ovation."

In addition to taking care of her children, Reckless was kept busy at Camp Pendleton, but in a way that she fully enjoyed. Whenever there was an important ceremony, ranging from changes in command to retirements to promotions, she was right there in attendance. The sorrel mare would be decked out in her special blanket after having undergone an extra-careful grooming. And, of course, she participated in every parade, both on and off the base, and was the center of attention. She marched along in a stately way, head bobbing slightly, tail twitching, eyeing the crowds and accepting the applause and other forms of adulation like any proud and accomplished dignitary would.

From time to time, Reckless was sought out by reporters and others wanting to "interview" or just meet the famous hero horse. She had missed her chance to be on Ed Sullivan's show, but she appeared on the TV program *House Party*, hosted by Art Linkletter. One producer proposed a twenty-six-episode TV show on Reckless and her days in the Marine Corps, but nothing came of it.

There were movie offers too. One was spurned immediately because it wanted to portray Reckless as a sort of chatterbox with a human voice dubbed in, and the Marines thought turning her into another Francis the Talking Mule was undignified. More promising was a visit by the director Francis D. Lyon. He was a Hollywood veteran who as an editor had shared an Academy Award with Robert Parrish for the 1947 boxing film *Body and Soul*. His directing efforts included the 1957 western *The Oklahoman* with longtime leading man Joel McCrea. Lyon announced his intention to develop a feature film on Reckless. She may have been ready for her close-up, but the project never got off the ground and Lyon moved on to other movies.

That was the fate of one other promising project that would have had America's most famous horse team up on the big screen with its top box office star. A screenplay was commissioned by Batjac Productions, the company owned by John Wayne. Titled *The Outpost*, it would focus on the Battle of the Nevada Cities, with Reckless playing herself.

"She'll probably steal every scene she is in," Duke told reporters. She was never given the opportunity, however, as the movie was not made.

Despite all the hardships of her early years—first as Flame, then as the true-life warhorse in the 5th Regiment—Reckless had a long life. Clearly, the loving care of the Marines extended her days, and they were healthy as well as happy ones. One of her caretakers was Jesse Winters, and Reckless kept him hopping.

"There were times that some of the Marines after a night on the town would turn her out to run free," Corporal Winters reported. "On one occasion while she was out running free she found her way to the flower garden of the wife of the base commander. I'm sure there were a lot of snickers about that, but let me tell you I was one PFC sweating bullets getting her out of there with the general standing in front of his house. I remember he was saying something—I don't think it was good. I do remember throwing him a salute as we took off at a trot up the trail."

Age finally caught up with even the fun-loving and resilient Reckless. On a beautiful spring day in 1968, while out for a walk, the elderly sorrel mare stumbled into a barbed-wire fence. To treat her bleeding wounds, she was put under sedation, and then she slipped away.

Staff Sergeant Reckless of the U.S. Marine Corps died on May 13, 1968. She was buried with full military honors near the Stepp Stables.

Today, one can find at the entrance to the Stepp Stables a headstone that was dedicated to Reckless by the 1st Marine Division Association in 1971. The ceremony included heartfelt remarks by a retired Marine Corps captain, Eric Pedersen, who nineteen years earlier had bought a horse and begun a remarkable journey with her.

The stables themselves are modest wooden structures where more than a hundred horses are boarded and riding lessons are given. It is a favorite destination of children from the surrounding area. One sign advises them about the horses: "Don't feed them your fingers." The Stepp Stables is surrounded by brown hills sporting yellow and pink flowers and the occasional outcroppings of gray rocks. Winding through the hills are narrow brown-dirt trails formed by the hooves of thousands of horses over the years.

Among them had been a heroic Marine and her children. One has to be looking for the headstone at the gate to the stables because it is not large or the least bit pretentious. It is a simple, loving tribute to a courageous, loving horse named Reckless.

AUTHOR'S NOTE ON SOURCES

The books listed in the Selected Bibliography were of much help in providing information about the Korean War and the life and times of the horse who would be named Reckless. Especially useful were the books by Lee Ballenger, who as a Marine sergeant served in the war; the fifth volume of *U.S. Marines in Korea*, the official account produced by Marine Corps historians; James Brady's memoir, which provided eloquent insight into the experiences of a Marine rifle platoon lieutenant; and both books by Andrew Geer, another Marine who saw combat in Korea.

Geer's book *Reckless: Pride of the Marines* has been described both as "heavily fictionalized" and full of leaping conclusions. As Geer points out in the book, he did not meet Reckless until June 1953, nine months after she had "joined" the 5th Marines. However, because of his interviews with men of the regiment and other research conducted for two *Saturday Evening Post* articles he authored, and given that Geer's expanded account in *Reckless: Pride of the Marines* is the only one written during Reckless's lifetime, I have relied on it. It is reasonable to wonder how much of the portion of the tale covering the life of Flame/Reckless before she was bought by Lieutenant Eric Pedersen and brought to the regiment in October 1952 is based on facts. At best, that portion must be read with a grain of salt, as some of it is based on hearsay and anecdotes from unidentified sources. Kim Huk Moon (whatever his real name) may well have existed and Pedersen did indeed purchase Flame from him, but there is no way today to verify the boy's backstory. Readers should keep in mind that what makes for a heck of a story can be highly speculative.

I first found out about Reckless when I received an e-mail message from Dick Bonelli. As a corporal and a member of Fox Company, 2nd Battalion, 7th Marines in the Battle of Toktong Pass in November 1950, Dick earned a Silver Star and a Purple Heart. He is one of the major characters of *The Last Stand of Fox Company*, a book I cowrote with Bob Drury, and he is the very active president of the Fox 2/7 Association. I am honored to be a friend. A few years ago, Dick sent a message with a YouTube video of Reckless attached. I wanted to know more about this remarkable Mongolian mare, and a journey began.

Along the way I encountered Robin Hutton and others who have devoted countless hours to having Reckless recognized for the hero she was. Readers who wish to learn more about these efforts can go to the Sgt. Reckless and Official Sgt. Reckless Fan Club pages on Facebook. Hutton has been compiling photographs, recollections, and other material for a book of her own, and no doubt when that is published it will be a sincere tribute to Reckless and her fellow Marines.

I cast as wide a net as possible to find sources of information beyond the books listed below. Particularly helpful were *Leatherneck* magazine, *Cowboys & Indians*, the newsletters of various Marine Corps units and organizations, 1st Marine Division after-action reports, Web sites, and the archives of the *New York Times*, the *San Diego Union-Tribune*, and other newspapers around the country. With some veterans having passed away or otherwise not available, in some cases interviews published over the years in hometown weeklies as well as major city dailies and regional magazines were the only ways to include their recollections of Reckless and her life during and after Korea. I am grateful also for the efforts and resources of the Korean War Project. The outreach it provides to Korean War veterans is very valuable. Please give it your support.

Every effort was made to ensure that the myriad details from October 1952 onward in this book are based on fact, and I am responsible for any inaccuracies that have slipped through.

SELECTED BIBLIOGRAPHY

Ballenger, Lee. *U.S. Marines in Korea.* Vol. 1, *The Outpost War, 1952.* Washington, D.C.: Brassey's, 2000.

——. *U.S. Marines in Korea.* Vol. 2, *The Final Crucible, 1953.* Washington, D.C.: Brassey's, 2001.

Barrett, Janet. *They Called Her Reckless: A True Story of War, Love, and One Extraordinary Horse.* Chester, CT: Tall Cedar Books, 2013.

Blair, Clay. *The Forgotten War.* New York: Times Books, 1987.

Brady, James. *The Coldest War: A Memoir of Korea.* New York: Thomas Dunne Books, 1990.

Crawford, Danny J., Robert V. Aquilina, Ann A. Ferrante, and Sheila P. Gramblin. *The 1st Marine Division and Its Regiments.* Washington, D.C.: History and Museums Division, U.S. Marine Corps, 1999.

DiMarco, Louis A. *War Horse: A History of the Military Horse and Rider.* Yardley, PA: Westholme Publishing, 2008.

Drury, Bob, and Tom Clavin. *The Last Stand of Fox Company: A True Story of U.S. Marines in Combat.* New York: Atlantic Monthly Press, 2009.

Edwards, Paul M. *The Hill Wars of the Korean Conflict.* Jefferson, NC: McFarland, 2005.

Farley, Walter. *The Black Stallion.* New York: Random House, 1991.

———. *The Black Stallion Returns.* New York: Random House, 1991.

Fehrenbach, T. R. *This Kind of War: The Classic Korean War History.* New York: Macmillan, 1963.

Geer, Andrew. *The New Breed: The Story of the U.S. Marines in Korea.* New York: Harper & Brothers, 1952.

———. *Reckless: Pride of the Marines.* New York: E. P. Dutton & Co., 1955.

Halberstam, David. *The Coldest Winter: America and the Korean War.* New York: Hyperion, 2008.

Hastings, Max. *The Korean War.* New York: Simon & Schuster, 1987.

Hermes, Walter G. *Truce Tent and Fighting Front.* Washington, D.C.: Center of Military History, United States Army, 1992.

Hillenbrand, Laura. *Seabiscuit: An American Legend.* New York: Ballantine Books, 2001.

Knox, Donald. *The Korean War: Uncertain Victory.* New York: Harcourt, Inc., 1988.

Letts, Elizabeth. *The Eighty-Dollar Champion: Snowman, the Horse That Inspired a Nation.* New York: Ballantine Books, 2011.

Meid, Lieutenant Colonel Pat, and Major James M. Yingling. *U.S. Marine Operations in Korea, 1950–1953.* Vol. 5, *Operations in West Korea.* Washington, D.C.: Historical Division Headquarters, U.S. Marine Corps, 1972.

Morpurgo, Michael. *War Horse.* New York: Scholastic Press, 2010.

Nalty, Bernard C. *Outpost War: U.S. Marines from the Nevada Battles to the Armistice.* Washington, D.C.: U.S. Marine Corps Historical Center, 2002.

Orlean, Susan. *Rin Tin Tin: The Life and the Legend.* New York: Simon & Schuster, 2012.

Russ, Martin. *The Last Parallel: A Marine's War Journal*. New York: Rinehart & Co., 1957.

Smith, Charles R., ed. *U.S. Marines in the Korean War*. Washington, D.C.: U.S. Marine Corps, 2008.

Stanton, Doug. *Horse Soldiers: The Extraordinary Story of a Band of U.S. Soldiers Who Rode to Victory in Afghanistan*. New York: Scribner, 2010.

Varhola, Michael J. *Fire and Ice: The Korean War, 1950–1953*. New York: Da Capo Press, 2000.

Williams, Ted, and John Underwood. *My Turn at Bat: The Story of My Life*. New York: Simon & Schuster, 1969.

Wilson, Arthur W., ed. *Korean Vignettes: Faces of War*. Portland, OR: Artwork Publications, 1996.

ACKNOWLEDGMENTS

I was very fortunate to receive the cooperation of many people during this journey with Reckless. In some instances, I conducted interviews with people who knew Reckless and/or were involved in combat in Korea in 1952 to 1953. Otherwise, I depended on oral/written sources, the kindness of family members and others who had stories to share about Reckless, and researchers generous with their time and efforts. It is my sincere hope that all those who offered their cooperation to me will see in this book a tribute to the courageous men who fought for their country in Korea as well as to a special horse.

In this regard, I want to offer my thanks and respect to Gwenn Adams, General James Amos, Ted Barker, Anthony and Mary Caputo, Jennifer Castro, Theodore Chenoweth, Kay Coyte, Beth Cullom, Fred Donovan, Patty Everett, Walt Ford, Carolina Gusman, Robert Hall, Arlen Hensley, George Hines, Bernard Hollinger, William Janzen, Don Johnson, Faye Jonason, Michael Keenan, Corey Kilgannon, Hana Kim, Ted King, James Larkin, John Melvin, John Meyers, Sinyoung Park, Billy Rivers Penn, Major Amy Punzel, Holly Reed, Bob Rogers, Richard Rothwell Jr., Art Sickler, Harold Wadley, and Jesse Winters.

No author of nonfiction could survive in this business without librarians, researchers, and others at various archives who give generously of their time and courtesy. I've been blessed to experience that thanks to the staffs at Camp Pendleton, the John Jermain Library, the Korea Racing Authority, the Marine Corps History Division, the Marines Heritage Foundation, the National Archives and Records Administration, and the National Museum of the Marine Corps.

Extra thanks to Megan Gambino for tossing her lasso and rounding up most of the images found in the book. Also providing vital and courteous help were Janet Barrett and, especially, Alisa Whitley.

And no author turns in a perfect manuscript. This one had its share of flaws, but thank goodness that in my corner was an especially fine editor, Brent Howard. He and others at New American Library/ Penguin—including Melissa Broder, Lorna Henry, and Loren Jaggers— did yeoman work in elevating the quality of *Reckless*. I am very grateful to Scott Gould and the rest of RLR Associates for making this collaboration happen and for all the hand-holding along the way.

There were friends, maybe a few Romans, and fellow countrymen who lent me their ears during the sometimes difficult period when this book was being researched and written. Their knowledge, their patience, and especially their support did and continue to inspire me. Thank you to John Bonfiglio, Debbie and Roby Braun, Heather Buchanan, Michael and Shelly Gambino, Peter Israelson and Yvonne Wibbe, Christopher and Eve Jarrett, Phil Keith and Laura Lyons, Bob Martin, Denise McDonald, Ken Moran, Jacqueline Reingold, Tony and Patty Sales, Lynne Scanlon, Joe Shaw, Maureen Tompkins and Peter Hoops, Tom Twomey, Larry Wagner, Rebecca Wilson, and David Winter. More thanks go to my mother, aunt, and siblings, Gertrude Clavin, Joan Geroch, Nancy Bartolotta, and James Clavin. And to Bob Drury, a fine friend who is also the best writer I know.

As always, to my two heroes, Kathryn Clavin and Brendan Clavin.

INDEX